GW00775922

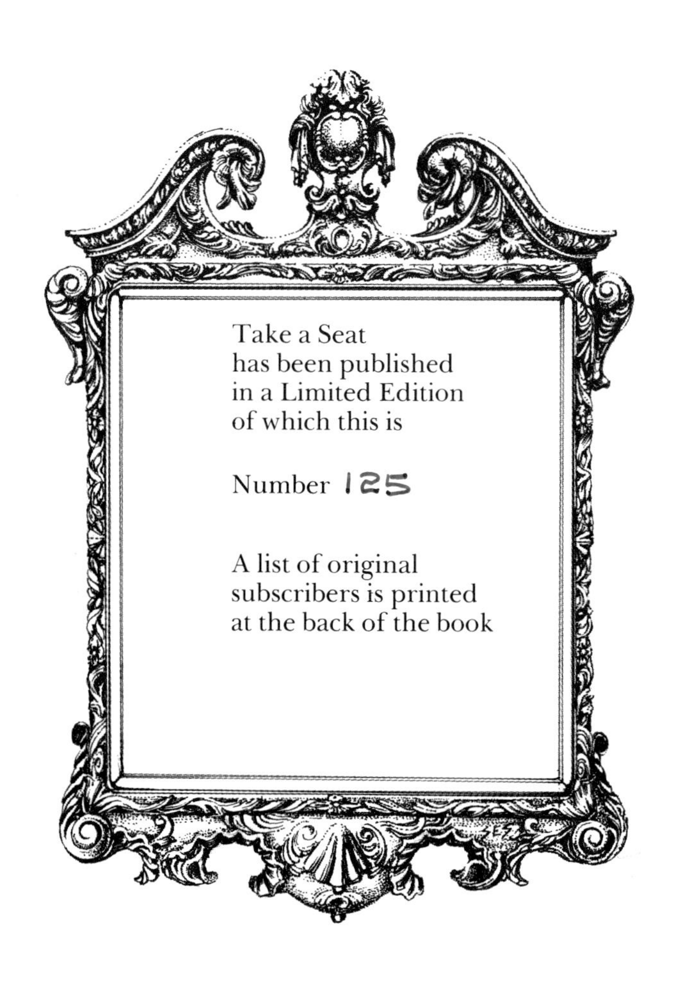
Take a Seat
has been published
in a Limited Edition
of which this is

Number 125

A list of original
subscribers is printed
at the back of the book

END PAPERS - LEFT: Bodiam — a design derived from 18th century English needlework and RIGHT: Cornucopia — a design taken from a fine example of petit-point needlework of 1710; the originals are in the Parker Knoll antique collection.

TAKE A SEAT

FRONT COVER: Frederick Parker and the Parker Knoll York chair in Cottesbrooke claret. BACK: Upholstery and chair caning shop, Temple End 1921.

Frederick Parker, founding father.

TAKE A SEAT

The History of Parker Knoll 1834-1994

Researched and compiled by
STEPHEN BLAND
Edited by Clive Birch
Assisted by Jonathan Arnold

BARON
MCMXCV

PUBLISHED BY BARON BIRCH FOR QUOTES LIMITED IN 1995
AND PRODUCED BY KEY COMPOSITION, SOUTH MIDLANDS LITHOPLATES,
HILLMAN PRINTERS (FROME) LIMITED, CHENEY & SONS AND
WBC BOOKBINDERS LIMITED

ISBN 0 86023 504 1

CONTENTS

FOREWORD *by Lucian Ercolani*

It was with a deep sense of privilege that, as a fellow furniture maker, I accepted the kind invitation to write this foreword to the history of Parkers, undoubtedly one of the most famous names in our industry, a position they have earned and held for well over a century.

The inspiration for this invitation stems from quite a romantic family association. It was the legendary Harry Parker who 'discovered' my father, way back in 1907, inviting him to join their design team in High Wycombe, thus giving him the golden opportunity of starting his career with the finest of furniture makers.

Some 10 years later, my father founded his own company in High Wycombe, but there is no doubt the location and history of our company and family could well have been very different but for that intuitive and friendly invitation.

I would like to tell that story, as it really was an extraordinary chapter of events:
my father was nearing the completion of his studies at the Shoredtich Tech (of hallowed memories), evening classes five nights per week for 5 years.

Arriving home by train at about midnight, carrying with him an unfinished drawing, he debated with himself whether to go straight to bed, as he certainly wanted and deserved to do, having given his best through a long day, or to push himself way beyond sensible limits, stay up and finish it off. This he did.

The next evening, taking his finished drawing into class, most fortuitously the Editor of the *Cabinet Maker* was making a rare visit. He saw the drawing, was impressed, and gave him a double-page spread in the next issue. Harry Parker, seeing this editorial, said to his colleagues 'There is the young man for us!', and arranged an immediate meeting. Within a few days, my father was installed in his design team at High Wycombe.

Luck certainly played a vital role but, as I like to tell aspiring and ambitious youngsters, nobody ever achieved anything because he or she was lucky. It is only those with a perceptive mind and who prepare themselves with dedication, who can recognise and take advantage of 'Lady Luck' when, perchance, she smiles upon them.

For my part, although I was nearly born in in father's workshops, my earliest memories are the stories he used to tell us, and continued to tell us throughout his life, of his early days with Parkers, of his daily visits around the works with Harry Parker, learning from him, and how he guided the skills of their craftsmen in the creation of beautiful furniture. Most certainly, I was brought up with the understanding of what those early days meant to him, the joy of witnessing, and the privilege of being allowed the opportunity to help to bring to life, what he always described as 'the Jewellery of Furniture' — a tradition of excellence which we, particularly in our industry, should value beyond measure.

Since those days, there have been two world wars and vast changes socially and economically; we now live in an entirely different world. Education and a more even spread of wealth give the great majority of people the opportunity to exercise their taste and judgement rather than just a privileged few.

This can present a great divide in the manufacturing world — to just go for the market in purely commercial terms, or go for the market with an understanding of the commercial problems but also with a mission to lift the level of aspirations. Furniture, I truly believe, can make an important social contribution towards a better life.

This book describes how Parker's have progressed through immense changes, how they have steadfastly translated and maintained the ethics involved with the Jewellery of Furniture of those early days, for the needs and requirements of today.

I salute them, and commend this book to you.

Preface

This record was written between 1987 and 1991, and my labours end with 1976, when the fourth generation took control. That is now a long time ago and many important developments have since taken place.

Patric Baker was asked to write the history in 1980 but, shortly after commencing his research, he died and the project was suspended. It was revived in 1985 when I retired. During my long service I accumulated many relevant records and became the only one who remembered the old days. By building upon Patric Baker's original notes and my own experience since 1936, I have been able to write the story.

Many of those intimately concerned with the business have died or retired and new people have taken their place. They have inherited the accumulated labours of their predecessors, who gradually built the one of the few surviving major upholstery businesses in the United Kingdom.

I wish to express my thanks to all who gave me advice, information and assistance. Space has not allowed individual mention of many who were, or still are, employed by the Company. It is hoped that they will find this a true and accurate record of the times they shared, and that it will give them some pleasure in recalling their service and contribution.

I am indebted to Martin Jourdan, first for his encouragement while I was writing the manuscript and then for making its publication possible. Derek Stewart patiently read through the manuscript and was able to make several corrections and useful suggestions. I also wish to express my particular thanks to John Arnold who has worked with great enthusiasm and energy on my behalf with the Editor and Publisher, thus relieving me of the onus and problems involved in finally bringing the book to print.

S. C. Bland, Pant, Oswestry, 1994

William Parker, Son of William [illegible]
was admitted into the Freedom aforesaid and sworn in the Mayoralty of [illegible] Mayor
and Sir James Shaw Bart. Chamberlain and is entered in the book signed with the Letter [illegible] relating
to the Purchasing of Freedoms and the Admissions of Freemen (to wit) the [illegible] day of
in the 4th Year of the reign of King William the Fourth, And in the Year of our Lord [illegible] In
Witness whereof the Seal of the Office of Chamberlain of the said City is hereunto affixed Dated in the Chamber
of the Guildhall of the same City the day and Year abovesaid.

FREDK PARKER & SONS LTD

~ SHIP FURNITURE ~

CHAIR & CABINET MANUFACTURERS

UPHOLSTERERS ANTIQUE DEALERS

·20·NEWMAN·ST·OXFORD·ST·

LONDON.W.

TELEGRAMS:
JOINDERING, RATH,
LONDON.
TELEPHONE: MUSEUM 0771
(3 LINES)
PRESENTED BY

FACTORIES { HIGH WYCOMBE, BUCKS. COWLEY PEACHEY, UXBRIDGE. MIDDX.

ABOVE: William Parker (1810-1879) and CENTRE: his City Freedom of 1 January 1831. BELOW: Frederick Parker's calling card.

GENESIS – 1834-1869

The Parker family was first associated with the furniture trade in 1826; Charles Dickens had just completed two years' rudimentary schooling and obtained his first position as a solicitor's clerk. Many landmarks with which we are familiar, had yet to be built — the old Palace of Westminster still stood (it burnt down in 1834), Nash had just built Regent Street, and Trafalgar Square was not laid out. Slavery in the British Empire was not abolished until 1833 and it was still customary to drive little boys through the soot-choked chimneys of large houses. The steam train had just arrived and so had the electric telegraph. The Co-operative Society was founded in Rochdale and Queen Victoria ascended the throne.

Unhappily and with a few notable exceptions, the standards of British design were pretty poor. In the 1840s the Government finally yielded to public opinion and set up a select committee to consider ways of promoting the fine arts. This may seem strange when one considers that the late 18th century was the heyday of Sir Joshua Reynolds, Thomas Gainsborough and George Romney and a time of prosperity for the London furniture industry, inspired by such men as Chippendale, Vile, Hepplewhite and Manwaring.

Household accessories were also a joy to behold — the miniatures of Richard Cosway and Andrew Plimmer, the ceramics, jewellery and portrait medallions of Josiah Wedgewood, the silver of Paul Stoor. Yet within forty years of their creation, good taste had virtually been lost.

British industrial art had declined, furniture and woodwork attracted little attention and there was no attempt to maintain style or harmony. As a critic in *The Times* put it: 'It was the age of artificial graining of woods, of heavy draperies, black horsehair covering of chairs and sofas, terrible effigies in cross-stitch worsted work and wallpapers and carpets, crude in colour and bad in design'.

1840 has been described as the 'low water mark of taste in England'. But there were those who rebelled. Examples of their work can still be seen in some of the older West End clubs and the halls of the City Guilds, furnished about that time, when a few outstanding cabinet makers ensured the best of British furniture survived. It was the Great Exhibition of 1851 which turned the tide, and in this encouraging atmosphere Parker furniture interests took root.

It must have been quite a momentous change in the life of William Parker the Younger when his father, a market gardener near Chingford in Essex, sent him to be apprenticed to the furniture trade in the City of London. At the age of sixteen, to be transferred from rural Essex to the hurly-burly of London, was a tremendous challenge. Hoxton, on the eastern edge of London, had become a noted centre for furniture making in the late 18th century. William Senior frequently drove his horse and cart to London to sell produce. Some association there may have led to an acquaintance with the established furniture making community, facilitating his son's apprenticeship. That area has maintained its assocaition with furniture making ever since.

Apprenticeship was essential for proper training. Indeed, the craft guilds, later City Livery Companies, had always guarded the interests of individual trades and made themselves responsible for quality of training. Parents of an intending apprentice, having found a suitable Master, paid him a premium and were given an indenture setting out the conditions. Often the trainee lived with his Master and family. When the term (usually seven years) was finished, samples of the apprentice's work were inspected by the Livery involved and, if satisfactory, and none of the other members objected, the apprentice was elected and sworn in as a freeman. Election following servitude was the accepted way for an experienced trainee to gain admission to a City Livery and London training was considered the best. By the middle of the eighteen century the system was under severe attack. As is often the case with standards based on achievement of a difficult skill or ability, easier ways of gaining admission were sought by the less able. For centuries, the privileges of City and Guild freedom were sought by those who wished to prosper. Privileges included immunity from tolls at markets and fairs, freedom from impressment into the armed forces, and the right to vote at ward or parliamentary elections. Most of these advantages disappeared in the nineteenth century, but Freedom is still a necessary qualification for admission to a Livery Company, and Liverymen still elect the Lord Mayor and Sheriffs.

Until 1835 all Freemen were admitted through membership of a Livery. It was common for a Freeman to follow a trade unrelated to the practices of his Company. The numbers admitted by servitude steadily declined and there was a great increase in admission by patrimony (children, usually sons of Freemen), and also by redemption (by paying a 'fine'). By resolution of 17 March 1835 persons could be admitted to the Freedom without intervention of a Company.

Historic London, embracing Finsbury, Shoreditch, Spitalfields and Hoxton had, by the end of the 18th century, become the home of the silk weaving and furniture industries in which many immigrants worked. Increasingly through the Victorian period there were more and more small furniture workshops there. By the end of the 19th century, Hoxton was 'Second amongst Eastern area Boroughs in the percentage of persons living in poverty'. Trade must have been competitive and some firms of high repute emerged, but generally the reputation of much Shoreditch-made furniture was 'cheap and cheerful'. This was the environment in which William Parker the Younger started.

From early boyhood William showed a marked interest in wood-carving, and spent much of his spare time whittling instead of attending to his farm duties. This gave him an interest in cabinet making even though his family background would have assured him a comfortable living.

On 1 February 1826 William was bound apprentice to Matthew Wild, of the Grange Road, Bermondsey, Surrey, a cabinet maker, Citizen and Goldsmith, to learn the art of a cabinet maker. Wild died intestate before William completed his apprenticeship, and he was then turned over to another City Freeman to complete his term, either on 6 April or 16 November 1831. His new master was Thomas Risdale of 4 Swan Street, Minories, City of London, a brass manufacturer, Citizen and Wheelwright.

It was long believed that William served his apprenticeship under William Farrer of Bunhill Row in the City of London, and indeed copies of an indenture to this effect have been cherished over the years. It is duly signed and witnessed, and records a £25 fee paid to William Farrer. The document is dated 18 January 1826, less than two weeks before the date of the actual apprenticeship was taken up under Matthew Wild. Servitude under Farrer did not take place, perhaps because of the late realisation that Farrer was not a Citizen and Freeman, so William would not become a Freeman himself through servitude.

The wording of the Farrer indenture shows how things have changed. What young man today would accept conditions such as 'not to commit fornication or contract matrimony within the said term, nor play at cards, dice tables or any other unlawful games whereby his said master may have any loss with his own goods or others'? As the indenture shows, apprentices in those days were not supposed to 'haunt taverns or playhouses' and could not 'absent themselves from their Masters' service day or night unlawfully'. William Parker senior paid '£25 of lawful money of Great Britain' for the privilege of apprenticing his son. He also undertook to provide 'proper implements and tools' during the last three and a half years of the seven year term. As to salary there is no mention. His Master merely undertook to 'find unto the said apprentice sufficient meat, drink, lodging and all other necessaries' during the 'said term'.

It appears that, despite the temptations of his period, William proved an assiduous worker. By the end of the seven years he was a skilled cabinet maker, Citizen and Freeman of the Goldsmith's Company of the City of London and thus well equipped to set up his own business. This he did in 1834, as William Parker, Master Cabinet Maker, at 5 Queen Street, Finsbury.

He then had to establish connections and build up a clientele. There is no known evidence of his furniture or his customers, but he soon came to be considered one of the best cabinet makers in the area. Of his original premises there is also no trace, as Queen Street disappeared in the London Blitz of 1940 and post-war development. William's business lasted longer, finally becoming A. J. Parker of Camomile Street in the 1950s.

In 1838 William married Esther Greenhill (born in 1815) who came from a remarkable landed family from the Kings Langley district. After marriage, believed to have been in Harrow, the coupled lived comfortably at 5 Queens Street until 1860. Their first son, Edward, was born in 1839. Then came Henry in 1842, and in 1845, Frederick, who eventually founded the family firm upon which the present Parker Knoll concern is based. Walter Parker, born in 1846, also became an upholsterer. Esther Parker bore eight children, all boys except Mary Anne, who died aged 23. The last two children, William, born in 1853, and Thomas, born in 1856, unfortunately only lived a few months.

William's business was expanding by 1860, along with his family, and this brought a move to a larger house in Bracklyn Street not far away. Again it had a factory, stables and a yard at the rear. A good stock of specialised timbers was kept, and all types of cabinet work and upholstery were made as well as chair frames for the trade. The labour force numbered about fifty, quite large for those days, including his own polishers and yard men.

As the young Parker boys grew up in Bracklyn Street, they were surrounded by and probably involved in the family business. Edward, Henry and Frederick must have been familiar with the factory behind their home and the skills and processes involved. Their father, no doubt, encouraged their interest but there is no record of the two eldest boys taking up outside apprenticeships. Frederick was apprenticed in 1862, his fee paid by a charity held by St Dunstans-in-the West. With the two older boys already in the business, it was perhaps a way of occuping Frederick elsewhere. His brother Walter also learnt the skills of the upholstery trade.

The two older boys, Edward and Henry, worked with their father, Henry eventually becoming responsible for design. They were both admitted to the Freedom of the City by patrimony in the Goldsmiths Company on 1 March 1865. Henry died in 1876 at the early age of 34.

Frederick's indenture of 1862 happily still exists, giving us a clear picture, not only of the terms under which he was bound, but also the extent to which conditions had changed in the last thirty six years since his father started. No longer were there stipulations regarding matrimony, gambling or taverns but instead, quite detailed specifications as to the hours of work and mealtimes, as well as payment to Frederick's father 'for and to the upkeep and maintenance outdoor of the said apprentice'. We do not know why Frederick was not apprenticed to a Freeman of the City. His father was himself a Freeman and was aware of the advantages. Three years after Frederick was indentured, his father applied for admission to the Goldsmiths' Company by patrimony for his two older brothers. He did not obtain admission for Frederick when he was twenty one in 1867, possibly because his apprenticeship was incomplete. In 1869, when Frederick did complete his servitude, he was not admitted. Perhaps he was too independent and more concerned to earn a living. There is no record in the City Freedom lists of any application.

Nonetheless, his father allowed him to take over the floor above the stables behind his factory and it was there that Frederick immediately started his own chairmaking business. He remained there for three years, until 1872, buying in his frames and selling chairs and settees. Like his father he worked hard and long. He was rewarded by steady expansion with a reputation for quality.

William Parker died in August 1879 aged 69, and is buried in Abney Park Cemetery, Stamford Hill. His son Edward then took over the business which continued for many years, final control passing to William's grandson A. H. Parker.

The transition from late Victorian market for which Frederick Parker made only the best cabinet and uphostereed furniture for the gentry, great country homes and public buildings, to today when Parker Knoll supply a wide spectrum of customers including the contract furnishing market, is the stuff of social history.

Over 45 years William Parker prospered and no doubt with contacts through the Goldsmiths' Company, built up a sound connection with large City banks and institutions. In those days it was the custom for City businessmen to have furniture made for their offices by City craftsmen. Parkers earned an enviable reputation in styles consistent with the imposing interiors required by international companies.

William had also brought his sons into his trade and business. Frederick independently achieved considerable success far into the twentieth century, maintaining the family tradition and founding a company which far exceeded his hopes and ambitions — a far cry indeed from William's early Chingford days.

1872. Marriage solemnized at the Parish Church in the Parish of Drypool in the County of York

No.	When Married.	Name and Surname.	Age.	Condition.	Rank or Profession.	Residence at the time of Marriage.	Father's Name and Surname.	Rank or Profession of Father.
109	Jan 8th 1872	Frederick Parker	27	Bachelor	Upholsterer	Hoxton	William Parker	Cabinet Maker
		Sarah Ann Gale	21	Spinster		Drypool	Henry Gale	Joiner

Married in the Parish Church according to the Rites and Ceremonies of the Established Church, by ________ or after Banns by me, J. [illegible] Vicar

This Marriage was solemnized between us, Frederick Parker, Sarah Ann Gale

in the Presence of us, Henry Gale, Jennie Seward

ABOVE: Frederick Parker's original sign, still displayed at Bellfield, High Wycombe and BELOW: his marriage certificate, 8 January 1872.

ABOVE: The family — back row left to right: Thomas Cornwell, Dora, Mary, Frederick George, Kate and Harry Gale; centre: William, Sara Ann (Gale), Frederick (Parker), Louise; below: Harold, Septimus, Hettie and Phillip Harvey. BELOW: The product — Chippendale style chairs with inverted fan backs, made by Frederick Parker & Sons, pictured at Cowley in 1904.

EARLY DAYS – 1869-1897

By 1871, Frederick Parker had established his own furniture business. The Bracklyn Street premises were getting cramped for the men and boys employed. Larger workshops, which also had a shop frontage, were found in Blomfield Street off London Wall, and production was transferred there that year. The original William Parker business continued in Bracklyn Street.

Frederick was 26 years old and one of his specialities was upholstery on board ship. While supervising installation of furniture in the cabins of a new liner in Hull he met his future wife, Sarah Anne Gale. Her father was the foreman shipwright at C. W. Earle's shipyard; during his visit Frederick lodged with the Gales. His courtship was something of a whirlwind affair, with a short engagement, particularly for Victorian times. The wedding took place on 18 January 1872 at St Andrews Church, Drypool, now part of Hull, and the newly-wed couple were soon back in London in their new home at 17, Almorah Road, off Downham Road, Islington. This was a quiet street of Regency houses. It was the first time that Frederick had lived away from his factory, although it was within walking distance — a sign of his improving prosperity. His first two children were born here, Mary on 16 January 1873, and Frederick George on 4 March 1874.

Furniture was supplied to most of the leading London retail companies, several of which also had their own factories. Prominent among these was John Maple & Co Ltd, Tottenham Court Road, set up in 1841 under the sign of the 'Hen and Chickens'. After a short partnership with a James Cook, on a Knightsbridge site which subsequently became Harrods, John Maple rebuilt his Tottenham Court Road stores as an emporium with large workshops in Tottenham Place. John Blundell Maple joined his father in 1861, and soon, as furniture warehousemen, they were supplying furnishings for everyone from Queen Victoria and the Czar of Russia to the more modest Victorian middle classes. In 1884 they offered 'ten thousand bedsteads in 600 styles for immediate delivery'. Their claim to 'the largest furniture establishment in the world' is easy to understand.

To meet the ever-increasing demand, Frederick Parker needed more space. In 1875 he bought a large house and additional factory premises at 16 Wenlock Street, between Shepherdess Walk and New North Road, and moved his wife and home back over the shop.

At the same time he took his brother, Walter, into partnership and traded as F. & W. Parker, an arrangement which continued for some years. Indicative of increasing prosperity and the fact that Frederick was becoming a man of some substance, is the purchase he made in 1879 of Welton Villa, St Annes Road, Tottenham. This substantial house on the rural fringe of northern London was one of a dozen built in a row. Each had nine rooms but no bathroom. Frederick caused quite a sensation by having one installed. This move represented a change in lifestyle for the Parker family. The Great Eastern Railway was built in 1840, terminating in Shoreditch. When Liverpool Street Station opened in 1875, offering cheap workman's tickets to the City, great building activity followed quickly, and commuter life began.

Frederick made his daily journey to work by train from either Seven Sisters or Stamford Hill Stations to Shoreditch, followed by a short walk to Wenlock Street. The London General Omnibus Company was established in 1855, and gradually increased its horse-drawn services outwards from the centre, but it is doubtful if by 1875 they had reached the far suburbs of Tottenham. The first motor-bus was licensed in 1897, but horse 'buses remained in use until 1910. The tramway system, horse-drawn at first, started in 1869, but it took ten years and more for the network to cover the whole Metropolis. Electric traction did not arrive until 1900.

As Frederick Parker's life-style improved, so did his family. His second son, Henry Gale Parker, was the first to be born in the new house, on 3 March 1876. He was quickly followed by five more brothers and five more sisters, at one or two year intervals. Of the boys, Frederick George (born 1874), Henry Gale, to be known all his life as Harry, (born 1876), William (born 1879) and Thomas Cornwell (born 1881) were destined to join their father's business and it is around them that the growth of the firm in the first half of the twentieth century took place. There is no record of their having to serve apprenticeships to other Masters. Such was the success of the business that the boys learnt their trade under their father's guidance.

The partnership with Walter Parker continued, and in 1880 another move took place. This time it was to Curtain Road, near Old Street, EC, the extensive workshops there having a basement used as the chair-makers shop, and a front shop window. Now management included a Scotsman called Robert Smith. Frederick was the 'outside man'; Walter looked after the upholstery output, while Smith attended to the accounts. The style of the firm was changed to Parker Smith and Parker. As there was no living accommodation at Curtain Road the family still lived at Tottenham.

The three-way partnership was not a success. In 1898 a disagreement developed when Walter Parker and Robert Smith refused to accept Frederick's eldest son, Frederick George, into the business, even as a fifteen-year old employee! The partnership was disolved. As Frederick George was enrolled in the City of London Volunteers, and had been spurned by the family business, he joined the regular army and served in the South African War. When he left the army in 1902 he joined his father's business, and later became Company Secretary until his death in 1942 at the age of 69.

After the breakup Frederick continued under his own name, and his brother Walter eventually took premises in Southgate Road, N. Both added in brackets under their business style 'late of Parker Smith and Parker'. The two businesses had no further connection. Frederick appears to have had some difficulty as a result of the separation as a lot of his money was locked up in the partnership. He had to seek external backing and managed to borrow £250 from George Gale, his father-in-law. His suppliers also helped by allowing him extended credit. Within two years the business was back on its feet.

Frederick was the one who had to find new premises and this no doubt added to his difficulties. Walter and his sons continued at Curtain Road and, although their 'Novelty Productions' including the Compacture folding cot, and the Duplex-Spring Easy Chair, were described with enthusiasm in the *Cabinet Maker* of October 1891, sales did not equal production, and in 1893 Walter Parker decided to emigrate to New Zealand with his family, to take up farming. He left his eldest son to do the best he could; he moved to 2 & 4 Rufus Street, Hoxton Square but, in a few years he too, sold up and joined the others in New Zealand.

Frederick Parker was by then (1889) aged 43, and had twenty years of business experience behind him. He also has his growing sons coming into their teenage years and could see that, with his trade connections and hard work, a prosperous firm could be built up again. In 1889 he established his workshops away from the Hoxton area, at West's Place, 1169a, Drummond Street, Hampstead Road.

Frederick was both a draughtsman and inventor. He took out several patents for adjustable box ottomans, a staple product of the firm as far back as 1880 when the first was reputedly made. One of these was 'Couches Patent 7086, F. Parker, for improvements in or relating to box ottoman couches and the like, and their fittings'. Dated 6 April 1893, this patent referred to an ingenious hinge which enabled the ottoman top to be raised from either side, the hinge engaging automatically on the side opposite to the one lifted. This product became known as the Ambidexter couch, which won a Gold Medal for Parkers at the 1884 Inventors' Exhibition at the Crystal Palace. However, when Frederick was informed that he was expected to pay for the medal, he politely declined. The retail price of these couches was about £4 2s 6d. Frederick would have been pleased, if not astonished, to know that the estimated price today for one of his ninety-year-old couches is between £750-£800.

The photographic records of some of the furniture made by Frederick Parker, the earliest from about 1880, have survived, and cover the ensuing years without break till 1940. Line drawings of all the 'Specials', that is the thousands of pieces made specially to order for clients in addition to the standard production range, are preserved as well. A copy of Frederick's first catalogue dates from 1889; it offers 'Improved Adjustable and Reversible Box Ottoman, Couches and Lounges. Adjustable and other Easy Chairs, with or without Cradle Springs'.

Although the records of the furniture made by Frederick Parker are extensive, they do not cover the period from 1869, when he started, until 1880. As it was not until 1871 that a satisfactory dry photographic plate was made by Maddox, it is quite likely that any earlier records would have been hand drawn, if they existed at all. The first box Kodak camera did not appear until 1888. Busy furniture makers were possibly unable to take advantage of this technology.

Thomas Cornwell Parker, who became affectionately known in the business as TCP, recalled that at the time his father moved into Drummond Street, the main business was upholstery and chair and couch frame-making, some for sale to other upholsterers. Any polishing was done by a visiting master polisher, who came when required, finding his own materials, and charging 1s for four legs. He often had to attend twice a day, as the work could not be completed in one sitting. Harry Parker also recalled some of the rates of pay and hours of work. His job was to pay the workers: a chairmaker or upholsterer cost 9d per hour, and a polisher, 8d.

The hours were long — 9½ hours a day plus 6½ hours on Saturdays, making 53½ hours a week. Holidays were unpaid, and there was often short time with no public assistance.

The newly sited factory quickly found customers, especially for the Box Ottomans, which had top quality horse hair stuffing and were mostly covered in Cretonnes. The costing book for 1900 shows that materials for such an Ottoman in customer's own cover cost £1 1s 6½d. The frame-making cost 4s 5d, sewing 1s 4d, and the finished job sold for about £2 15s each at factory prices. The first customers were those London stores to which delivery could be made with the minimum of difficulty: Maples, and Schoolbreds, just around the corner, with Army and Navy Stores, Marshall & Snellgrove, and Oetzmanns a little further afield. Delivery was by hand truck, hired at 2d per hour from Joseph May. Harry fetched the truck and, when it was loaded, two people had to accompany it, probably to take turns pushing. When a job was urgent and no truck was available, a workman was induced to hoist the ottoman on his back — they were fully 6ft long — and carry it into Maples, or Schoolbreds which was a bit further on. TCP recalls that he did this while on school holidays, before he joined the firm. For longer journeys a horse-drawn van was hired from the same source at the high rental of 1s 6d per hour.

By 1891 the quality of the Parker products again brought its own reward and steadily increasing demand meant another move. This caused many complications for it was not at all easy to find premises with the required layout and space. The first salesman had just been engaged, Mr A. J. Springett, whom TCP recalled as a wonderful character with energy and enterprise. Eventually, in 1892 the firm moved to 280 Euston Road, the front of which was occuplied by George Ell, a ladder-maker. Ell told Harry Parker about what happened when Maples were building their first shop, just across the stret. The ladder-maker could hardly believe his eyes when, due to faulty construction, the whole edifice suddenly collapsed into Euston Road.

The Parker property at Euston Road was rented from Schoolbreds, the famous house furnishers, whose premises fronted Grafton Way. The Parker boys thought their father's factory was not exactly desirable. There were two floors, the first used for chairmaking, timber store, and showroom, the floor above for upholstery. The top floor was reached by an external, vertical ladder, attached none too securely, Not only was this inconvenient, but it greatly increased fire danger. Any polishing work was still done by a master polisher who came when needed. The timber was selected and marked out at the factory, but had to be sent out to Hampstead Road to be cut. This cost 5s per hour and must have been a complication, but obviously there was neither space nor facility on the spot.

About then Harry Parker joined. He was not more than 16 and, so started at the bottom. The property included a number of stables behind the factory in which lived a number of unsavory characters. One of Harry's first jobs was to collect the rents and he went there in fear of his life.

Harry's younger brothers, who would eventually join him, were still at school, but were put to work as soon as they reached their teens. Both William and Thomas had clear recollections of the end of their schooldays. William was a singer and at the age of eight was a member of the choir at St John's Stamford Hill, where his brother, Frederick George, was head boy, William was paid 3d a week, which he gave to his mother. At Christmas he asked her if he could have some of it back to buy presents. The answer was a beating, his mother demanding to know where he thought his food and clothes came from. His contribution to the family well-being was to rise at 6 am 'to rake out the kitchen grate, light the fire, and cook father's breakfast of bacon and cocoa'. Although there was nothing accomplished about William's singing, when he was 10½ his father saw an advertisement for a choirboy with a strong voice, at the American church in Paris. Much to his surprise William got the job. His choir duties left little time for schooling and Will reckoned that his formal education finished when he went to France. Unfortunately, his voice broke after only eighteen months, a fact noted by the Choirmaster one Sunday evening. In Will's own words 'he packed me off on the train that night and I arrived at London Bridge Station with only 20 centimes in my pocket'. No-one came to meet him. After waiting for four hours he asked to see the Station Master, who felt so sorry for the boy that he took him all the way home in a four-wheeler. The fare came to 7s 6d. When he arrived he was met with scant sympathy: 'Better take this apron and go and see Mr Hill, the factory foreman'. Soon Will was picking horse hair for the upholsterers, and thus joined the family business.

Will was later reprieved by apprenticeship to Colbourne & Co, a large drapery business in London and Birmingham, where he gained an expert knowledge of fabrics. When his apprenticeship finished he brought his knowledge to Parkers, and was given the job of buying fabrics for upholstery, an important function not previously given special importance. Will soon got rid of the saddlebag (Turkey rug) and velvet business and the firm soon became widely known for the excellence of its fabrics. He also took over his father's job of calling on top London customers to help with their problems, which he continued until 1940.

Thomas Cornwell Parker (TCP) left school in 1894 when he was thirteen, and was just looking forward to his summer holidays when he 'had no sooner arrived home than my father said "Are you ready for work?". Well I can tell you that in those days there was only one answer and that was "Yes father". "Well, come up with me tomorrow morning", and that was how I got down to work! I had to be there first in the morning to open up the workshops, and stay to shut up at night'. His first pay was 1s per week, Saturdays included. 'I had in some way to augment this vast sum. We used to dine at a Cooks Shop in Hampstead Road, this was just around the corner, with the old fashioned benches back to back. I was given 7½d, for this repast, that was beef and potatoes and ½d, for bread. I did without the bread, saving 3d in a week'.

He frequently went to the City to match up patterns of fabrics and buy materials. 'It was a hell of a job and I hated it! Travel by 'bus helped. I used to walk to the bottom of Tottenham Court Road and take a 'bus to the City, the horse 'bus, the old knife board. I used to like to sit up with the driver for a 1d to the Bank. It used to take a long time and it was hard work.'

Harold Parker (born 1886) and his brother Phillip Harvey, (born 1889) did not join the family business, Harold first worked as a hardware salesman at Harrods, later setting up his own retail business in Eastbourne. He gave this up at the outbreak of war in 1914, and at 28 joined the Royal Flying Corps. As he was too old to fly, he went into the transport section as a driver, becoming a Flight Sergeant before being commissioned. After the War, he opened a garage across the road from the Cowley factory gates and looked after the firm's motor vehicles. When his father died in 1927, he was left a little money, and bought a small furniture business. At premises in Mile End Road, he started making Parker-Loom from woven papier-maché stiffened with wire, which he sold to restaurants and hotels. He eventually moved his factory to Weymouth, where he obtained the contract to furnish the Forté brothers' cafés.

Phillip became a tea-taster and eventually emigrated to Canada. In correspondence in 1978 when he was 83, Phillip recalled how his father 'came home one night saying that he had to go to Buckingham Palace to measure King Edward VII for a chair. He said they had not a comfortable chair that gave him rest. I can see him now, in his drawing study, preparing a sketch, which was eventually made up in cheap wood and finished, then sent to Windsor Castle for His Majesty to try. He was very pleased with it and ordered the chair to be made up for him. Dad kept the pattern chair for himself; if fitted him very well.' (Enquiries of the Lord Chamberlain's Office have unfortunately failed to identify any relevant chair at any Royal home today.)

The annual company accounts survive, hand-written in elegant copperplate, from the year 1893. Until the turn of the century, all creditors and debtors at year end were listed, highlighting the names of many famous suppliers and retail concerns, some still trading. The trading balance for 1893 was £507 8s 3d. By 1900 it had increased to £4,572, and continued to increase steadily each year until the outbreak of the First World War. In 1893 the value of plant and fixtures was £30, and by 1898 it had tripled to £100.

It is not widely known that Parkers Furniture were also antique dealers from the end of the last century until 1930. A ledger in the company archives records all the transactions between 1910 and 1929, giving details of the source of each purchase, the eventual buyer, and both purchase and resale prices. Every type of antique was handled, including china, porcelain, rugs, chandeliers and pictures, as well as furniture. The names of many famous personalities and dealers can be found both as buyers and sellers.

During his years in the trade Frederick had come to realise the importance of skilled design in chairs with both elegant and slender proportions, and robust construction. He was convinced that, in order to train his craftsmen to produce work of the highest quality, he needed to study, and show them, how chairs were made by master craftsmen in earlier years. The demand for high quality reproduction chairs in the best designs since the sixteenth century remained strong, and Frederick, a craftsman himself, resolved that his business would make only the highest quality reproductions.

Thus he purchased fine examples from the classic periods and many reproductions can be found in the company's photographic archives. Gradually these antique models began to form a collection, which spanned the late 17th century to the 1900s, and these now form the unique collection of some 350 antique chairs which the Company still treasures.

The market in the last quarter of the 19th century was much the same as today's, general styles in greater volume at lower prices, but also something better produced and bespoke to a customer's special requirements, at a much higher price. Frederick Parker developed his business to supply furniture for both the middle price and highest quality sectors. He earned a reputation for quality cabinet making and upholstery work which he never lost.

A portable photograph album of 1893, possibly carried by Mr Springett, the salesman, on his visits to London customers, gives a clear idea of the furniture made and sold by the firm then: Chesterfield settees, Box Ottomans covered in Crestonne at 55s each, alongside popular seven piece suites. These suites were available in various styles: 'in green silk at 7/9d per yard and with brass mounts' at £40 the set, or 'in silk tapestry', at £31; also winged and buttoned three piece suites on cabriole legs in tapestry at £14 15s 0d. A large and deep-seated club chair cost 90s. Anticipating today's reclining chairs by sixty years, was an easy chair covered in Morocco leather at £6. It had an adjustable back, operated by pulling on a tasselled cord at the front of the seat. A wide variety of other pieces was offered including stools, and a faithful reproduction of the James I settee at Knole, with ends adjustable on ratchets at £20 — altogether a first class selection. Compared with what else was available for the cheapest market, this was high quality and more expensive furniture, but it is a clear indication of Frederick's belief in making the best. By contrast, a firm called Clozenburg and Son, 19 Curtain Road, were in 1892 advertising seven piece suites in superior finish for £10. The competition from cheap imported furniture is indicated by an advertisement by The Austrian Bentwood Furniture Co, 85 Great Eastern Street EC, for 'No 58 suite in leather or Frieze Velvet, stuffed all hair, polished Walnut, Mahogany or Ebonised For £8-0-0'.

An album of Parker models sold by Liberty & Sons around that period shows some of the standard items in the Parker range but, in addition, some much more elaborate pieces, including many Chippendale-style side chairs and a fine reproduction inverted fan-back in Morocco, at £11 7s 6d, plus a finely carved riband back arm chair with the seat covered in silk for £7 17s 6d. This album is coverstamped 'Liberty Studio Regent Street London. NOT TO BE TAKEN FROM THE STUDIO'.

Suddenly, at the end of 1894, Schoolbreds told Frederick they were going to pull down the factory and he would have to go! He did not take them seriously and took no action. Then, arriving for business one morning, he saw to his amazement that the roof was being taken off. Something had to be done. Frederick got in touch with Hewitson, Milner and Thexton, Furnishers and House Agents in Tottenham Court Road, who had some workshops to let at 44a, Whitfield Street, which apparently were known locally as 'the flea pit'. The building had been used as a German Club — a place where waiters used to come for an evening's entertainment. Faced as they were with Hobson's Choice, the firm decided to move in, and took over the place together with a house which took in waiters as lodgers. Some slept in the beds during the day and others at night. It was too late to back out when Frederick discovered that the buildings were condemnded by the local authority, and due for demolition. A cheque for £250 to the estate agent sufficed to get the order withdrawn. The whole sorry episode smells of sharp practice as well as insufficient attention to detail by Frederick himself.

TCP recalled 'We moved in early in 1895; it really was a dreadful place to work in, rat-infested and lacking the space required. We had to rent a building in Charlotte Street to act as a store and showroom but this was exactly the same'. Despite all, orders continued to arrive, compounding the difficulties. Extra premises were taken in Ockenden Road, Islington for frame-making, but this was several miles away. On top of all this the firm ran into serious labour problems. The Amalgamated Union of Upholsterers was particularly militant, campaigning for higher wages. They came into strong conflict with Frederick because he refused to increase the hourly rate from 9d to 1s, an increase of 33%! Harry Parker recalled the conversation his father had with the union secretary, Alexander Gossip. 'You really do want to shut us up don't you Mr Gossip?' asked Frederick. 'Yes we do!' was the reply. And so more than 50 employees went on strike in 1896 and this was the first of many.

Frederick was nothing if not resourceful. During the spate of strikes he advertised in the *Morning Post* for young men wishing to train as upholsterers. There were scores of replies and he engaged sufficient men to be back in business again after only a few weeks. Frederick always acknowledged the loyalty and support in these troubled times of his foreman, William Hill, who had been with the firm many years. But the union troubles continued. It was this that made Frederick consider moving the whole business into the country.

By hard work, attention to detail and quality products, he had developed a business recognised in the trade as one of the best. He had built up a good reputation with the retail trade, both for designs and trading practice. When his father started in the East End trade was just beginning to expand for, until Victorian times and the effects of the Industrial Revolution, most furniture was made by trained craft workers and only the wealthy could afford to buy. Journalist Henry Mayhew noted in 1850 that some 200 miles of new streets had been added to London since 1839 and over 66,000 new houses built. He pointed out that these homes 'must have required new furniture'.

At the same time there was an influx of immigrants from Eastern Europe, many of them Jews and, many with furniture-making skills. They settled in large numbers in the East End, while the London Docks, virtually on the doorstep, and the network of canals and waterways radiating from them, enabled imported timbers to be delivered easily by barge to local saw-mills. This all contributed to the rapid increase in workshops producing furniture, many in attics and alleyways. Those with the skill and energy set up on their own and even employed a few men. Little machinery was used, so the costs of opening a workshop were limited to finding a small rented space, a few tools and the materials. The Jews were known as 'greeners' and the large number of boys paid next to nothing, were 'learners'.

These trends ran counter to traditional methods of manufacture, increasingly so if the new markets were to be satisfied. Competition was cut-throat and often the large middlemen, wholesalers and retailers, would dictate prices, causing wage rates to be 'sweated' to get the job. All this meant much cheaper furniture for the working classes than had previously been possible and in greatly increased quantities. Even so, they wre often unable to afford it on their own low wages, until the hire purchase system was introduced in the last decade of the century. At first it was considered 'low class' to buy this way, and furniture was delivered in unpainted vans to prevent the neighbours from knowing.

Inevitably the East End furniture trade earnt a reputation for poor quality. For the first twenty years that Frederick Parker worked in the East End he was surrounded by often shoddy output of the 'garretmasters' and this stiffened his resolve to do better, for both he and his father had served their apprenticeships and were skilled craftsmen.

In those days the retail furnisher or middleman was very much the arbiter of the quality of merchandise he would sell and to whom. It was unthinkable that any manufacturer would sell direct to the public, (yet many did) and retailers liked to foster the idea that their furniture was made for or by them. Some applied their own names and continued to do so until quite recently.

The *Cabinet Maker* of July 1927, reporting an address given to the National Association of Retail House Furnishers by President C. A. Richter, described the retailer's function thus: 'He should be the furnishing artist par excellence. Unless he makes some attempt to be this, he does not justify his existence. He should do something more than rent a few thousand feet of showroom space and fill it with a miscellaneous assortment of articles culled from manufacturers, leaving his salesmen to sell what it is easiest to sell, or to his customers to select what their uninstructed fancies suggest. Like the tailor, the couturier and the maitre-d'hotel, he must sell something more than "goods". He must make himself known as an artist whose rare natural endowments and long years of careful training have fitted him for exceptional service; whose taste, judgement and experience are worth paying for.'

The best class of retailer at the end of the last century required staff who themselves had undergone apprenticeships in their own specialist field, be it cabinets, upholstery, carpets or soft furnishing. As a result, customers were assured of expert advice on all furnishing problems and the retailer built up a satisfied and loyal clientele. In those days it was also no problem to translate a customer's own ideas into practice by having a special piece made up. Sketches and estimates were submitted and to be able to do this a manufacturer had to have adequate studio resources. Not many did. A large quantity of Parker's studio books still exist, showing the special work done over 50 years. They are beautifully hand-drawn in indian ink and cover every conceivable style and type of furniture.

The second half of the nineteenth century saw sweeping change. In 1872 UK foreign trade was more than that of France, Germany and Italy put together and nearly four times that of the USA. There were five dollars to the pound sterling and income tax was down to 4d in the pound, which itself comprised 240 penny units.

The more prosperous sections of the working class had begun to share in the prosperity which urbanisation had brought. From the middle classes a new intermediate group — the lower middle class — emerged to service the demands for white collar workers in the rapidly expanding bureaucracies of manufacturing industry and trading sectors. The lifestyle of the aristocracy and gentry was not greatly affected. They continued to enjoy political power nationally, in the Empire and in local Government. After the losses caused by agricultural depression, they reinvested in urban lands which created new wealth as new suburbs were built around the still expanding towns. In the 1870s urbanisation itensified and by 1900 only one fifth of the population of England and Wales lived in rural areas. The population of London had grown from 2.3 million in 1851 to 4.5 millikon in 1911, 7.3 million including the suburbs. Against this background the Parker furniture interests developed. Frederick had a choice of markets; his inclination and interests led him, in the main, toward top quality hand-crafted cabinet work and upholstery for the wealthiest customers. Their tastes ran mainly to traditional styles derived from the great designer craftsmen of the previous century and it was in this field that the Parker craftsmen capably produced their best work. Yet, at the same time, a less expensive range of simpler furniture was produced, and catalogued in 1902 under the title of 'Inexpensive Furniture'.

FREDK. PARKER,

(Late of the firm of PARKER, SMITH & PARKER.)

UPHOLSTERER & FRAME MAKER,

West's Place, Drummond St.,

HAMPSTEAD ROAD.

Specialities:

BOX OTTOMAN COUCHES (Lids open both sides, with or without Adjustable Scrolls).

ADJUSTABLE LOUNGES. ADJUSTABLE EASY CHAIRS, &c.

ABOVE: Box ottoman couches with adjustable scrolls were advertised by Fredk. Parker in the *Upholstery & Decorating Journal* in June 1892. LEFT: Grandfather wing easy chair in tapestry, 1894; cost £3 10s and RIGHT: adjustable easy chair in saddlebag and velvet; the tasselled cord on the seat operated the reclining action.

ABOVE: Three piece suite including a lady's and gentleman's seat, all in striped linen plush; the chairs sold for £4 10s, the settee £6 10s — in 1894. LEFT: Based on a Chippendale design of 1735, this Morocco leather-covered chair sold for £9 in 1904. RIGHT: This carver was finished in Morocco leather, brass studded and sold for £6 6s 0d.

Industria Ditat

The motto on High Wycombe's crest seems to typify the attitude of Frederick Parker toward his business. A long established centre of chair-making, Wycombe, though rural, offered an appropriate environment.

Although only thirty miles from London, Wycombe compared favourably with the congestion and bustle of Tottenham Court Road. It had been connected with the manufacture of chairs since the last quarter of the eighteenth century. Set among the Chiltern Hills on which the beech tree grew so abundantly that it was known as the Buckinghamshire Weed, it could, by the middle of the nineteenth century, claim undisputed leadership in its field. In the eighteenth century stage coaches from London to Oxford changed horses at the Red Lion and Falcon Inns. The staple product was the 'Windsor' chair in its many forms, made entirely from local beech; there was also plenty of elm in the valleys and ash for bending — materials idealy suited to the making of simple chairs for kitchens and servants' quarters, as well as for the working population. In the 1750s the town had a population of 2,000, and an area of 126 acres.

The chalk hills have always been hard to work and so it is likely that farmworkers found winter work under shelter, making stools and benches, initially for use in local farms and inns. This eventually led to manufacture on a larger scale, with different groups specialising in a particular type of article. Thus, what started as a cottage industry gradually evolved into full-scale manufacture. The Industrial Revolution opened up a commercial market for Wycombe-made chairs and this increasd with urban growth.

Initially, various components were supplied for assembly by specialists, working in villages and woods. Many were known locally as Bodgers, often living in the woods alongside their crude workshops. Parker Knoll, in the 1960s, made a film based on the life of Sam Rockall, a Bodger all his life until he retired at 80. The film shows how Bodgers produced sets of turned chair legs and stretchers for the base of a Windsor chair. These were turned on a rudimentary pole-lathe erected in the woods and the sets of parts were then taken into Wycombe by horse and cart to be sold to the Chair Masters for assembly in their factories. (The film won an Industrial Film Society Diploma and a copy is held in the National Film Archive.)

By 1890 there were over fifty factories producing wood-seated and Windsor-style chairs as well as rush-seated and caned varieties. They were turning out 4,700 chairs a day at an average price of 3s 4d. One famous order was that for the Moody and Sankey Revivalist meeting at the Crystal Palace in 1875, when 19,200 chairs were delivered in a matter of days. Wycombe chairs were increasingly exported, but little upholstery was made there until after 1850; indeed, *Kelly's Buckinghamshire Directory* of 1903 only listed eight firms making upholstery, including Parkers. A small amount of cabinet work was also made by the mid-nineteenth century.

To reach the market, early salesmen loaded horse-drawn drays with chairs stacked ten feet high and toured the towns of the Midlands and West, calling on drapery shops and ironmongers until all their chairs were sold. A new method was evolved in 1836 by Benjamin North — a Wycombe chairmaker. He was the first to have a picture album showing his wares.

These albums, which were hand-drawn in Indian ink and watercoloured, still survive in the local museum. They were taken by his agents to potential customers, who placed their orders for subsequent delivery from the factory. This was helped by the growth of the railway.

Wages were low, but nonetheless workmen often took Monday off work — Saint Monday — and spent all day at the pubs, drinking and playing dominoes. They opened from 6am till 11pm, and beer was 2d per pint.

A Chairmakers Protection Society had been formed in 1855 with the motto 'We stand for the right to work'. Then in 1857 the Vicar called a meeting of chair manufacturers in the Guildhall 'to consider what could be done to stop the growing source of depravity from the constant association of young persons in our factories'. This was solved by separating the sexes and appointing 'respectable Christian men to supervise the youngsters'. The end of the working day was staggered by half an hour between men and women.

The Parkers had contacts with several Wycombe chairmakers, one of whom was Alan Janes, who had supplied the firm with chair frames for some years. The two men met in Maples one day in 1897. Janes suggested Parkers move down to Wycombe and mentioned a property in Frogmoor, available and possibly suitable. Frederick Parker was reputed to take risks for business and family which always paid off. The move from London was probably one of the biggest but, after deliberation with his sons and an inspection of the property, he decided to go ahead. Number 9 Frogmoor Gardens consisted of some sheds and a row of cottages, with a house fronting onto the street which was to become the new Parker home for the immediate future. In the early part of the century the site had been a farm, although one of the sheds had been used by John Hunt, a coachbuilder. The purchase was made and the move from London took place in January 1898. Vacant possession of the cottages was obtained by paying a year's rent for the occupants to move elsewhere. This is the site which the sales and administration headquarters of the company still occupies today. Frogmoor Gardens lived up to its name with a garden and several trees enclosed by a hedge, whereas today the central island is paved, with new trees, a fountain and statue.

TCP recalled that Dickson, an upholsterer, and he were the first to arrive with a vanload of equipment. It used to be said that it was easy to set up as a furniture maker as so little equipment was required. Plant, fixtures and stock of the Parker business were valued at £2,931 in 1897, a sizeable sum, so the move must have taken several days with horse-drawn transport. Frederick did his best to encourage his London workers to move to the country and a few did come on trial with their families. It seems, however, that the wives could not abide the rural atmosphere and the majority returned to London within a few weeks. Mrs Kit Morris, Frederick's daughter, described the Wycombe of 1900: women carried loads suspended on yokes over their shoulders and walked the unpaved High Street. By day cows wandered through the town, forming a procession to wend their way home along the High Street in the evening. There was no street lighting. The area of the Borough was less than 150 acres and the population was about 5,000.

The firm recruited from local sources under the supervision and training of foreman Mr Hill, until his death in 1904. At that time it was normal for all hired hands to bring their own light to work by and men taken on at Frogmoor brought their own candles by whose slight light they produced exquisite carving and inlay.

Although wages were slightly below London rates, there was an adequate supply of sufficiently skilled labour. The new workforce was trained in Parker's methods, under the supervision of the foremen moved from London. The 'experts' in Wycombe, however, were soon shaking their heads and saying that the newly arrived Parker organisation would be unable to get upholstery made. In their view, only the Wycombe staple — wood-seated chairs — could be made satisfactorily. Despite that, Frederick, then aged 53, his young sons and Mr Hill were soon producing high quality upholstery — the first in the area to do so.

ABOVE: The family home at Frogmoor, in 1908, with Cubbage Bros stores and, a sign of things to pass many years later, H. Locke & Co — not furnishers, but restaurateurs. BELOW: A six foot antiqued and distressed 'old oak' table with baluster, made in 1910; price £15 10s.

LEFT: Lacquered and decorated Chinese style display cabinet, 3 ft 6 ins and £30 new in 1912; in the white for £18s 10s, RIGHT: gilded carver, and BELOW: reproduction 5 ft 6 ins oak settle with turned legs and carved panels; 1911, £10.

ABOVE: Chaise longue, stuffed all hair, in calico at £5. BELOW: Mahogany tilt-top circular table, 1911 — £17 10s.

LEFT: Carved walnut side chair, calico covered for £7 17s 6d and RIGHT: carved mahogany grandfather chair, in calico for £5 10s, part of a batch made for George V's party in the Royal box at the International Horse Show of 1911. CENTRE: This lacquered, decorated cabinet had ten drawers and a gilt stand and cost £66 in 1911. BELOW: A mahogany carved tub chair in Morocco leather for £7 5s — still used by John Arnold.

LEFT: Porter's hall chair, with a carved mahogany frame — £12 10s and RIGHT, BELOW: Mahogany adjustable chair with pullout footrest, stuffed with best hair and down, and covered in Morroco leather; the cord and tassel worked the action. This forerunner of the modern recliner cost £15 17s.

Parker's canalside factory at Cowley Peachey, Middlesex, from 1906-1936.

On the Move – 1899-1909

Soon, extra space was needed, The Frogmoor sheds were replaced early in 1900 by the present three storey buildings, around the central yard in which timber was seasoned. New machinery, including burnishers and planers of the latest design, as well as power-driven lathes and bandsaws, were installed – the first machinery used by the firm. When A. E. Barnes went to work at Frogmoor in 1900 he saw a gas engine, recently installed near the entrance to drive the machinery. Before that, there was only a treadle-lathe, operated by an old man named Bicknell, who lived in the present cottage at 23 Frogmoor. Planks, when marked out, were sent to be cut at a sawmill behind the Technical School, at the top of Frogmoor, recently restored as offices and once the Town Swimming baths as well as the Wycombe Repertory Theatre.

Kit Morris, when single, worked at Bulls Drapery and China Stores in Southsea. When Frederick moved his business to Wycombe she gave up her job and moved to Wycombe 'to work in the office and keep house for Harry and Tom – two hungry men'. She was the first woman employed in the Parker office and was mainly concerned with accounts. It was her duty to pay the men on Saturdays – the wages bill was about £100 a week. Frederick once forgot to give her the cheque on Friday evening and she worried until he arrived at the office just before the bank opened on Saturday. All he said was 'They would have given you the money anyway', for it was one of Frederick's principles never to be in debt.

Her move to Wycombe was also to bring romance and she stayed only three years from 1899 to 1902, for then she married William Morris, a farmer at Handy Cross Farm, and lived there until 1929. Soon after the firm moved to Wycombe it obtained an order for eighty Chippendale-style chairs for the dining salon on the *Ophir*. This converted P&O liner was impressed into the Navy as the Royal Yacht in 1902, to enable the Prince and Princess of Wales to sail round the world visiting the Dominions, the first-ever Royal tour. The covering for the chairs was of such fine silk (deep cream with pink rosebuds) that it could not be sewn on the standard factory machine. Mrs Morris took the work home to sew the covers on her own sewing machine and kept a few inches of the material for some years as a memento. A little later she machined covers for chairs supplied to the first Royal Yacht, the *Victoria and Albert*.

By 1900, new factory premises were being built at Frogmoor. Until this time Frederick had run the business single-handed with the help of his workforce and a growing contribution from his young sons. Frederick was now aged 57, and his sons were of an age – Harry 24, Will 21, and Tom 19 – to make a fuller contribution. That contribution was paramount in maintaining and increasing the reputation of both the firm and its products.

In 1901 a private limited company was formed with the title Frederick Parker and Sons Ltd, and capital of £10,000 in £1 shares, of which £7,077 were issued. Each of the three sons received a portion – Harry 25; William 22; Thomas 20, and they all became directors. At the same time Kit Morris received some shares together with the two foremen, Messrs Hill and Vincent, and the salesman, Mr Springett. Frederick as Chairman held the remainder and controlling interest. Limited companies at the time were regarded with a certain amount of suspicion. One supplier of long-standing wrote to Frederick congratulating him on the change, but stating that he felt unable to give such extended credit as in the past. Frederick decided to buy elsewhere 'not wishing to cause them any anxiety'. When the limited company was formed all existing accounts were given new account numbers. This appears to have been done by numbering all debtor accounts at that time from zero, leaving all names not then linked to be added as new transactions occurred. By 1940 account numbers issued were 6500.

Many of the largest Wycombe manufacturers were opening showrooms in London: William Birch had showrooms at 370 Euston Road and B. North and Sons Ltd were at 42 City Road. After the move to Wycombe Parkers also felt the loss of contact with the capital market. In 1903 they bought the leasehold of a new four-storey building at 20 Newman Street off the eastern end of Oxford Street, for £11,316 19s 10d. This fine building provided the company with ample space. Initially they only required one floor, and occupied the basement. The upper floors were let to Bourne and Hollingsworth, the large store in Berners Street. It was usual for all large London stores to recruit shop staff, mostly female, from outside London, and to do so they provided accommodation; the upper floors at Newman Steet began life as dormitories. This arrangement continued until 1908, when the lease was transferred to Mary Clark of the Hotel York in Berners Street. This building, on the corner of Eastcastle Street, is now the Nurses' Home for the Middlesex Hospital.

The Newman Street and Berners Street areas had long been associated with London's artistic community, and indeed, the adjacent Tottenham Court Road and its adjoining streets, throughout the eighteenth and nineteenth centuries, were known as the Latin Quarter. Newman Street's northern end gave onto open country in 1775; John Bacon RA the prolific sculptor, lived at number 17 from 1777, and filled Westminster Abbey with his immense classical monuments. Thomas Stothard RA lived in Newman Street for forty years from 1794. While there, he is said to have produced between five and ten thousand pictures and book illustrations. James Heath, the well-known engraver, lived at number 42 and executed his version of Gilbert Stuart's full length portrait of George Washington. The actor Charles Kemble lived in the street in 1809, and the famous art school, Heatherleys, was long domiciled at number 79. It was still there when Parkers arrived at number 20.

William Parker, still at Colbournes of Birmingham, moved to London to take charge of the new showrooms and his brother Frederick George also joined the company, after his service in the Boer War, as Company Secretary at Wycombe.

Moving to Wycombe brought a problem of delivery to customers. Many of the most important were in London. The railway from London to Oxford had missed Wycombe altogether and it was 1847 before a single spur line from Taplow was connected to the town. Although this did help deliveries and imported timbers, it was not sufficient. The direct rail link to London was not opened for 59 years, in 1906, and in the meantime Wycombe makers found it easier to make door-to-door deliveries by road to London.

This resulted in long convoys of horse-drawn vehicles leaving Wycombe several times a week, and often on Sundays, to deliver to their West End customers. Various firms' vans would join a convoy, which would leave late in the evening to plod the thirty odd miles to London. The journey was too much for both men and horses to do in twenty-four hours, so two nights and part of two days were occupied by the round trip. Spare horses were kept at the bottom of White Hill to help pull the heaviest waggons. The official crew was one man to a wagon and the drivers arranged among themselves that only the man on the front wagon stayed awake, while the rest curled up with their loads to sleep. The convoy would halt every few hours to rest, water the horses and change pilots. It generally worked well unless the pilot fell asleep. Even so, the horses had a good sense of the route and seldom took a wrong turning. It is said that they would put into the Coach and Horses at Gerrards Cross automatically. In the early days, Parker wagons always broke their journey at Frederick's home at Hayes End, where there were four acres of land on which they could graze. Parkers used their own vans and hired horses from Worley's Stable near Frogmoor. The 1902 balance sheet shows the value of 'Vans and Harness' at £100. This item is entered every year at slowly declining value until 1924. Fred Collins frequently drove in this wagon train and later was the driver of the company's first motor van in 1912.

It was said that, when a new horse was being used on the London run, the driver had to hold its head all the way from Wycombe. When they arrived they had the misfortune to meet one of the new electric tramcars. It is not difficult to imagine the effect this had on a nervous horse. This long journey often had to be made in winter with snow on the ground and all the attendant hazards of horses falling on ice or being unable to move. The firm of William Keen introduced the first mechanical transport in 1904. This 'Motor Trolley' was in fact a steam wagon, which also pulled a trailer. On its first trip it took 700 chairs, leaving Wycombe at nine in the evening and arriving in London at three the next morning. The chairs were delivered early and the vehicle was back in Wycombe fourteen hours after it set out.

The Parker business settled down rapidly in Wycombe and grew at a steady pace. The annual accounts show that turnover increased from £13,095 in 1902, to £46,963 in 1912, and profits increased year by year, from £3,233 to £15,741. Retail price was a matter for the retailer but was generally 50% more than the factory price.

Frederick lived at the house in Frogmoor until in 1904 he moved to Hayes, which was conveniently between Wycombe and London. In 1908 he purchased a substantial house with several acres of land at Cowley Peachey, near Uxbridge. Cowley Peachey House, or Clock House as it was known in the family, with eight or nine bedrooms, was spacious, rambling and ivy-clad. The elegant gardens had tennis lawns and conservatories as well as plenty of extra undeveloped land. This sloped down to the Grand Junction Canal which joined the Thames at Brentford. Harry continued to live at the house at 9 Frogmoor Gardens in Wycombe, where he was always on hand for the factory. He also purchased some land at Temple End, on the outskirts of the town. Harry had taken on full responsibility for running the Wycombe factories and TCP, whose interest was on the sales side, decided that he could function best if he based himself at Newman Street. He joined his brother William there, where they assumed joint responsibility for Sales. TCP had Springfield, a new house, built in the grounds of Clock House at Cowley.

It was in this way that the three Parker brothers each assumed responsibility for an aspect of the business, setting the pattern of operations until 1941. This *modus operandi* worked well.

William is remembered as the most generous, kindest and jolliest of the Parker brothers. He made daily visits to London customers, dealing with estimates and quotations as well as putting suggestions forward as to which models would best suit a particular job. TCP stayed at the Newman Street showrooms where he was available to buyers and visitors. As a salesman acting in his customers' best interests, William would often promise delivery without consulting the factory and many an argument ensued. All who knew him remember his personality, wide knowledge and experience, particularly on fabrics, which endeared him to London buyers. When he was explaining something, his discourse would be interspersed with 'J'un-osee?' — which left his listener puzzled, feeling he had not properly grasped the point.

Early in the century it was not normal for upholsterers to carry stocks of fabrics beyond their immediate needs. Parkers were unique for they thought textiles were as much a part of their product as timber. They went to immense pains to acquire old types of covering materials which were kept in store until the opportunity came to use them. Harry Parker always liked to experiment. In 1908 he bought some special skins from Pickled Herring Wharf in London and had them soaked in a tank, so that they took on the appearance of moleskin.

In 1907, Harry had heard of a young freelance designer named Ercolani, who was living and working in London. He sought him out and asked the young man to pay him a visit. The meeting is recorded in Lucien R. Ercolani's autobiography *A Furniture Maker* in which he recalls three years at Parkers: He though the workshops 'were dark, untidy, and disorderly but was extremely pleased to see the variety and supreme quality of the work. These men were making what could be well described as the "jewellery of furniture".'

One does not normally think of furniture-making firms having initiation ceremonies for new recruits, but the young Ercolani discovered that he was expected to prove himself by racing one of the best runners among the men along Birdcage Walk. Whoever came last would buy a bottle of port for 10½d from a shop in Frogmoor and drink it on the spot! Unfortunately, he does not tell us who bought or drank the bottle!

Mr Ercolani gives an insight into Frederick's character when he recalls the daily ritual at half past ten, when Frederick and he would go around the workshops and closely inspect everyone's work:

'He would listen to what his men had to say; and I noticed that he understood them and that they had confidence in him . . . Behind me I knew there was the critical eye of a man who is certain of himself. Beyond that, life was very free . . . Always from the simplest article upwards, our work had to be in its best form, one might say in the grand manner. I do not mean to say that Mr Parker was always right; he was so impressive that everyone felt satisfied with his judgment.'

Mr Ercolani also remembers having access to a large library of books on interior decoration as well as the design books of the Masters such as Chippendale, Hepplewhite and Sheraton. This library is still carefully preserved by the Company. Later Harry Parker followed with interest his young designer's success, as he started his own business, itself based on the same tenets of quality. It was Frederick who suggested that Ercolani should answer an advertisement for a lecturer in design at the Technical Institute and it was this that eventually led to the opportunity to found his own business.

Mr A. E. Barnes joined the firm at Frogmoor as foreman woodcarver in 1900. His father, also a woodcarver, knew the Parkers in London and considered them 'very fine people and cultured folk'. Frederick Parker was 'a great man for truth and tradition'. This is borne out by other long-serving employees. One said 'he was a very kind old gent with very high standards; you always got a pleasant word but he was a stickler for accuracy'.

According to Mr Barnes, there was 'nothing of the parish pump' about the Parkers. They were not wedded to a particular style and would 'go in for anything'. When he joined the firm he earned the same wage as his men although he was foreman. 'I did the job for a price' he said 'and paid the men what I thought was right'. This method was quite common practice then — an early form of sub-contracting.

Mr Barnes also recalled the occasion when Parkers received an order from Scotland for a set of twelve small and two arm chairs with elaborately carved frames. 'Frederick came down from London for this important job and personally chose the log to be cut; it was Cuban Mahogany. This was so beautifully figured — almost like a fiddle back — that it would have been more suited to veneer. The task of carving it was a difficult one because of the "rowey" [rippling in the grain]. One had to be careful that little pieces did not come out of the carving.'

Between 1907 and 1909 turnover once again increased by 25%, demanding urgent increases in production. Frederick had a large amount of land next to his home at Cowley Peachey and some of this was already on lease to the Company. The contract to build a new factory there was made with Try & Hancock on 2 July 1907. The land was purchased outright on 24 June 1909 together with the factory property at Frogmoor, which had hitherto been leased. All debts on the two properties were discharged before financing the new buildings at Cowley. These were built and fully operating by 1909.

By then turnover had increased by a dramatic 50% and the firm was working at maximum capacity. Harry Parker recalled that one reason for going to Cowley was the problem of getting best quality upholsterers and cabinet makers in Wycombe. Because of the wide diversity of the quality of furniture made in Wycombe, a system had grown up of grading pay according to the type of work. As a result there were differing payrates for best framers as opposed to ordinary framers, best cabinet makers and best chairmakers as opposed to those less skilled. This was favoured by the higher paid, but strongly opposed by the Union.

Frederick also suffered from the old problem of having successful designs copied by others, 'having the guts knocked out of it and sold at a lower price' as he put it. He saw the Cowley factory as offering some protection from Wycombe copyists. But labour problems arose at Cowley too. Nearby was the HMV factory, making gramophone cabinets and, when this was working at full pressure, Parker's men were tempted away, presumably because HMV found it difficult to recruit skilled cabinet makers, and offered higher rates. They often came back to Parkers, reflecting the ebb and flow of work at HMV and continuity at Parkers. Upholsterers were not tempted to move until later, when the film studios opened at Denham and the same situation arose. Initially about 25 men were employed at Cowley, which had an output of twenty or so chairs a week.

One advantage of the Cowley site was the adjoining Grand Junction Canal. This provided a direct route to the factory from the London Docks and greatly facilitated delivery of timber, mostly mahogany, with the minimum of handling. This was an important consideration since few motor vehicles existed, let alone suitable roads. The factory site enclosed a dock at which the barges unloaded. The Parker children asked the friendly bargees to let them take the tow horses under the canal bridge next to the Paddington Packetboat. Both this and the dock and bridge are still there, but sadly — and ironically — the Cowley factory site is now covered by an MFI warehouse.

Parker furniture was becoming known to the shipping companies and was also appreciated in Europe and North America. Germany, Belgium and France were particularly good markets, especially for top quality upholstery. This success in overseas markets gave Tom and Harry the idea of opening a factory and showroom in Berlin. Frederick would have nothing to do with it. In his view it was a bad thing to take the actual manufacture of Parker products outside the United Kingdom. Nothing daunted, Harry went to Berlin in 1912, and opened a business at 183 Orenstrasse. The original idea was to buy in the frames, partially upholstered, from Wycombe — thus avoiding import duty — and finish them in Berlin, Al Brinkman, a skilled upholsterer and son of a Wycombe policeman, was sent over to work with Wilhelm Knowers, a German in the textile trade who acted as salesman.

Everything went well until war broke out in 1914. Brinkman was at once interned and the landlord received permission to take what he wanted from the stock in lieu of rent. Knowers kept an accurate record of what occurred and sent a final statement after the war showing the disposition of all the goods involved and a DM.2 balance due to Frederick Parker & Sons. This was finally cleared in 1922 when £247 15s 4d was repaid.

Had the War not intervened, the Berlin operation might have done well. There was a strong demand for both best quality cabinet work and upholstery, possibly because of its 'English' styling. Many of the Parker chairs sold on the Continent were faithful reproductions of 18th century designs, and the collection of original period English chairs was put to good use, enabling Parkers to appeal to the best continental furnishing houses.

In Wycombe things continued to progress. Steady growth and the need for better transport to connect the factories at Wycombe and Cowley with Newman Street led in 1912 to the company's first motor van, shown in the accounts at £230.

HIGH WYCOMBE & DISTRICT
FURNITURE MANUFACTURERS' FEDERATION.

The under-named members of the above Federation in General Meeting held the 28th day of November, 1913, unanimously resolved that in face of the facts

(1) That the Union men rejected the Employers' proposal that with a view of assisting an amicable settlement the men on strike should return to work last Tuesday;

(2) That the strikes continue;

(3) That the Union men rejected the Employers' principle of grading which through their delegates they were informed was a vital principle with the Employers;

(4) That the Union men have rejected the Employers' offer of a Standard Wage as per Schedule sent them;

(5) That the alternative proposals of the Union are impossible for acceptance by the Employers,

negotiations by the Employers be no longer continued, but that the Members terminate at once the engagement of all Members of the Union in their employ.

Messrs. W. Birch, Ltd.
,, Wm. Bartlett and Son
,, Birch and Cox
,, Caffal and Keen
,, J. Cox and Son, Ltd.
,, Castle Bros.
Mr. Walter E. Ellis
Messrs. James Elliott and Sons
,, Thomas Glenister, Ltd.
,, H. Goodearl and Sons
,, Goodearl Bros., Ltd.
Mr. John Gomm
,, C. Gibbons
,, William James Goodchild
Messrs. R. Howland and Sons, Ltd.
,, Hill and Butler
Messrs. R. J. Howland and Co., Ltd.
,, Joynson and Co.
,, Joynson, Holland and Co.
Mr. W. Keen
Messrs. G. H. and S. Keen
,, V. M. Millbourne and Son
,, Nicholls and Janes
,, B. North and Sons
,, F. Parker and Sons, Ltd.
,, Randall Bros. and Co., Ltd.
,, W. Skull and Son, Ltd.
,, Stratford and Brion
Mr. Cecil Smith
,, R. Tyzack
,, C. P. Vine

E. Gomm

In accordance with the above resolution ALL UNION MEN employed upon this Firm are hereby given ONE HOUR'S NOTICE to terminate their respective engagements

DATED this ~~2~~4th day of ~~November~~ December, 1913.

(Signed)

All pieceworkers may finish their work on contract.

The industry takes a serious stand against the unions on 4 December 1913.

In Dispute – 1913-1914

The decade after the formation of the Company in 1902 was something of a heyday, broadening all aspects of the Company's activities. Further impetus was given to the cabinet side when Walter Ferry joined the company in 1913. He was a skilled designer and a talented artist. Ferry lived in Whitstable and had an office in Newman Street where he trained as a boy with Christopher Gill, who was a freelance designer for furniture and interior decoration. When Ferry was eighteen, Gill decided to give up his business and told him he could continue it if he wished. He decided to do so and stayed in Newman Street until he joined Parkers. He occupied number 5, a large warehouse, which he filled with antiques. His interests were in designing classical interiors based on his wide knowledge of fine eighteenth century furniture and decoration, both English and Continental.

In 1900 Ferry made a copy of a bed in the Victoria and Albert Museum for his own use. It was in mahogany with carved decoration head and foot, and he soon sold several to Heals. They placed the orders for making the design with Parkers and that led to the addition of a dressing table and wardrobe to match. Through their association, TCP and Ferry became close friends and it was TCP's appreciation of Ferry's design skills and understanding of period that led him to suggest he joined the company. Ferry saw this might relieve his worries and, when Parkers offered the handsome salary of £1,000 a year, he decided to move. He continued to travel daily to Cannon Street until he was settled, and then moved into lodgings near the factory at Cowley. He left Whitstable when war broke out and bought the Corner House at Cowley. Eventually the opportunity arose for him to buy Cowley Grove House, a large Georgian property with four acres of ground and he lived there for fifty years.

There is no doubt that Ferry's contribution was to give added design impetus to the foundations established by Frederick himself. TCP stated that Ferry's designs enabled the Company to produce some really fine work, carved and decorated furniture of all types, needlework, lacquering and painting. Beautifully drawn books of 'specials' survive, mostly Ferry's work. After working at Cowley until 1924, he then moved his studio to the Wycombe factory which was becoming the main centre of operations. Not only did he prepare all the sketches required but, with his head assistant Smith, who was good at constructioin, produced all the full-sized working drawings. These were on large sheets of plywood so they were permanently available. Sad to say the complete collection was destroyed by fire in the 1950s.

Typical of the 1920s craftsmen upholsterers at Cowley was Edward Belcher. He was apprenticed at Parkers in 1913 on six months' trial and served from 1916 in the Royal Ordnance Corps. When he returned in 1919 there were three shops at Cowley including one for apprentices, of which there were five to ten at any one time. Belcher lived at Iver and cycled to work, when the hours were 7.30 am to 7.00 pm daily. His father paid Parkers £5 per annum for his tuition and after three years he became a qualified upholsterer. He was a good button worker, with hands which did not sweat. Parkers did a lot of work in Morocco leather and Nigerian goatskins which would show the lightest finger print and could only be handled by people with dry, non-greasy hands. All workers had to supply their own tools and Frederick used to carry out tool inspections without warning. His philosophy, often stated, was 'Good tools made good workmen' and 'Fitness is the order of the day'. Harry Parker always walked round the benches every day to inspect work in progress, exchanging a few words with each man.

Belcher moved to Wycombe in the thirties, when Charlie Tapping was manager and worked on many jobs for shipping lines, including the *Gripsholm* and *Samaria,* to Ferry's designs — covered in finest silks and tapestries, upholstered in best hair and swansdown. Belcher worked for the Company until 1941 when, due to shortage of work, he went to London, where he worked for Percy Bass doing high-class upholstery for Aspreys of Bond Street.

Jobs carried out under Ferry's supervision included furniture for the Council Chamber in Wycombe and the reredos in the Parish Church, designed by an architect. The fine work on the reredos, erected in 1922 as a war memorial, was executed by Len Michael, foreman carver. George Lane and Jim Hathaway also produced some notable work including the thrones for the Emperor of Abyssinia, while Wilf Layton carved the pulpit at West Wycombe Church. With the outbreak of War in 1939, production of this fine quality work ended, unfortunately never to be resumed. Ferry left the firm in 1941 and established a successful antique business in Uxbridge, before retiring in the sixties. He lived to the aged of 101 and died in 1982.

A feature of this period was the number of apprenticeships. These are recorded in the company minutes throughout the first two decades of the century, covering cabinetmaking, upholstery, chairmaking, woodcarving, draughtsmanship and woodturning. Periods varied between 3½ and five years for upholsterers with four or five years for other trades. Indentures covering a four year period in 1913 specified rates of pay to the apprentice of 3s in the first year, 5s in the second, 7s in the third and 9s per week in the last. Only occasionally was any premium paid; when it was, it was usually in £5 instalments over a four year period.

Peaceful working conditions within the Company were disputed in 1913 by Parkers carvers' strike. This broke out in mid-April and was extensively reported in the *South Bucks Free Press.* The dispute revolved around the practice of sending carving work outside the factory. This was done when the workload exceeded the Company's own carving resources and was to ensure that excessive delivery delays were kept to a minimum. Thirty woodcarvers were employed and, stated Harry Parker, 'all the carvers at the factory have been full of work, and the men have no cause to lose time. If they arrived late that is their own fault'. There were occasions when the rush of business compelled him to get carving from outside sources so that orders might be fulfilled. The polishers joined the strike and, when the press asked the men to state their case, they said their lips were sealed. This engendered a good deal of local heat with a well-attended public meeting by the Fountain on Frogmoor reported on 21 April. Notice of this was given 'by means of writing on the pavements of the principal streets of the town'. One local firm was reported to have 'taken note of the splendid example of the Parker polishers and had given their own polishers an extra ½d per hour'.

The dispute was settled on 2 May 1913 but not before some of the firm's cabinetmakers had also stopped work. One aspect was the publication of correspondence between Alec Gossip of the National Amalgamated Furniture Trade Association in London and Harry Parker, as well as that with the strike committee. Settlement came when 'the men admitted that occasions might arise when it was imperative that work should be put out, while the firm on their part agreed that the practice should not be used to the detriment of carvers employed at the factory' . . . 'After a meeting on Frogmoor the men decided to return to work on the next Thursday' . . . the men then conveyed their tools back to the factory from the Union headquarters at the Swan, 'the scene en route being lively and amusing'.

Whether in connection with this dispute or not, the Directors resolved on 27 May 1913 'to form a partnership association which shall indemnify each and all the members against all liability to pay compensation to workmen'. Members were: Henry James Castle and William John Castle of Castle Bros; James Cox of Birch & Cox; James Elliott, Harry Elliott and Frank Elliott of Jas Elliott & Sons; Walter Edwin Ellis, Ebenezer Gomme, John Gomm; Frederick Joynson the younger and James Holland of Joynson Holland & Co; George Keen, Sidney Keen of Keen & Son; George Albert Large of Large & Sons; Harry Stratford, Charles Brion of Stratford and Brion; Ralph Tyzack, Christopher Percy Vine, John Williams; and Harry, Thomas, William and Frederick Parker of Fredk. Parker & Sons.

Frederick had for some time been interested in schemes to distribute a share of profits to selected employees. He had studied papers drawn up by the Rowntree organisation in York, and John Knights' profit sharing scheme of 1911. As a result a sum was set aside each year from 1912. We do not know who the recipients were, or how many, but the arrangement required them to invest one third of the sum in the Company, on which they were paid interest at 5% per annum.

The peace of the whole Wycombe furniture industry was shattered on 28 November 1913 when a major dispute broke out which involved the whole town. Settlement was not achieved until 23 February 1914, and most of the town's production was curtailed. The reasons are well documented by L. J. Mayes and extremely detailed verbatim reports in the *South Bucks Free Press*. Unrest over wage rates had existed for some time and resulted in the Union drawing up a proposed scale for minimum wages. This was submitted to a meeting of the High Wycombe and District Furniture Manufacturers Federation on 21 November. On the 25th a stoppage occured at William Birch as a result of which the majority of their employees 'left their employment'. On the 28th, thirty-one of the thirty-two members of the employers' federation decided against the demands of the Union and resolved to give one hour's notice to all Union employees. Thus the scene was set for a long and bitter dispute that caused a lot of hardship and bitterness. Several firms, such as Goodearls, Glenisters, Edgerleys and Parkers, where Union membership was only a small proportion of the employees, were able to continue without too much difficulty. By mid-December it was reported that 130 workers had left the town to obtain work elsewhere. Many of them went to Scotland, where the furniture industry was booming. The London makers were also pleased with the increase in orders. A football match played for the benefit of the fund for women and children raised £2. As time progressed feelings ran higher and higher until violence broke out. During a Union meeting at the Town Hall, Goodearls, whose non-union employees were still working, managed to get a load of furniture out of their factory and escorted out of town by police. This led to an attack on Goodearls' workers at closing time next day, with bottles thrown and police injured. As a result, the Police Superintendent decided to ask for support from the Metropolitan Police. Twenty-five police, ten of them mounted, arrived in Wycombe to supplement the local force, a move not likely to appeal to the hotheads. The mounted police stayed until the dispute ended but the rest returned to London on 9 January.

A report inthe *Uxbridge Gazette* of 26 December states that 'pickets are watching Parker's chair factory at Cowley day by day. A party of fifty cyclists came over from Wycombe on Wednesday with a view to inducing the employees to make common cause with them, but were unable to effect a meeting with the latter. It is stated that about twelve or thirteen men at Parkers had joined the Union and had been given an hour's notice. Later, other employees were told that the same would apply to any who joined the Union or encouraged others to do so'. Attempts to arrange a meeting in a local hall fell through; the explanation — 'it was hoped to persuade the women employees to join, but the women preferred not to attend'.

There were frequent clashes between Union and police and on 9 January a large crowd assembled at the railway station to head off a reported 'train load of blacklegs coming from London'. When the train arrived no blacklegs were found and it was thought to be a hoax. Magistrates' courts were overloaded with breach-of-the-peace cases and a display of missiles and weapons used against the police was held.

Amid the extremely acrimonious climate, it is refreshing to find a report in the *South Bucks Free Press* of the Annual Dinner held by Parkers' employees at Cowley, which was attended by one hundred people. Relations locally were clearly excellent and not affected by the anger generated in Wycombe. Four directors were welcomed at the dinner and pleasure was expressed at 'seeing so many of the Wycombe firm with them'.

Events in Wycombe were going from bad to worse with attacks by Union women on the cottages of two young women, one of whom was a cripple, in Desborough Street. A load of chair seats belonging to Edgerleys was set upon in Oxford Road and the driver overwhelmed. The load was thrown into the river. Later in Desborough Road a march came face to face with the police where 'the hostility of the crowd reached a culminating point. The officers were pelted with stones, bottle and lumps of coal taken from a passing vehicle. Eventually the Police drew batons and charged the hostile crowd and only with difficulty broke up the demonstration and made arrests. The trouble continued all day in the market where, in the midst of it all, a Liberal Speaker was endeavouring to speek in connection with the current election. Half way through the afternoon the Lockout Band arrived on the scene "playing a lively tune" and in a subsequent speech to the crowd not to throw stones, Mr Bramley informed them with some anticipation that "a few days from now, those who control the large London Warehouses will be placing their Spring orders and would want guarantees that delivery would be completed on time, or they would go elsewhere". If Wycombe firms could not promise Maples or Schoolbreds that they could meet the orders they would lose the business "and that would bring them to the point if anything would".'

Meanwhile meetings with both sides were being held in London by Sir George Askwith, at the offices of the Chief Industrial Commissioner, 5 Old Place Yard. The first meetings were adjourned, but eventually a settlement of the dispute was reached. Finally, a detailed document, setting out the wage rates for all classes of work and defining terms of employment, was signed by representatives of both sides. The acceptance by the Union of the principle of grading wages for different classes of the same type of work was greatly welcomed by the employers as it was the Union's strongest objection at the beginning. Agreed wage scales for women workers were defined for the first time, but the actual rates agreed for the men differed only marginally from those proposed by the employers before the trouble started. In any case a lot of leeway had now to be made up and lost business recouped. Most of the men had assumed that they would go straight back to work, but many found that this was not the case, as insufficient orders and disorganised production schedules had to be overcome. It took several months for things gradually to get back towards normal. Hardly had this happened than a great catastrophe arose with the outbreak of War on 4 August 1914.

The Wycombe troubles do not appear to have affected Parkers' activities; the accounts show that turnover increased again that year, although the nett profit was down for the first time for many years. Early in 1914 Parkers were settling the details of a large and important order with the Cunard Steamship Company. Since Frederick Parker's earliest days, the firm had developed contacts with large shipping lines. The largest retailers, Waring and Gillow, Hamptons and Wylie and Lochead also had specialist ship furnishing departments which could cope with the often mammoth job of preparing complete interior schemes for furnishing the largest and most luxurious ocean liners.

Ever since Brunel's paddle steamer *Great Western* first crossed the Atlantic to New York in 1837, commercial passenger lines had rapidly developed. Fares at £31 10s for a cabin and food were considered high but there was no shortage of passengers. Samuel Cunard founded his shippping line in 1840 with a contract to carry mail and passengers, and this was followed by a race between Germany, France, Italy and Britain to put the fastest ships onto the North Atlantic crossing. This opened lucrative and prestigious contracts to those furniture makers who could deal with the specialised requirements.

Early in 1914 it was the pride of the Cunard line, RMS *Aquitania*, that was fitting out, and engaging the Parker factories in Wycombe and Cowley. Many firms contributed furniture for such a large project, which was co-ordinated by Davis, the consultant designer, and the shipping company. Although all the third class passengers on the *Aquitania* were in two and four bunk berths, the first class accommodation was equal to anything the age could produce. The Palladian lounge was the height of interior design afloat. The shipping magnates of the day planned their liners as they did their own homes, in all manner of periods and styles. Inspiration for a furnishing scheme would be derived from as diverse sources as a Louis XVI library at the Trianon, or the Orangerie at Hampton Court. It was a case of creating the atmosphere of the great English country houses and baronial halls, so that tradition-starved Americans flocked to join the passenger lists.

Over two hundred Hepplewhite style chairs were supplied by Parkers for the Second Class Dining Salon, and various elegant Georgian styles of upholstered chairs for the famous Palladian Lounge — 'one of the most elegant rooms afloat'. Other saloons and smoking rooms were furnished luxuriously in baronial styles with tapestries and portraits under elaborate plaster ceilings.

Parkers supplied a wide assortment of styles for the liner, several of them exact reproductions of period chairs in their collection. The 45,000 ton vessel sailed on her maiden voyage from Liverpool on 30 May 1914 *via* Cobh for New York. Apart from her luxury service on the regular North Atlantic crossings she saw service as troopship and hospital ship in both World Wars before being retired and scrapped in 1950. The *Cabinet Maker* of 6 June 1914 gave a somewhat cursory mention of the furnishings, without photographs. The way in which the article is written suggests that it was done in the office from a Cunard press handout and not by a reporter who had been to see the ship.

A new vogue in upholstery covers arose from the Company's close working relationship with Cunard. They told TCP that a large quantity of undyed Niger goatskins was lying at London Docks in bales wrapped in undyed cow hides. Although the goatskins were too small for normal upholstery, the leather was soft and at a giveaway price, Harry and TCP worked out a method of joining the small skins together for upholstery on three piece suites, making the seams a feature of the design. The skins were dyed and polished in the factory and, as they were too small for use on seat cushions, brown velveteen purchased from Libertys was used instead.

Hide and Velveteen Suites became a standard term in the trade and enjoyed great popularity. Eventually competitors unable to obtain the Nigers started to produce imitations at lower prices, using plain hide and even early plastic pegamoid. The hides from the bales in which the original consignment was wrapped were unusually thick, sufficient to allow them to be used on Cromwellian style upright side chairs.

At the annual meeting of the Wycombe and District Furniture Manufacturers Federation, reported in the *Cabinet Maker* on 2 May 1914, new officers were appointed. Harry Parker was elected as one of the Trustees together with Walter Birch. In resolving the membership of the Federation council by ballot, council members' firms were classified in grades — Grade 1: William Bartlett & Son, Frederick Parker & Sons Ltd, W. Skull & Sons; Medium Grade: James Cox and Son Ltd, Thomas Glenister Ltd, Goodearl Bros Ltd, and B. North & Sons (West Wycombe); Suite Manufacturers: R. Howland & Sons Ltd, Randall Bros and Co Ltd;

Wycombe Trade: James Elliott & Son and Jonson Holland & Co. This classification continued well into the 1920s.

Parkers went to the High Court in September 1914, seeking an interim injunction to restrain G. H. & S. Keen of High Wycombe from publishing in their catalogue a photograph of a chair which they contended was their own copyright. Mr Justice Shearman said he could not grant the interim injunction, although he expressed the opinion that there was a question to be tried. He thought an undertaking should be given by the defendants not to continue publication pending the trial. His own view was that it was a 'rather trumperey proceeding'. It may well be that it was from these proceedings that TCP received this cynical advice from his friend Marshall Hall KC: 'Never go to Law Parker!'.

In London on 25 September 1914, furniture makers met representatives of the textile industry, G. H. Cooper of William Lawrence of Nottingham was in the chair and Harry Parker was among many furniture makers. The meeting examined how the British textile industry might provide the covering materials which had previously been purchased from Germany. A long and not very useful discussion took place before the following resolution was agreed: 'That this meeting of British manufacturers and wholesale buyers are of opinion that the present opportunity of making the majority of goods hitherto imported from Germany and Austria should be seized upon wholeheartedly. We thereby pledge ourselves unreservedly to do everything that lies in our power to secure this trade for British workers, and that the Board of Trade be asked to give every facility in this most important matter. That copies of this resolution be sent to His Majesty the King as Patron of the National Patriotic Association, to the Prime Minister, the Lord Chancellor and the President of the Board of Trade'.

However well intentioned, the provision of covering materials was of small concern against the fighting in France. The significance of this had not yet become apparent when in November 1914 a conference was held between the High Wycombe Manufacturers and Mr Gandell of the Commercial Intelligence Unit of the Board of Trade. This was to find out how far Wycombe might capture the trade in bentwood furniture formerly supplied by Austria. This furniture was sold throughout the world. Mr Gandell pointed out that manufacture of this distinctive type of chair required considerable investment, with specialist machinery and moulds for bending. This was confirmed by Mr W. Birch who had visited the Austrian factories before the War. Mr Gandell thought that Wycombe manufacturers would be better advised to consider a chair so made that it could be knocked down and assembled at destination by unskilled labour. Pointing out that no means existed in Wycombe to bend the circular hoop which formed the underframe of Austrian chairs, he produced an example of a circular seat, and a ring made in England of compressed paper. Rather than copy the Austrian article, it might be better to create something original to benefit from local skills. As to high costs of packing and freight charges, he suggested that, if knock-down furniture was made, packing cases could be so designed to convert into useful articles of furniture on arrival, instead of going for firewood.

He offered to exhibit samples to prominent exporters and shippers. The meeting bore no Austrian fruit, but much thought and design work was put in on knock-down models, of which an exhibition took place in London 1915. Parkers contributed what was described as 'A most ingenious folding chair' but no illustration survives.

Though 1914 closed unhappily as the casualty lists increased, the War had little immediate effect in Wycombe, and Parkers carried on almost normally. New designs went into production throughout the first years of the War, and undoubtedly stocks of timber and materials in hand were sufficient. There was however, a sharp decline in business after the end of the year. Such indicators as wages and salaries fell by 50% while turnover and gross profit also fell. After twenty years of unbroken growth and prosperity, the Company made its first nett loss since 1893.

ABOVE: Parker made the reredos installed in 1922 at High Wycombe Parish Church, in memory of the town's Great War dead. BELOW: First of the great steamship contracts was for the *Aquitania*.

ABOVE: The magnificent lounge of the *Aquitania* where BELOW: Parker's Hepplewhite style chairs graced the ship's reading room.

BEHIND THE LINES

Early 1915 saw British commerce and manufacturing desperately trying to adjust to the demands of the War, although the popular ethic was business as usual. As conscription was not introduced until May 1916, it was up to individuals to join up. Many thousands did flock to the colours, but initially, firms were able to carry on without too much disturbance. They needed to seek War contracts as swiftly as possible, in order to make their own contribution.

Initially Parkers continued to make high class cabinet and upholstery goods. They already supplied the Office of Works with quality furniture for coronations and embassies, as well as for the Houses of Parliament and other Government buildings. They were therefore in close contact with the sources of Government contracts and it was not long before their production facilities were turned over to the national effort.

An early order placed by the War Office was for twenty thousand kettle stands and two million tent pegs. The trade press of the time is full of notices of 'War Contracts awarded'. These show, by early 1915, the extent to which the furniture industry was contributing. The diverse list of products was defined in a list issued in March 1915:
'Bedding: Bedsteads, Barrack; Bedsteads, Folding; Blankets: Cases, Packing; Chests; Doors: Deal; Flags; Furniture; Ladders; Matresses, Spring; Poles, Tent; Rugs, Hearth, Rugs, Goatskins; Tables, Operating; Tents; Tables, Trestle; Web, Webbing; Wood, threeply; Woodware (Misc); Shelters, Ready made; Pegs, Tent; Boxes, Ammunition; Etc.'

Parkers took on as much war work as they could obtain and ran this alongside such normal production as could be sold. Tenders were issued early in 1915 by the Governors for the furnishing of the new High Wycombe School and the firm won a large part of this.

In view of the unsatisfactory outlook, the Directors prudently decided to declare no divident for the years to August 1914 and 1915. By 1916 the results had improved sufficiently to yield a dividend of 15% plus bonus payments to selected staff members. By 1918, however, the Directors had reduced their salaries by 33% compared to 1915, which indicates a tightening of the Company's trading position as the War progressed.

The fire of 1970 destroyed the Company's records of how many employees served with the forces in either of the two world wars, but it is known that from the outset TCP had insisted he was the one brother who should undertake military service when required. By that time he had a family of three daughters aged between four and eight but, despite this, he volunteered as a private in the Artists Rifles (2/28 London Regiment). His pay was 1s 2½d per day. He then went to Officers Training College, Cambridge and in March 1917 was commissioned as a Second Lieutenant in the East Yorkshire Regiment. He soon arrived in France and, after only seven weeks, on 22 June 1917, as a member of the 13th Battalion, took part in a raid by 200 men and four officers on enemy trenches between Oppy and Gavrelle. As one small action in the Battle of Arras this was no doubt a routine affair, although the account of the action, published in the *Daily Mail* of 14 February 1929, gives a vivid impression of the horror and futility of this type of trench warfare. TCP emerged unscathed, but only two days later was severely wounded by shrapnel in the chest.

One can imagine the shock to Mrs Parker and her family of young daughters when the War Office telegram arrived on 2 July. Couched in stark language it gave little information, but merely said that 2nd Lt Parker was wounded on 28 June and promised to send further news. A second telegram arrived 8 July. TCP had been admitted to 20 General Hospital, Camiers, with a wound in the left chest 'penetrating and severe'. His daughter, Nancy, recalled how she was in the garden when the telegram arrived and 'everybody was crying and sobbing by the sundial'. TCP used to recount how, at the field hospital after examining and dressing the would, the doctor said to him 'There's no more I can do for you'. TCP said 'Well, if that's it — O.K.' and turned over and went to sleep. Whatever the doctor had intended to convey, to everybody's amazement TCP gradually recovered sufficiently to be invalided home. After a long period of convalescence he returned to duty and spent the rest of the War as a Messing Officer at Withernsea. The wound cost him one of his lungs, and he survived on the other to draw his disablement pension of £52 10s a year. Following the Gavrelle action, TCP received a poignant letter seeking information from the parents of one of his brother officers on the raid, who was posted 'missing in action'. Because of his wound T.C.P. was demobilised in 1918 and was back in the Company boardroom for its meeting of 7 January 1919.

The Wycombe section of the High Wycombe furniture trade had been kept busy throughout the War making 'basic' furniture for barracks and other similar needs. The best end of the trade had found times increasingly difficult and to offset this several makers took up work on aircraft. Their simple construction in fabric-covered wood enabled furniture craftsmen to use their skills. Manpower was an increasing problem, and workers from furniture firms took every opportunity to move into munitions, where the pay rates were higher. As the aeroplane increased in use, the Government decided in 1917 to open a large aircraft factory in Bellfield near Parkers, and buildings were rapidly erected. Local manufacturers were expected to co-operate by releasing their remaining skilled cabinet and chairmakers to work in the new factory. Advertisements appeared in lcoal papers for 1,000 power sewing machinists and a large number of woodworkers. The War ended before the project started and not a single 'plane was produced. The buildings were eventually used as a sawdust processing plant before being pulled down.

Parkers' Cowley factory contributed to the Royal Air Force by producing hundreds of mainplane leading edges for the famous Sopwith Camel and Pup fighter planes, while the Wycombe factory made untold quantities of ammunition boxes and anything else the military required in wood. The annual accounts show that the business remained in good health, both turnover and profits reaching an all-time high in the year ending August 1918, and even better in 1919. Dividends of 15% were paid to ordinary shareholders with a bonus to Directors and key staff members.

The upheaval caused by four years of War would be felt for a long time. The flower of British manhood had died or been mutilated — 75,000 dead and 2,500,000 wounded — apart from the drain on the country's wealth. The War had a profound impact on cultural and social life and the Ministry of Munitions had taken central control of all production in all spheres, often riding roughshod over many sacred cows in labour relations. Women played their part in munitions production and, incredibly, had served at the Front. Those over thirty had also been allowed to vote for the first time and British agriculture enjoyed a new lease of life. The National debt, which in 1914 stood at £707 millions, had six years later soared to an incredible £7,875 millions.

It was in this dramatically changed climate that commerce had to re-establish itself as controls were removed. Pay disputes broke out in Wycombe in the autumn of 1918, mainly because the women's section of the Union wanted the same pay as those in munitions. The men also wanted an increase of 5½d per hour. Strike notices were issued to employers in 'munitions and aircraft' as well as furniture. The Defence of the Realm Act was immediately invoked, preventing those in munitions from striking, but some 300-400 furniture workers did strike at the end of September. Union membership had increased enormously during the War years, so that a strike call now had much more impact than in 1913. By November, the matter had still not been settled despite an enquiry by the Ministry of Labour but, on the 5th, agreement was reached on the promise that the disputed pay rates would be sent to arbitration. An award was finally made in February 1919, giving workers over 18 an increase of 23s 6d above the rate prevailing in February 1914, plus 12½d for workers over 21.

The immediate post-war effect of rapidly rising prices for food and other necessities led to still more labour disputes in August 1919, when the national Union strove for an improved national wage and shorter working week. The Manchester Employers Federation did not agree and locked out all Union members. The Wycombe Federation decided to give support and also declared a lockout. The London Federation ignored the dispute entirely, with the result that their members enjoyed boom conditions, while in other areas only non-federated firms were working. In Wycombe, it was almost a repeat of the 1913 situation and things became ugly. Once again, police were drafted into the town, this time from Oxford. The dispute dragged on beyond the 14 week record of 1913, and the rest of the country had gone back to work long before the factory gates reopened there. The result was the final scrapping of piece-work and the setting of a standard rate for all journeymen, with lower standard rates for all less skilled trades.

It looked then, as if the 'Peace' for which everybody had so earnestly fought was to be somewhat fragile.

LEFT: 2nd Lt Thomas Cornwell Parker in the uniform of the East Yorkshire Regiment in 1914. RIGHT: This reading table was popular in the 1890s and for many years after — it flatpacked for delivery at £1 8s in 1913.

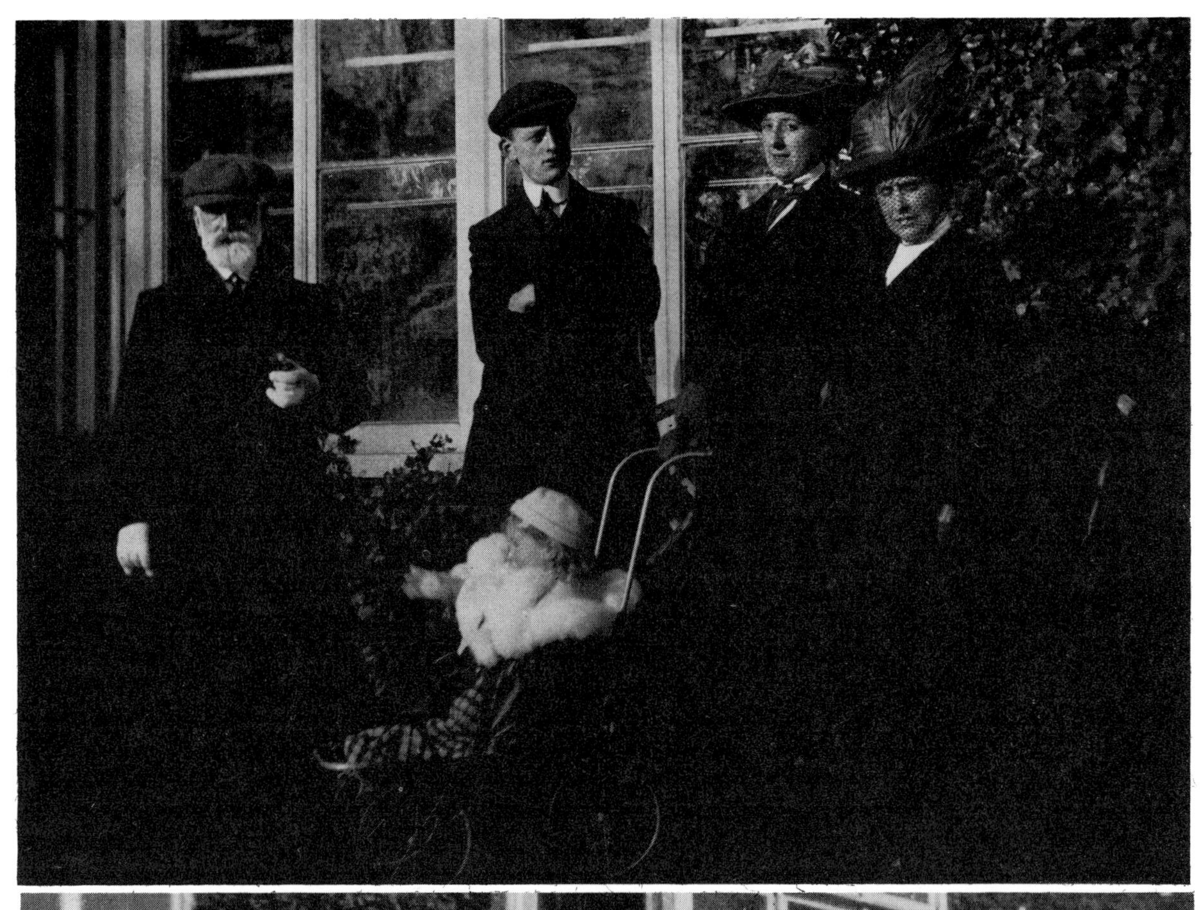

ABOVE: Frederick Parker, two daughters and a son-in-law, with one of his grandchildren and BELOW: Frederick Parker and his grandchildren in his car, c1917.

STEAMING AHEAD IN THE '20S

From the first, the twenties were marked by bitter and ever-increasing political turmoil. The heavy industries, in such demand during the War, slid into decline as foreign competition grew and overseas markets turned to other suppliers. For the North of England, South Wales, Clydeside and Belfast this was a time of mounting despair and poverty. Prosperity divided increasingly along class lines, exploding into the General Strike of May 1926. For much of southern England and the Midlands, the twenties were a period of growing contentment and prosperity. A much larger part of the population emerged from the War years with middle class aspirations — home ownership and a quiet family life with more leisure pursuits. New technology in the factories of Herbert Austin and William Morris generated over a million cars by 1930, while domestic comforts and mechanical aids for the housewife were removing some domestic drudgery. The invention of wireless was bringing all households, especially those who did not read newspapers, almost immediate information on politics and world and home affairs as well as providing entertainment. For members of the white-collar administrative and professonal groups which had expanded so dramatically, the twenties were not such a bad time. There were many suburban housing developments with consumer prices starting to fall. 'Easy terms' became more widely available, and acceptable.

Furniture manufacturers now had to find new customers. Although the market had grown larger and offered all sorts of opportunities, it did not require the type of furniture in vogue before the War. New, simpler styles that could be manufactured in volume and sold for less were wanted, as against the fine hand-made products. More machinery was available for woodworking, executing jobs formerly done by hand, swiftly and accurately. New designers and home stylists showed in home magazines how new interior effects could be achieved, lighter, simpler, and less cluttered with bric-a-brac. Many of the largest London manufacturers, finding their premises too small, moved away from Shoreditch and Hoxton to new sites in the Lea Valley to the North. There they were able to plan for much larger runs, taking advantage of machine production.

At the end of 1919, at an extraordinary general meeting, the Parker board decided to increase the Company's capital to £80,000 by creating 20,000 preference shares of £1 each, and 50,000 ordinary shares of £1 each. This was achieved by the capitalisation of £44,602, part of the undistributed profits and reserve funds. The new shares were distributed proportionately among holders of the original 7,077 ordinary shares issued in 1901. It was also decided to promote a limited liability company to be known as The Cowley Garage Ltd. Its shares of £5,000 were held by Harry and Frederick George Parker. This venture, opposite the Paddington Packet Boat Inn, which is still there, was run by Harold Parker and provided Parkers with maintenance and service facilities for their motor transport, which consisted of three vehicles valued at £591. The Canalside Dock adjoining the Cowley factory was also bought.

Frederick Parker was taking a less active role day to day, although he remained an active Chairman. Harry had two daughters, William had two sons, George and Richard, and TCP had his three daughters. Although George did work for the Company and managed the Wycombe factory through the Second World War, he left in 1947 and went to Canada. Richard spent only a short time at Newman Street in 1938-40 and did not return to the business after the War. It was in this way that future control evolved through TCP's daughters, not directly, but *via* his future sons-in-law.

TCP's daughters were growing up by 1920, Marion aged 12, Peggy aged 10, and Nancy aged eight. They all lived at Springfield, the house TCP built before the War in the grounds of the Cowley factory. The three girls recall their schooldays there with pleasure, as they were able to roam the grounds and dockside at will. TCP had a billiard room in the cellar which was used as a store for fragments of antique furniture and carving that he acquired wherever he went. Nancy recalled that, whenever they went out in the car, they always stopped at antique shops and often bought a piece of 'rubbish'. She also remembers the barges full of timber floating into the dock after delivery by canal from London.

Peggy remembers the adjacent factory and grounds of Clock House where her Grandfather lived — strictly out of bounds. She remembers Frederick as rather a stern but kindly man, who took all his grandchildren on an annual outing by 'bus to London. This was for a visit to the Coliseum, followed by a fish and chip tea afterwards. Peggy also recalls that Frederick was the first in Cowley to have a motor car. 'When he came up the drive past our house, out of the big gates, it was quite an event, there were people waiting with flags. Everybody in Cowley Peachey was terribly interested in the car.' A photograph of 1917 shows Frederick and several grandchildren in a large open Crossley Tourer.

Another childhood memory was of the factory hooter which woke up the whole village at 7.25 am each day. It was known locally as 'Parkers Dog Dying' and gave only five minutes' warning. Nancy remembers the men 'rushing and scuffling to be there on time'.

Business returned to normal in the early twenties. By 1920, war contracts finished; the turnover that year of £131,112 was the highest yet and probably all from furniture. There was a record profit of £37,696, lending confidence to further expansion. On 3 June 1920 the Board authorised the purchase of land at Temple End from Harry Parker for £1,408. An adjoining piece was also bought from the Marquess of Lincolnshire for £1,650.

This site is an historic one. There appears to have been a 'Manor of Temple of Wicombe' before the Norman Conquest. In the reign of King John a grant of the Manor of Temple was made to the Knights Templar, from whom it passed to the Knights Hospitaller. In 1532 it was granted to John Cock and in 1628 the Manor came into the possession of Richard Archdale, who sold it in 1700 to Henry Petty, Lord Shelburne. His newphew, John Fitzmaurice, inherited and was created Earl of Shelburne in 1753 and 'Brion of Chipping Wicobe' (sic) in 1760. Later he became Earl of Chipping Wycombe. In 1784, the then Earl Wycombe of Chipping Wycombe and Marquess of Lansdowne sold the Manor in lots which were, about 1794, all purchased by the then Lord Carrington. In 1862 'The Temple Manor House is now converted into a farm residence occupied by Mr Edwin Phipps who holds Temple Farm'.

New administration and factory buildingts were soon erected, enabling some production to be moved from Frogmoor where space was limited. The new workshops were extensive, and soon busy. Parkers were manufacturing upholstery of the finest quality and re-introducing down-filled cushions for the first time for many years. The shortage of working space at Frogmoor is remembered by one of the workmen of the time: 'I was in the chair shop as a boy. It was on the third floor. At that time Hall and Clay were the makers and Dunning the foreman. My duties were to add starch particles to a machine and to take the wood round to be planed and shaped. We had just the one band saw, but later new machinery was introduced. When I joined the company we were making chairs, some cabinet work and best upholstery. The chairs were made twelve at a time, but there was just nowhere to put them. We had to go outside for storage space — to the loft above Belchamber and Evans' slaughter -house in Coronation Place. In between humping the chairs we watched the sausage machines and got a bit of free sausage'.

Special models for the Cunard Steamship Co were in hand, especially those for the steamships *Tyrrhenia, Samaria, Askania,* and *Scythia.* (The author sailed from Capetown to Suez on this boat in 1942.) A considerable amount of ship work followed, and furniture was made for a string of Cunard ships in succeeding years. These were *Lanconia* (1921), *Tuscania (1922), Franconia (1923), Transylvania, Aurania,* and *Andania (1924),* with *Albania* (1925).

Their interior designers usually called for traditional styles. For instance, for the First Class Smoking Rooms on the *Franconia* and *Lanconia,* Cunard's drawings specify five items. These were an open/arm wing chair, a Cromwellian style, a folding top table, an elaborate 'X' chair, and an oak joint stool (all in MacQuoid). Chairs for the *Aurania* included a reproduction of an attractive, painted Hepplewhite chair of 1785. The original on which these were modelled is in the Parker Knoll antique collection.

Uncertainty about the future is reflected in the minutes of the annual general meeting of 21 March 1921, when it was agreed to pay no dividend. The previous 31 May a dividend of 2½% had been declared on the Ordinary shares, but 1921 saw a sudden fall in turnover which, after tax, produced a loss of £5,606. This proved only a temporary setback.

Frederick, who was now 76, expressed the wish in December 1921 to retire as Chairman and Managing Director. He was asked to stay on as a consultant to the Board for life, at a salary of £250. During the 52 years since he first set up in Bracklyn Street he had created a substantial, successful and respected company with a reputation for honest dealing and excellence.

This table was designed for the *Aurania* smoke room in 1924, price £11 10s.

ABOVE: The 'new' office block and factory at Temple End, High Wycombe in 1920 and BELOW: the best chair frame shop a year later. OPPOSITE ABOVE: The decorated furniture studio at Cowley in 1920 and BELOW: Parker chairs in a London showroom.

ABOVE: Another vista in an elegant London furriers and BELOW: Parker's London showrooms in Newman Street.

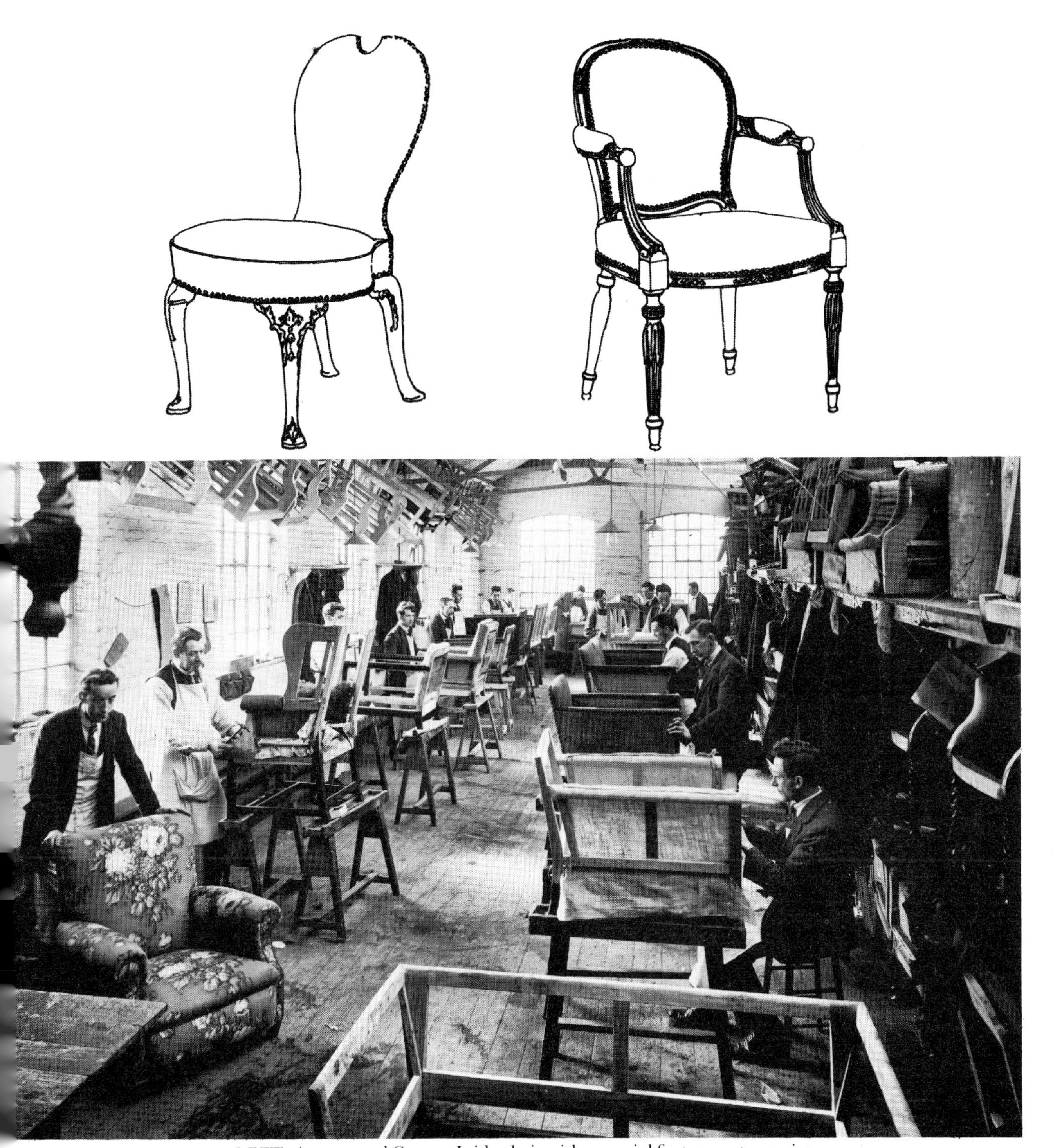

LEFT: An unusual George I side chair with a special feature — to receive a man's tie wig. RIGHT: This 1795 Hepplewhite design was the model for the *Aurania* chairs of 1923. BELOW: Upholstery and partly finished goods at Temple End in 1921.

MODERN FACTORY FOR SALE AT HIGH WYCOMBE · FREEHOLD · HAS ELECTRIC LIGHT & POWER

FOR SALE AT
HIGH WYCOMBE
HAVING MOVED INTO LARGER PREMISES
FREDK PARKER & SONS Lᵀᴰ
HAVE FOR DISPOSAL
A FREEHOLD FACTORY
ABOUT 15000 Fᵀ SUPER · ELECTRIC
LIGHT AND POWER INSTALLED &
WITH DWELLING HOUSE ADJOINING

Apply F. PARKER & SONS Lᵀᴰ
20 Newman St, London, W

WHF

THIS AGREEMENT made the Sixth day of February One thousand nine hundred and twenty-two BETWEEN FREDERICK PARKER & SONS LIMITED whose Registered Office is situate at No. 20 Newman Street in the County of London (hereinafter called "the Company") of the one part and FREDERICK PARKER of No. 20 Newman Street aforesaid of the other part WHEREAS the said Frederick Parker is the Managing Director of the Company and he is desirous of retiring from active participation in the general control of the Company's business but the Company are desirous of retaining his services as Consulting Adviser to the Company upon the terms hereinafter expressed NOW IT IS HEREBY AGREED by and between the parties hereto as follows :-

1. THE said Frederick Parker shall retire from the Office of a Director of the Company asfrom the ~~Seventh day of August~~ First day of December One thousand nine hundred and twenty-one and shall as from that date relinquish all claims to any remuneration or emolument as Managing Director of the Company. *(initialled: FP, FBP)*

2. THE Company shall engage the said Frederick Parker and the said Frederick Parker will as from the ~~Seventh day of August~~ First day of December One thousand nine hundred and twenty-one give his services to the Company in the capacity of Consulting Adviser during the term of his natural life at a salary at the rate of Two hundred and fifty pounds per annum to be paid quarterly but to be treated as accruing from day to day. *(initialled: FP, FBP)*

3. THE said Frederick Parker shall be required to devote only such time and attention as Consulting Adviser of the Company as he shall think fit and shall not be responsible for the management or conduct of the Company's business or for any act matter or thing in connection with the Company's affairs.

4. THE said Frederick Parker shall be at liberty to retire from his position as Consulting Adviser to the Company at any time on giving to the Company one calendar's month 's previous notice in writing and shall also be at liberty whether during his continuance in such position or after his retirement therefrom to engage in any other business profession or vocation not directly antagonistic to the interest of the Company.

AS WITNESS the Common Seal of the Company and the hand of the said Frederick Parker.

WITNESS to the signature of the said Frederick Parker.

Witness Harry Blick
Draper
89 High St North
East Ham E.6.

LEFT: Frederick Parker & Sons Ltd advertised their Cowley premises in the *Furnishing and Ladies Organiser* of 1921. RIGHT: The agreement with Frederick Parker on his retirement tried to stop him meddling without spelling it out.

IN THE FRAME – THE '20S

As is often the case in the furniture trade, when business is slack, it is not the quality makers who suffer for they are not operating on volume production, but treating orders more or less individually. Lower price makers must maintain a large order book to work to capacity. This was probably true of Parkers' experience during the difficult twenties. Sometimes trade was frantically busy while at others it was extremely slow. Parkers' turnover and profits show they were not much affected by the depression, until 1926, when there was a slightly lower turnover.

An advertisement in *The Furniture Trades Organiser* during 1921 implies the planned sale of Frogmoor, perhaps due to the success of the factory at Cowley, and the new Temple End factory. The Frogmoor factory had served for twenty three years and was cramped. However, the idea must have been dropped for nothing more is heard. In 1928 those premises were extended by a fine two-storey half-timbered building, which today houses accounts.

The most difficult year, which affected the whole trade, was 1926. After the Government declined to renew its subsidy to the mining industry in April, the crippling General Strike occurred from 3 to 13 May. Trade shrank rapidly in the face of middle class fears of 'red revolution', but there was no really serious violence. The working class having shown its solidarity and despair, the TUC called it off without achieving change, and life for the middle classes returned slowly to normal.

The way prices moved was reflected in the story of the Stuart Marriage Chest. This seventeenth century chest, covered in all-over appliqué work on a a base of red velvet, was purchased by TCP as the basis for a covering material he wished to use on some chairs sold to America. The chest was bought from Mawers of Fulham Road on 17 May 1927 for £80. It was quite well-known already — Herbert Cecsinsky illustrated it in his books on English furniture. He was a frequent visitor to TCP at Newman Street, and on one such visit on 3 June 1927 Cecsinsky saw the chest, greatly admired it and purchased it for £200, later selling it in the States. One day in 1932, Basil Mawer telephoned TCP saying he had just purchased a chest and thought it was the same one he sold Parkers in 1927. He was right — Mawer's agent had picked it up at an auction in France and it still had the French Customs marks. TCP said he would like to buy it back: 'How much do you want for it?' 'Well,' said Basil Mawer, 'with trade the way it is I would be glad to get £24 and that would show me a good profit'. TCP bought the chest and it was returned to Newman Street. Ferry designed an elaborately carved and silver-gilt stand which was made for £6 19s 6d in October 1938. The chest and stand remained on view at the showrooms until September 1939, when they were sold to Gill & Reigate for £47 10s.

During the twenties Walter Ferry was encouraged to develop his own ideas for cabinet designs, working on the assumption that the market no longer wanted exact reproductions, but something sympathetic but less elaborate and possibly less expensive. Thus he adapted traditional designs within a more functional idiom, resulting in some superb pieces. Frederick himself kept an eagle eye on finished goods. If he found the slightest defect he would delay even urgent deliveries. Sometimes this meant starting all over again. The craftsmen were as proud of their skills as the firm and, although Frederick was a hard taskmaster, respected him for it.

Another young apprentice to upholstery was 'Cosh' Belson, who joined in 1924. Over many years Cosh saw many changes — he recalls Harry Parker as the RSM keeping everyone on their toes. Outlets for the finest quality work were steadily declining, but there was still sufficient demand from the wealthy for something special, and this provided Parkers with steady work through leading firms like Maples, Harrods, Hamptons, Heals, Warings, Gill and Reigate, Mallets, Hammonds, Tozers and Haines. Special furniture was made for the RAC and Masonic Club and the new AA building at Fanum House, where the Boardroom was furnished with special chairs and table to an unusual design. The large Chairman's chair still exists at the present Basingstoke offices. The frames for these chairs were made by a firm of Belgian carvers, Levasseur of Malines. Old friends of the Parkers, they were reckoned the best in Europe, and had a showroom and office in Poland Street just off Oxford Street. Malines was the home of many fine Flemish carvers and produced a lot of ecclesiastical work, although wages were said to be as low as 3d to 4d per hour. Parkers effected a business tie-up with Levasseurs early in the twenties, and imported a variety of beautifully carved chair and mirror frames from them. Frames for chairs supplied to Grosvenor House were from Belgium, and gradually Belgian influence in carved work spread into Walter Ferry's designs for elaborate bed-heads made chiefly for Heals, Hamptons and Maples. The high quality work on the mirror frames made them much sought after. Nothing of this type is available today. Customers visiting the Newman Street showrooms were often tempted by a small, elm milking stool which always stood by the door. They would see it on the way out, having completed their order, and many a time one was added as an extra as they departed — price retail 37s 6d.

TCP's eldest daughter, Marion, was 18 in 1926 and, after boarding school at Eastbourne, obtained a place at Girton College, Cambridge. Her artistic temperament led her to forsake Cambridge for the Slade School of Art. Her parents were not pleased for, apart from the expense, they were not happy about the elegant young men their daughter brought home. Marion was removed from the Slade and sent to the lesser Central School of Art. Family relations became a little strained, especially when, on her first night at the school, she was brought home by the President's son in his Rolls. TCP in a display of parental control removed Marion from the school and put her to work in the Parker design studio. Even then, Marion was picked up each morning by 'the skilful and charming Walter Ferry' in his Bugatti.

Walter does seem to have lived in greater style than his employers, enjoying his large Georgian house, Cowley Grove, which he filled with many beautiful artifacts. The studio was run by Miss Ferry, Walter's sister, who was also artistic; with Marion's developing skills in this field they did excellent work, creating needlework and dealing with all the decorative painting of furniture then greatly in vogue. Painted and decorated bedroom furniture was particularly popular, with bedheads covered in leather and hand-painted with large floral bouquets. Also in demand were decorated and lacquered cabinets in the Chinese or Japanese style, all requiring great attention to detail and skill. Peter Jones had a special department for many years. Furniture was often painted to designs created for specific customers. These often came back annotated 'gold lining is too dark' or 'too wide' or 'the ground colour is too grey; it is to be a little more blue and a little deeper in colour'.

A complimentary article appeared in the *Daily Telegraph* on 28 March 1924, which described the Parkers' work in ship furnishing. It referred particularly to the *Aquitania*, by then in service for ten years. Another article in the *Cabinet Maker* of 2 November 1929 drew attention to the Company's collection of old chairs. Commenting on the Wycombe tradition, the writer pointed out the value of preserving fine old chairs. A first-class reproduction should have the individual touch and refinement in its execution; it should show appreciation for the modelling of the chair, and that subtle variety in surface treatment, whether carved or plain, which cannot be observed without close inspection of the original. In short it should be a work of art. After complimenting Parkers on having formed a collection covering so many styles and periods, the article ended with a plea for the creation of a Wycombe Museum of Chairmaking: 'Chairmaking is much closer to human requirements than cabinetmaking, for chairs must always be made to accommodate the unalterable proportions of the human frame, whereas cabinets have no such limitations and may be made to whatever scale and structural design the architect pleases'.

An exhibition of art treasures took place at the Grafton Galleries in 1928 under the auspices of the British Antique Dealers Association. There were many famous names among the exhibitors and to this display Parkers contributed three chairs from their antique collection, which still carry the exhibition labels today.

One of the secrets of Parkers' escape from the worst effects of slumps was their ability to keep costs at the lowest possible level by constant monitoring. Nothing was ever wasted and, when materials were collected from stores, with what meticulous care storekeeper Mr Hill issued only the exact quantity. Economy was practised from management downwards and everyone learnt to adopt an attitude of care towards use of the Company's assets and time. Punctuality was of the essence and no staff or departmental heads took liberties by using the telephone for private purposes or to receive incoming private calls. The tone was set by the Directors.

Business through the last years of the twenties was such as to justify expansion at the Wycombe factory at Temple End. In 1928 a large four-storey buiding was added, together with the first drying kilns, which simplified timber buying and reduced stocks held.

The Parkers found time to be involved in various trade activities outside the firm. At a meeting of the Governors of High Wycombe Technical Institute in February 1827 Harry Parker, together with Lucien Ercolani, representing the Federation of Furniture Manufacturers, agreed to help set technical questions and inspect the final work of apprentices at the Institute. Seventy were attending classes several evenings each week, and the Federation offered prizes for the best specimens of work in previous years. Messrs Parker, Ercolani and Gomme formed a sub-committee to consider how the trade could support the apprenticeship classes.

It was a sad day when Frederick died on 2 February 1927, aged 82. After resigning his chairmanship, he had retired to live in Leigh on Sea, and died after a short illness. The funeral was attended by family and large numbers of staff from both Cowley and High Wycombe and was held at Cowley, where he was buried alongside his wife in the churchyard.

A large gathering of the High Wycombe & District Furniture Manufacturers Federation took place at the Red Lion Hotel for the annual dinner in early February 1927; Mr J. P. Birch was Chairman and expressed members' sympathy to both Harry and Tom Parker following their father's death. The toast 'The Town and Trade of Wycombe' was proposed by G. A. Locock CMG as the representative of the Federation of British Industry. Alan Janes responding, commenting 'that Wycombe was famous for chairs, chapels and children'. He deprecated the constant cry for lower priced goods and said that a few extra shillings was the cheapest purchase in the end. Later the following year, a thoughtful and detailed article on eighteenth century Windsor chairs, by A. E. Reveirs-Hopkins, appeared in the monthly *Old Furniture* in November 1928, extensively illustrated with items from the Parker collection.

28 November 1928 was to prove an important date although it was not significant at the time. A brief notice in the trade press each month gave details of newly issued patent specifications, applicable to the furnishing industry. Among new issues for mattresses, bed

settees, trays and so on is a one line entry — 'Knoll W. Spring Upholstery, November 28th, 1928, 322638.'.

As the decade drew to a close, the Wycombe furniture trade was enjoying a period of prosperity. This is illustrated by speeches at the 1929 annual dinner of the Wycombe Manufacturers' Federation. Among the guests was Sir Lawrence Weaver KBE who had recently published his book *High Wycombe Furniture.*

Lord Riddell, proposing the traditional toast 'The Town and Trade of Wycombe', noted how pleasant it was to visit such a prosperous place. There was no unemployment in Wycombe and 'several of the biggest Wycombe factories leap gaily over the tarriff fence of the United States, with upholstered chairs which are the best in the world and without which the American millionaire declines to live'. (A glance at Parkers' model record books shows that many prices were quoted in dollars as well as in sterling.)

Lord Riddell regretted that few Technical Institutes gave lessons in salesmanship and how to manage men. He suggested the Governors of the Wycombe Institute might consider this; it was a mistake when things were going well not to re-examine methods and consider if by altering or improving them, they could do even better. The Americans did this constantly, but we were not much given to it, especially in the older businesses.

It was with this mixture of congratulation and advice that Wycombe manufacturers left their 1929 dinner to face the trials of the approaching thirties.

The famous, and much transacted, Stuart marriage chest, bought for £80 and sold in 1927 for £200, bought again in 1932 for £24 after if had been to France and America.

1926 studio designs for room settings in the latest vogue — an uneasy marriage of old and new.

ABOVE: Miss Margery Ferry decorates by hand and BELOW: the Parkers relax in the garden at Cowley, Peachey House (known to the family as the Clock House), c1910.

THE TURBULENT THIRTIES

The crash of the American Stock Market in October 1929 had repercussions throughout the world. The banking crisis precipitated a world industrial crisis and social and political unrest in all European countries followed. In Britain, the downward spiral of trade and employment was beyond the power of the Government to control and unemployment rose with alarming rapidity to nearly three million in 1932. There was worldwide over-production against a vast slump in demand, and other factors increased the stagnation and social decay. The industrial structure had long been geared to the heavy industries of coal, textiles, steel and shipbuilding, and it was in these areas, essential for winning the War, that the depression bit deepest. The entire manufacturing base of the Nation contracted. This was not the most suitable economic background for a manufacturer geared to the best and most elaborate furniture that money could buy.

Yet, Society and the upper middle class were not so severely affected and those markets continued as before, albeit in a lower key. The Government resigned in August 1931 after taking Britain off the Gold Standard and devaluing the pound. A National Government was elected and set the tone for recovery. The depressed areas were given some assistance, but nothing significant was done to diversify or overhaul the industrial base, so misery and unemployment continued. It was not until the 1935 Defence White Paper, with its emphasis on engineering and aircraft for re-armament, that there was any significant rise in employment.

The majority elsewhere in the country found life slowly improved. There were cheap private housing, low inflation, and a growing choice of new consumer goods. An average of 345,000 houses was built each year between 1933 and 1937, presenting the furniture trade with a great opportunity for more sales. There was a continuing expansion of the service and professional sectors, typified by the spread of the London Underground to Cockfosters, Uxbridge, Harrow and Hendon. Midlands towns like Coventry and Leicester experienced growth and prosperity, all of which resulted in a pleasing and comfortable suburban life-style.

For those in furniture still making quality goods, largely by hand, it was like changing the scenery between acts in a play. What had gone before bore little relation to what was now wanted.

The Parkers had always welcomed new ideas, especially when abroad, and what happened next was perhaps fortuitous. It was certainlay to prove significant.

Frederick Parker had met the Knolls, furniture makers of Stuttgart, when he was in Germany in 1900 and the Company had occasional contact from time to time when they had bought covering materials and special leathers. Knolls produced high quality furniture too and some years previously had introduced chairs to the German market using a new type of springing. The method involved coiled steel wire springs which were attached laterally across both seat and back of the chair frame. Legend has it that in the First World War, a German fighter pilot, fed up with the uncomfortable basket seat in his fighter, got hold of some short coil springs and had a seat rigged up, using them as a base. The pilot was known to Willi Knoll and this set him thinking how to use the idea in domestic upholstery. In the mid-twenties he put it into production in Germany and later, in Sweden as well.

The Knolls were friendly with the Heal family who were one of several retailers with their own manufacturing facilities. Sir Ambrose Heal in 1890 was apprenticed to James Plucknett, a Warwick woodcarver. Now he was designing much simpler cabinet furniture, chiefly in light oak. This was a far cry from the design ideals of the Bauhaus movement on the Continent but, as the first attempt in England to break away from heavily carved and decorated styles, it interested a firm such as Knoll. They were designing and selling simply designed chairs of great elegance which made considerable use of bentwood arms; by the British standards of the day, they were extremely modern.

In 1929, Ambrose Heal telephoned TCP to say that he had a man in his shop who seemed to have a good idea concerning chairs, and he thought that Parkers would be the best firm to handle it. Nancy, TCP's youngest daughter, was working at Heals at the time, and recalls how Anthony Heal suggested she should ensure her father saw the sample chair. TCP discovered the 'man in the shop' was Willi Knoll, their old Stuttgart acquaintance. That chair incorporated the new springing that Knoll had patented in 1928. Willi had drawn up a list of three possible firms, including Parkers.

TCP soon realised this was a design with great potential. Its simplicity was in sharp contrast to the customary method. The simplest were stuffed over a base of jute webbing or, if sprung, involved various degrees of laborious hand-work building up the seat, fixing individual conical or cone-shaped coil springs in the base, and stuffing the whole over in first and sometimes in second cover. The materials and time involved were unfortunately reflected in the price. The Knoll chair consisted of machined show-wood parts for the frame, which was polished, plus a system of thin steel coil springs with hooks at each end. Inset into the chair side rails and upper back foot were rectangular metal blocks containing hooks on one side. By this means the seat and back springs were hooked into position horizontally, which took up no depth at all. This system was eventually modified and improved by Parkers with a strong and flexible eyeletted webbing to attach the seat springs, and metal buttons with hooked shanks, countersunk into the back feet of unupholstered models.

Loose seat and back cusions were all that was necessary to complete the chair. Consistent with Continental preference for firm seats, the square bordered cushions were filled with tufted Kapoc, with a stitched rolled edge. As a result they were extremely durable but lacked the softness that Parkers were used to building into their best upholstery.

However, the Knoll chair was exactly what Parkers needed. Capable of quantity machine production, simple assembly and thus strong but lightweight, it also provided a high degree of comfort. The springs moulded themselves to the shape and weight of the sitter, giving a firm but soft seat. Here indeed, was a revolutionary approach to the manufacture of chairs which also offered the prospect of lower prices without sacrificing quality. Willi Knoll had already shown his sample to Cohens who had turned it down; a decision Arthur Cohen rued for long afterwards. TCP was fired with enthusiasm and sought urgent consultation with his brothers. Willi Knoll was quite dogmatic that, if Parkers went ahead, they must make only German designs, which were clearly different from anything they had sold before.

William Parker was against this, as inconsistent with Parker tradition, and 'his Father would turn in his grave'. Considerable argument followed but finally, despite William's misgivings, it was decided that TCP should make an agreement with Willi Knoll to manufacture under licence. This was done in three days, Parkers agreeing initially to make 200 chairs a month. To give the new range its own market identity, the name of the new product in Britain was soon formulated: simply PARKER-KNOLL.

BRITISH INDUSTRIES FAIR

FEB 16-27 1931 FEB 16-27

EMPIRE HALL OLYMPIA
STAND J,4, SECOND FLOOR

PARKER-KNOLL FURNISHINGS

Do not fail to see this interesting exhibit

FREDK PARKER AND SONS LTD
20 NEWMAN ST., LONDON W1

Fredk. Parker & Sons Ltd.

UPHOLSTERERS & CABINET MAKERS.

FACTORIES,
TEMPLE END, HIGH WYCOMBE, BUCKS.
AND
COWLEY PEACHEY, COWLEY, MIDDSX.

TELEGRAMS. UPHOLSTERING, RATH, LONDON.
TELEPHONE. 0531 MUSEUM.

20, NEWMAN STREET,
OXFORD STREET,
LONDON, W.1.

30th March, 1932.

Messrs. Gibbs & Co.,
30, Gold St.,
Kettering.

Dear Sirs,

We are now stimulating interest in PARKER-KNOLL upholstery by means of a comprehensive advertising campaign.

Full page advertisements are appearing in all the leading home furnishing magazines - showcards are available for display in windows and showrooms - illustrated folders have been printed for distribution to the public.*

In your district there are many who will want to buy PARKER-KNOLL chairs. They will come to you and ask for them - your past experience of advertising tells you this is true. And there is no substitute for PARKER-KNOLL.

Increased profits are awaiting you if you stock PARKER-KNOLL upholstery. Stock it, display it, demonstrate it - and sell it.

Yours faithfully,
FREDK. PARKER & SONS, LTD.

*These folders will be supplied printed with your name and address - 500 for 20/-, 1,000 for 37/6, 2,000 for 70/-, upon application.

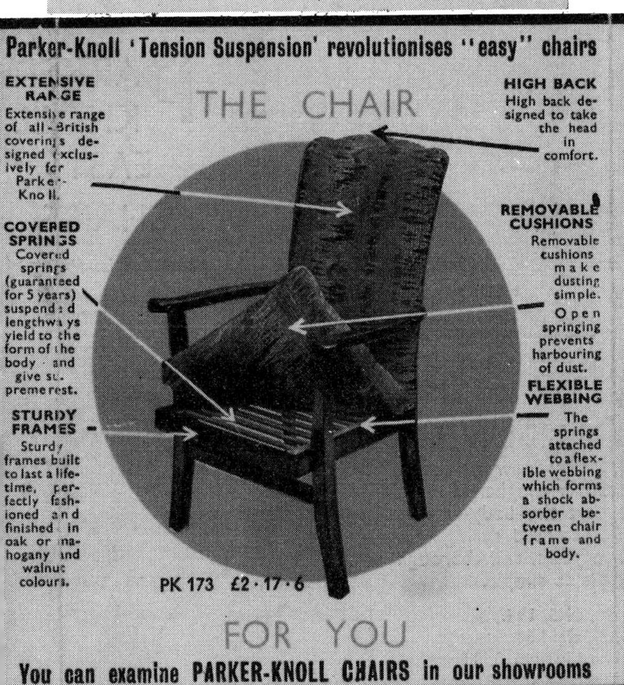

PARKER KNOLL IS THE CHAIR FOR YOU

PARKER KNOLL TENSION SUSPENSION

Fredk. PARKER & SONS, Ltd.,
20, Newman Street,
Oxford Street,
London, W.1.
'Phone Museum 0531

LEFT: It's 1931 and the British Industries Fair — Parker-Knoll issues its first-ever sales literature. RIGHT: In 1932 the firm pushed its wares by letter. BELOW: After retail criticism, the Company produced chairs with headrests and used this leaflet in 1932.

DIE
ANTIMOTT-Sessel
erfreuen sich überall größter Beliebtheit durch
unerreichte Bequemlichkeit
dauerhafte Konstruktion
praktische Reinigung
geschmackvolle Formen
niedrige Preise
Die umsponnenen ANTIMOTT-Stahlzugfedern haben sich in vielen Zehntausenden Sesseln hervorragend bewährt. Die Art der Federung bestimmt die Qualität des Sessels.
Die auf der ANTIMOTT-Federung liegenden elastischen KAFEDER-Kissen-Polster garantieren eine Doppelfederung von unerreichter Güte und Behaglichkeit.

Stylish 1930s chairs were made for the German market, but the home market was not yet ready for bentwood arms.

NEW PRODUCT, NEW PROBLEMS

It is strange that the Company minutes for 1930 make no mention whatever of the agreement with Knoll, especially as it involved giving various undertakings as to models and items of production, as well as royalties. After all, this was an important departure as well as a new venture.

The new range faced the Company with the need for a new marketing policy. Undoubtedly TCP was responsible for solving these problems, not all of which were immediately apparent. Initially the operation was small, but selling even fifty chairs a week posed problems. Parker's traditional production had to continue undisturbed, so separate space was needed for the new models. Different polishing arrangements had to be organised, although early models were hand-polished. The special spring-making and braiding machines had to be imported, and orders placed in England for special high tensile spring wire and webbing. Decisions were needed on pricing policy and on what types of cover ranges to offer. Thought had also to be given to the literature necessary to tell the trade about the new range. Many of these were new areas.

Meanwhile, the older Parker business continued. In India the formal architecture and wide boulevards of Sir Edward Lutyens between 1912 and 1930 created the new administrative centre of New Dehli. Parkers were involved in supplying upholstery and cabinet work for the luxurious and spectacular Viceroy's House. Another important job was the hand carved throne for His Majesty Haile Selassie, Emperor of Abyssinia and Lion of Judah. This was ordered for his palace in Addis Ababa following his proclamation as Emperor in 1930. The throne was carved from solid wood and took four months to complete. When the job was nearly finished, foreman carver Jim Hathaway found a flaw in the wood so a whole section had to be done again. A number of other chairs were also supplied each having the Royal coat of arms in the back, finished in gilt. Soon after these fine examples of Parker craftsmanship arrived at Addis Ababa they were destroyed by fire during the Italian invasion.

High quality upholstery was in continuous demand from wealthy Americans, many of whom used to pay visits to the Newman Street showrooms when in England. Apart from the more exotic three piece suites, many covered in the richest brocatelles, brocades and needleworks, the plain club easy chair continued a best seller. This type had been made in many styles since before the First World War. Lacking any elegance except for scroll arms, these chairs had long seats, the absolute epitome of comfort. Their secret lay in the high quality first and second stuffed upholstery, which used best white horse hair, with seat and back cushions of swansdown. It was a joy to rise from one and to watch the depressed cushions also rising to their normal shape as the swansdown expanded, and to hear the crackle of the cushions filling when they were plumped up. No less than 320 different styles were made in this special upholstery, known as the 'P Range', several large retailers each reserving a design exclusively. Coverings were often customers' own material or they supplied their own cretonne in which loose covers were made up and fitted to calico covered chairs. More expensively, Morocco with its warm, soft luxury, made a sumptuous and long-lasting chair.

One of the most popular was the P 139. Priced at around £10 in 1915, it still sold in 1938 for only £11 15s 6d when covered in print linen at 2s 6d per yard. The price in hide, with velveteen cushions, was £16 5s. This chair even today graces many country house drawing rooms, and many also went to British Embassies.

The development and extension of the Temple End factory at Wycombe in 1928 led to a gradual running-down of the Cowley factory in the early thirties. There were difficulties in obtaining the skilled labour required, and the distance from Wycombe created difficulties too. This increased the desirability of concentrating all production in one main factory. The machine shop and two-floor cabinet shop at Cowley were leased to the Sentry Safety Glass Company in 1930 and some employees moved to Wycombe. Among them was Mrs Nellie Woods, an experienced and clever sewing machinist. She supervised the sewing room at Wycombe for many years and, it is said, gave lessons on the use of the machines to Harry Parker.

The house at 21-23 Frogmoor into which the Parkers had moved in 1898 was leased in 1930 to Fleet's Dairy, who remained there until the 1950s; Frederick's house at Cowley was leased too, following his death and about then Walter Ferry moved his studio to Wycombe.

At Newman Street, the ground floor was let, but all the other showroom floors and basement were in use, crammed with every sort of cabinet and upholstery work, except for the cheapest end of the market. The top floor displayed some of the antique chairs sent to Wycombe when needed as models. At the rear of the showrooms, in Newman Passage, was another three storey building, connected to the front by the basement. This was inconvenient when buyers were touring the showrooms, and so a bridge was built in 1931 at third floor level.

The severity of the depression was increasingly felt. Parker's nett profits had run at a steady 9% each year since the nett loss of 1921 but there was a sharp drop in 1930 to only 6%. This might not have been too significant had a recovery followed. A small nett loss in 1931 was followed by a severe nett loss of £10,677 for 1932. It is difficult today to know how the Board saw the future in 1932 but, at the annual meeting in June, it was decided to pay no dividend on the 1931 results. No dividend was paid until 1934, and then only on the preference shares. Directors' salaries were reduced in May 1932 to £11 weekly and it was not until November 1934 that they were restored to the original level of £22. It must have been obvious that the Company could not maintain the same style of business, and this perhaps influenced TCP in 1930 when pressing for a link-up with Knoll.

TCP's daughters recall how worried both he and his brother Harry were then. They often had arguments over the 'phone about order levels — either too many of this, or not enough of that, or late deliveries. William, calling on customers, was anxious to satisfy them, and often gave promises without consulting Harry, who ran the factory. It all sounds so familiar today.

They also recall the scenes at the factory gate 'where these chaps in threadbare coats and terrible plimsoll shoes queued up for work on any icy cold day and were often turned away, there being no work to give them'.

As in any busienss, the factory may be short of work while the sales people are seeking orders, the two operations in apparent conflict. This was the situation in 1931, when the Company exhibited at the British Industries Fair at Olympia. This was probably the first time the new Parker-Knoll chairs were displayed to the trade. The *Cabinet Maker* preview concentrates solely on the new chairs and the Company's leaflet illustrates three different models. These are seen in a contrived domestic setting with some of the severe, modern occasional furniture then in vogue.

The Company exhibited at the British Industries fair every year throughout the 1930s showing Parkers' traditional cabinet and upholstery alongside the Parker-Knoll range, to which new models were constantly added. This provided a useful shop window for manufacturers, which moved to White City in 1934 where, for the first time, there was a Wycombe section, although Parkers preferred to show separately in another hall. Her Majesty Queen Mary was a regular visitor to the Fair, and paused during her 1934 tour to inspect the Frederick Parker stand.

There was increasingly a feeling that the worst of the depression was over and that business was getting back to normal. In their field of traditional furniture, Parkers in the thirties produced some of the best upholstery work ever. This is typified by the richly covered three piece suites always displayed at Newman Street as well as in the fine reproduction chairs. The results from the new Parker-Knoll chairs were somewhat disappointing and the hope that this new range would offset falling sales and lift the company out of the recession was so far unfounded.

P.K. 198
£3 . 17 . 6
P.K. 199
£3 . 17 . 6
The
PARKER-KNOLL Chair
arouses great attention everywhere through
Unsurpassed Comfort
Lasting Construction
Easy Cleaning
Tasteful Designs
Low Prices
The covered Parker-Knoll Steel Springs have proved their excellent quality in many thousands of chairs.
The type of spring governs the quality of the chair.
Patented.
DICKSON & BENSON, LTD.
THE ARCADES AND LINTHORPE ROAD,
MIDDLESBROUGH.
Telephone: 2855 (3 lines).

The English leaflet and these Anglicised chairs included the PK140, resurrected in 1975 and still selling.

LEFT: Harold Vernon, the man who revolutionised the firm's advertising with, among other things, RIGHT: the famous man on a spring, which encouraged BELOW: window displays like this one by Furlongs of Woolwich in the 1930s.

Tension Suspension

The trend in living standards by the mid-twenties had a marked effect on the style of living rooms. The boom in house building and the steady rise in hire purchase both led the development of mass-production, such as with Lebus and Dependable Upholstery, and large retail organisations selling on no-deposit credit. 'It's easier to pay Smarts the four year way' became a well known slogan, while full-page press advertisements by Drages, Bolsoms, Thomas Wallis and many more maintained the thrust of the message, 'buy your furniture now and pay later'.

Styles of furnishing at all price levels have moved a long way form the heavily overstuffed and ornamental Victorian taste towards lighter, simpler styles. A few shillings would purchase a simple wood-armed chair with upholstered back and seat. The small squat variety, with a simple fabric-covered seat and often an elaborately caned back, soon became known as 'Firesides', a description which eventually applied to any lightweight chair with open wooden arms. The adjustable backed chair with loose corduroy-covered cushions on wooden slatted seats and backs had been Wycombe's best seller in the late twenties. Many of these were priced at £2 or less.

Parkers never had to seek publicity for their products before, as they had always been in the position of 'making the better mouse trap' and 'the world HAD beaten a path to THEIR door'. When the new Parker-Knoll chairs were first introduced they were very much an adjunct to Parkers' main business. As they introduced their new product to their old trade friends they soon found they had moved into a area of which they had almost no experience. Their reputation for quality made it difficult to persuade traditional customers that their new product, untried as it was, had sales potential. Their traditional customers were conservative and reluctant to experiment.

TCP realised that it was up to him to convince the trade, and that to do so he had to formulate and apply marketing policies which required a completely different approach.

When Parkers decided to make chairs with the Knoll suspension they saw the Parker-Knoll chair as offering quality before price, built to last, using only the best materials. All frames were of solid timber and available in a choice of oak, mahogany, walnut, and sometimes cherry and sycamore. It is not surprising that the chairs did not appeal to the low priced mass market through which the bulk of furniture was sold.

While Harry Parker dealt with the initial production arrangements, TCP and William had first to obtain orders. They were both well-known to buyers and had many friends. They presented the long-established Parker tradition of honest dealing and value for money. The Company had long been recognised for its pursuit of new ideas, and was renowned as the firm to go to with a difficult problem. It was said that Harry Parker would make up a design even if it was on the back of an envelope.

Thus, it was expected that customers would back the firm's judgement and enthusiastically support the new springing. TCP described their first efforts as a complete flop:

'The buyers of course, who are experienced in everything, looked at it, (we had spent a long time studying it ourselves you know,) and they said nobody would buy it — "won't last ten minutes" — Well, what could you do? The customers stated that this time we had made a mistake and refused to hold stocks'.

Despite all, trial orders were obtained from customers who took a pair of chairs out of friendship rather than conviction, and this was enough to start production. The first models used frames from Germany but it was soon clear they were too modern in style. The Company developed more appropriate designs, including chairs with upholstered arms and loose seat cushions.

Lacking any promotional material, the first chairs failed to create a sensaton. Unless the retailer gave them some prominence, they were easily lost on the shop floor. TCP was not perturbed, for he had faith in the new springing, especially its comfort.

The selling points of the Parker-Knoll chair were clear to Parkers, even if initially not to the trade. The new springing system was quite revolutionary and offered a number of user benefits.

A cotton cover, woven closely around each horizontal steel spring, protected the cushion covers from damage, and limited the stretch of the spring. The flexible eyeletted webbing into which each spring hooked acted as a shock absorber between sitter and frame. There were no pockets to form dust traps. When the cushions were removed, the springs were exposed, making for easy cleaning.

The simplicity of the concept made it possible to manufacture at moderate prices while mechanical loading tests had established the durability of the system far beyond loads it would normally bear.

Obviously the most convincing way to demonstrate these features would be to show them a sample chair. This technique was used at an early stage when George Parker, William's son, loaded a selection of chairs into a lorry and presented himself to startled buyers. Bond's of Norwich, Wenleys of Chelmsford, and many others became customers in this way. In London, William persevered with the large furnishing houses, persuading them to visit the showrooms at 20, Newman Street to see for themselves.

Even so, it was an uphill struggle and the orders came in slowly. Parkers' original range of cabinet and upholstered furniture soon came to be described as 'best quality' and was in no way affected by the new range. Buyers from leading provincial accounts often paid visits to Newman Street and were then introduced to Parker-Knoll.

Due to Parkers' inexperience, the new range was initially brought to the market without promotional material or programme. It was recognised at an early stage that some means of identification was needed on the chairs themselves in the shops. This at first took the form of a red and white circular ticket which carried the legend: 'Parker-Knoll Furnishings Patented', but this was hardly sufficient or satisfactory. In addition, the words 'Parker Knoll Patent' were embossed in red paint into the back seat rail, to be followed by an oval red or silver metal label which also carried the Parker-Knoll name and the patent number 322638. In those early days, when there were no known furniture brands, Parkers failed to realise how much effort would be necessary to translate their confidence into a leading brand name.

TCP was always a man of imaginative mind, and the eventual success of Parker-Knoll owes a great deal to his vision and direct thinking in areas of promotion never before used by a furniture manufacturer. He was convinced that the Parker-Knoll springing system would sell. The more he thought about it, the more convinced he became that there was only one way to do this, and that was by advertising in the daily press. This was new, and Parkers had little idea of how to achieve it.

Initially, Walter Ferry was asked to prepare some draft advertisements in his studio, and space was booked in the *Daily Mail*. Ferry was an excellent Chief Designer, but he was not a graphic artist. An insertion in just one daily paper was not sufficient either. There was no immediate rush to the shops to buy the new chairs. The first advertisements in late 1931 were quite small and focused attention on the details of the new tension spring. Their visual impact was low and, surrounded by newsprint, the message did not stand out or arrest the attention.

It must have disappointed TCP and his brothers when they were unable to persuade reluctant retailers that they risked losing sales if they did not stock the chairs, especially as many had not seen the advertisements.

Other furniture makers were quicker to appreciate the merits of Parker-Knoll than the retailers. Other chairs began to appear, using the idea of horizontal springing. Some had systems of flat steel bands, others reinforced horizontal rubber springs. Although less expensive imitations of the principle they were noticeably inferior in many ways. To quote TCP:

'The first thing that happened as always in the furniture trade if you have a good idea, everybody copies it. They all looked up the Patent and got the idea that our springs were covered, and if they used springs without the covering or covered them in some other material, they would not infringe the Patent. Well, of course they did [make copies]. I won't mention the name of the firm who did it in Wycombe, but I telegraphed to Willi to come over because it was his Patent, not ours, but not Willi! He was wiser than we were. He left it to us'.

Again, because Parkers were unfamiliar with such matters they intially thought a patent number was sufficient to give protection from imitators. As distribution of the chairs increased and the Parker-Knoll name became more widely known it was not long before some retailers were using the term 'Parker-Knoll type' to describe those imitations. They probably did not realise that in doing so they were misusing the name and exposing themselves to legal action. No action could be taken against manufacturers of imitations, as their chairs differed in all sorts of ways from the patented specification. Any retailer who described or sold non-PK products either as 'Parker Knoll type' or 'style', or worse, as Parker Knoll, was infringing the law. It was not long before Parkers felt it necessary to act. In 1932 a North London retailer had passed off other products as Parker Knoll, and the Company asked the High Court for an injunction. This was heard before the Honourable Mr Justice Swift at the end of 1933, when a perpetual injunction was granted, enabling Parkers to publicise the case as a warning to others, that they would act to protect their trade name. Full page notices were inserted in the *Cabinet Maker, Furniture Record* and other trade papers, and that court action was the first of several.

TCP's eldest daughter Marion married John Arnold, who was a patent agent able to advise TCP. Stressing that the patent taken out by Knoll gave no protection, as it could be easily circumvented, he advised that the Parker Knoll name be registered as the Company's trade mark. This would provide absolute protection in law.

In 1932 TCP took a message on the stand at the British Industries Fair that a Mr Morgans had called. When Morgans returned, the nature of his visit was topical and of great interest. He had, he said, seen some advertisements in the *Daily Mail* for the new Parker Knoll chairs. Were Parkers satisfied with the resposne? When TCP admitted that there had not been any, Morgans went on to say that the design and layout was terrible and would never create the necessary interest. Morgans then introduced his Managing Director Harold Vernon, who said that he could prepare something for the Company. He also stressed that it was useless to advertise any product which did not already have a sufficiently wide distribution. Interest created by the advertising would soon be lost if potential customers could not find the product.

His challenge was taken up; after discussion and visits to the factory where they wanted to know every deail about the product, Vernons were asked to submit a detailed proposal. After what seemed a long dealy, at a meeting at Newman Street they presented their plan. This was for a six months' campaign, and TCP and his brothers were convinced that the proposal would succeed in bringing the Parker-Knoll chair to the attention of a wide public. When they asked how much it would cost, they were astonished to be told £10,000. In 1932 this was a lot of money, especially for a product yet to obtain wide distribution. First reaction was that it was ridiculous and beyond the Company's means but, after much consideration, and scaling down of both media and insertions, it was agreed to place the matter in Vernon's hads for a trial period. Thus Vernons became the Comany's advertising agents, an association which continued unbroken for fifty years.

At the same time, the trade mark was registered as 'Parker-Knoll. Tension Suspension'.

The next step was to create an easily identifiable logo, not only to establish the brand name but also to identify the Company and its products at a glance. It was James Fitton RA, Art Director of Vernons, who conceived and designed the simple but expressive 'Man on the Spring' emblem which became so famous in the 1930s. This stylised logo cleverly illustrated the tension chair spring, visually indicating the way in which it functioned by incorporating the descriptive words 'Tension Suspension'.

Once adopted, it appeared on all the Company's literature and products, and played an important part in creating the identity of Parker-Knoll with trade and public alike.

A second innovation from Vernons was a spring guarantee. As a means of testing the durability of both chair frames and springs, Parkers had set up a test rig. This consisted of a strong canvas bag filled with sixteen stones of sand which was raised and lowered by machine into the test chair, if necessary till destruction. It was thus possible to know with certainty how durable all parts of the chairs would be in normal use, resulting in Parkers' absolute confidence in their new product. This was expressed in Vernon's advertisements as 'New Springing. Guaranteed for 5 years'. It is a matter of record that rarely were claims received against this guarantee.

Parkers wanted to continue with their *Daily Mail* insertions, but Vernons wanted the money spent on magazines, which had a longer life, and would best attract the attention of people interested in furnishings. Initially, expenditure on advertising was small; £1,236 in 1932, rising to £2,007 in 1934, but it was sufficient to send the public into the shops for the new chairs, and thus Parker-Knoll became a household word.

On 3 June 1932 TCP wrote a note to Harry which illustrates his search for other ways to broaden the market and fresh ideas:

'Russell called here today commenting on P.K. He says all customers state prices are too high and until we get out a cheaper range no large business is likely. In no case can he find a customer who has had an enquiry through the advertisements. More models required high enough to take the head.'

TCP, wondering how larger production might be obtained, then put forward another idea:

'? P.K.s on the Ford plan? It is worth while going into ? say two models P.K.36 and P.K.37. – could 100,000 a year be produced to sell complete for 30/- each allowing cover (material) at 3/- a yard?

Willi Knoll's commission reduced to 1% (or purchased outright by instalments)'.

Harry's terse and pragmatic initial reply was:

'The question of producing a la Ford brings up a lot of questions. 1 Machinery 2 Premises 3 Stock.'

Such reactions to such bold thinking on TCP's part were understandable at a time when it was a struggle to get sufficient orders to avoid the failure of the whole project.

Parkers needed to capitalise in every possible way on their new tactics. Editorial writeups were much valued and a sales force was required to call on all retailers, to convince them of the potential benefits of becoming stockists, displaying this new and advertised product. An assortment of showcards and leaflets were produced and, to encourage retailers to advertise locally, blocks and stereos were supplied free.

The suggestion that the range would sell better with some high-backed models included, was soon implemented, with the introduction in 1932 of a set of four new models. Selling retail at £2 17s 6d, much lower than the average Parker-Knoll chair, these became the 'pot boilers' of the range and were an immediate success, and one of the largest volume groups until 1940.

Soon after the first Vernon advertisements appeared, TCP experienced a wave of protest and criticism from many of the oldest and most important customers. Until then, retailers had done all their own advertising and promotions; never before had a manufacturer advertised his furniture direct to the public. There was probably a good deal of misunderstanding of Parkers' motives including fears that they intended to sell direct. Nothing was further from their thoughts. The trade convention that a manufacturer never sold direct was long established and, as far as Parkers were concerned, absolutely correct. There was, however, in their view nothing to stop a manufacturer proud of his product from informing the public. Yet all furniture makers were supposed by the retail trade to be anonymous, and there had never been such a thing as a brand name.

Some retailers were so jealous of their position that they continued for many years to remove all labels and maker's marks if they could, pretending that the furniture was of their own make, or specially commissioned. When Parkers discovered that this was actually happening, they overcame the problem by having the name 'Parker-Knoll' woven into a wide tape sewn the length of the flexible straps into which the springs hooked. This clever idea, apart from being impossible to remove, had the additional advantage of making a Parker Knoll chair easy to identify.

Some of Parkers' oldest and most valuable customers threatened to close their accounts unless the advertising stopped. TCP made it clear that he would much regret it if they did so, but that he would not alter his policy. The response to advertising built slowly, but at a sufficient rate to show retailers that the public was noticing the advertisements and making enquiries in their shops for 'those new Parker Knoll chairs'. Opposition slowly faded as retailers realised the customers liked what they saw and sales were made. Another manufacturer, Buoyant Upholstery of Nottingham, had been thinking along the same lines and had also started national advertising. Their logo showed an easy chair from the depths of which only a pair of knees was visible, with the text 'Kenneth! let your Father Sit Down!' and this quickly became known. Thus, nationally advertised, branded furniture was established for the first time.

The marketing of Parker-Knoll raised other questions and required policy decisions on matters entirely new. With their traditional furniture they had no need to organise their retailers in any way. Their business was in effect a bespoke one, with retailers knowing that all they had to do was to submit general requirements, and Parkers would offer alternatives. There were some cabinent models in constant demand and made in larger batches, but the majority was made up to order. If nothing suitable could be found, then what was required could be made specially. The same was true of upholstery, with the largest stores keeping certain suites and chairs on display, knowing that they could always obtain details for potential customers from Parkers' vast selection. This service was based on a library held at Newman Street of photographs of some 3,000 models in both cabinet and unholstery ranges. As new models had been added over the years they had been photographed on glass plate negatives by Newburys, who then supplied prints as required. Glossy prints were sent out to customers through the post, offering a far more flexible servioce than for a smaller catalogued range.

The complete collection of plates posed a considerable problem of storage due to their fragile nature, as well as their vast weight. When Newburys closed down the plates were offered to the Company. These were destroyed in the disastrous fire at the Wycombe factory in 1970. All that now remains is the library of photographic prints, not entirely complete.

The philosophy behind the marketing of Parker-Knoll was different. The whole project was founded on the intention to produce a limited range of chairs and settees on a continuing and quantity basis. Initially the range of models was quite small, and retailers were to be encouraged to stock them all so that they could benefit from the advertising which would send customers to them. Standardisation in this way was new and took a bit of getting used to. This quickly raised the question of pricing. On traditional furniture, the retailer had taken the profit he thought it would bear, but advertising, and promotion at exhibitions, meant that some uniformity must be imposed. It was decided at an early stage to adopt a policy under retail price maintenance which would ensure a given chair was sold at the same price from Lands End to John o'Groats. This stopped retailers being undersold and increased their confidence. Retail prices were fixed at a level that gave the retailer the customary trade margin of 50% on cost, 33.3% on return, for all Parker-Knoll models. TCP believed that this was both necessary and fair, at the same time allowing Parkers to publish priced literature and catalogues, with which to further promote sales.

Other problems arose. The traditional trade in upholstery had always allowed for the customer's individual choice of cover. The choice was made at the retailers from a vast selection of pattern books. Parkers would then order the required amount, and carried only a small selection of covering materials in stock. Often customers would obtain material independently and this would be sent in by the retailer. If one of these methods met the customer's needs, Parkers would find suitable samples. This involved the employment of a young person known as a 'pattern matcher', who would spend every day touring the wholesalers' showrooms to obtain samples to match the often minute snippings sent in. Repeat size of the pattern had to be right for the job on which it was to be used and samples then had to be sent back to the retailer for selection by his customer, and finally ordered by Parkers. It was time consuming, but it did ensure that the most exacting requirements could be satisfied. Many a young person started in the trade in this way, and would agree that it was an excellent way of learning about the wide range of materials. A related problem was that of finding suitable trimmings — braid, cord, ruche, fringe and so on. Often only small quantities of gimp or braid were required, but it was essential that they should match or at least blend with the selected covering material. While trimming wholesalers held a wide selection it was not always possible to find a match and a special order had to be placed. Brook Bros & Dean in Rathbone Place and their obliging London representative, Mr Smith, will be remembered, as well as A. H. Lee of Birkenhead. All acquainted with the complex looms required to produce trimmings will understand what an undertaking it was to make a couple of yards of braid or ruche to special order. This is a service that the trade still needs, but which seems to have gone for ever.

The promotional techniques of advertising and pricing also brought the need to stock and offer a standard range of covering materials. It was essential to offer a choice of covering at the point of sale, as regards colour, style and price. Only by doing this could the opportunity to book orders be maximised, as the number of occasions on which a stock chair was exactly right were obviously limited. Also, selling the stock chairs reduced the opportunity to book further orders. Parkers selected a range of materials, put them into stock and issued pattern swatches to retailers. At the same time the old service of finding a special cover continued through the matching service. Keeping frames of the most popular chairs in stock meant delivery could be speeded up. Today it is recalled with envy that an order received on a Monday from London could be despatched by rail the following Friday!

About this time, Parkers started to recruit a larger sales force to cover the whole country, with regular calls on retailers and to obtain more stockists. This was another important part of establishing confidence and goodwill with retailers, as well as helping with their problems and booking repeat orders. Despite the fixed resale price, many retailers wanted to price according to 'what the customer will bear' which soon led to complaints from the public that they had been charged more than the advertised price, or from retailers that another shop was underselling them.

In such cases, Parkers quickly drew the offender's attention to their pricing policy, stressing that the account would have to be closed if they felt unable to comply. The majority welcomed the resale price policy and expected the Company do deal firmly with infringements. Complaints from the public were referred to the retailer.

There was one way round the fixed price policy — to supply their own covering materials for all stock chairs. They could then price the furniture as they wished, but had to suffer the inconvenience of obtaining and sending the covers to the factory. Chamberlain King & Jones of Birmingham followed this policy and yet remained good friends with the Parkers.

By 1934, the main hurdles had been overcome and most leading retailers and stores had settled down to regular business. The advertising policy had proved its value and a drive to gain more stockists developed. Two valuable orders in particular demonstrated recognition of the merits of Parker Knoll. The new BBC headquarters, Broadcasting House, in Portland Place, London was opened on 2 May 1932. Built on the site of James Wyatt's own house it had caused controversy. Required to blend with its Georgian and Regency surroundings and yet house twenty-two sound-proof studios, the building, designed by G. Val Myers, like a great ship, aimed its bow down Portland Place, and was intended to express the modernity of the new technology. Parker-Knoll chairs, equally modern in style and concept, were chosen for most of the rooms and studios, including the Council Chamber and Boardroom. This substantial order led to an association with the BBC which has continued to present times. The second order, which recognised the value of Parker-Knoll in the hotel business, was from the Trust House Group, which adopted Parker Knoll chairs as almost standard seating for their extensive range of hotels. It was common to see these chairs still in use in the 1950s, after almost twenty years' valiant service under exacting conditions.

By the mid-thirties the Parker-Knoll chair was firmly established in the marketplace. Many of Parkers' old customers had become enthusiastic supporters. It was thanks to TCP's clear vision in establishing policy, and his decision to advertise, coupled also with Parkers' reputation for integrity and quality that achieved this. Harry Parker had successfully reorganised the factory to cope with quantity production of Parker-Knoll, alongside bespoke furniture. Thenceforth, manufacturers assumed their share of promotion and the selling of good, quality, medium-priced furniture to the rapidly expanding middle class markets.

There was still a demand for Parkers' 'best quality', but for less flamboyant styles and on a declining scale. Nevertheless, this was still the major Company activity and relied upon by retailers whose business was selling top quality reproduction furniture.

Results were improving. Although turnover for 1934 was no better at £88,000 than in 1930, the net profit had recovered to £7,418 after the heavy losses of 1932.

Although some retailers supported the new range, many of Parkers' old friends had taken a more conservative view and only sampled one or two models or did nothing at all. Parkers knew from long experience the difficulties, nay impossibility, of galvanising the whole furniture retail trade to actively promote a new product on a national scale. It took a long time to persuade many that national advertising, far from threatening their interests, offered them an opportunity to convert interest into sales.

No examples remain of the original advertisements Parkers inserted in the *Daily Mail*. The first Vernons advertisement, CVS 1, was in ten inch high single column, but it was not long before that was increased, eventually standardising at twelve inch doubles. A study of the layouts developed over the years shows the message becoming gradually more sophisticated.

Much thought had been given to appropriate media. In 1932 advertisements were confined to *Woman at Home* and *Ideal Home* magazine, but by 1933 the *Daily Mail* was included again. Further widening came in 1934 with the *Daily Telegraph*. This association has continued. Initially, readers were advised to visit their retailers to see the chairs, but eventually this was modified to an invitation to write for a free catalogue and names of stockists, if one of 700 available could not be located.

As the campaign expanded, further additions were made including the *Sunday Times*, *Observer* and *Punch*. Campaigns were run in the spring and autumn of each year, designed to coincide with the peak buying seasons. The whimsical approach to domestic life situations in the copy was unashamedly designed to have middle-class appeal, and was tremendously successful.

Retailers were notified in advance of each campaign and given full details of media and dates. They were exhorted to make sure their stocks were adequate. Many retailers thought that Parkers would be inundated with letters from potential customers asking where they could buy. A frequent complaint was that no names and addresses were ever sent on for them to follow up. Parkers felt, if they did so, it would lead to embarrassment should they start knocking on doors.

Increasing public awareness became progressively apparent to reluctant or over-cautious retailers. It also led to a great increase in the number of retailers. Many had no call for expensive hand-made furniture, but were well able to sell this new range of moderately priced chairs. In the early and mid-thirties travel for most people was confined to holidays away from home, with car ownership at quite a low level. This meant that most domestic equipment was bought locally, especially in the less urban parts of the country. To serve this market each town had its own specialist shops, many of them long-established family businesses, with considerable expertise and their own inbuilt preferences.

It was from these High Street retailers that Parker-Knoll received such staunch support. Their customers were asking to see the chairs and liked what they saw, while experienced retailers could readily appreciate their merits. In larger departmental stores there was always more competition for floor space, and generally less emphasis on any one of many products.

By the middle years of the 1930s demand for Parker-Knoll chairs and settees was increasing. Advertising had created interest with both public and trade and had justified Vernon's confidence.

By 1935 the initial operations to sell Parker-Knoll had been completed. Credit for this is due in no small measure to C. Vernon & Sons.

A WARNING

Messrs. Frederick Parker & Sons, Ltd., the manufacturers of the well-known "Parker-Knoll" Chairs and Settees, have recently been granted by the Honourable Mr. Justice Swift in the High Court of Justice a perpetual Injunction restraining a Retailer from selling, offering or exposing for sale or causing to be sold, offered or exposed for sale any Chair or Settee not manufactured by Messrs. Frederick Parker & Sons, Ltd., under the name of "Parker-Knoll" or any other name or by any other description such as to lead to the belief that the Chairs and Settees or any of them sold by the retailer were the Chairs and Settees manufactured and sold by Messrs. Frederick Parker & Sons, Ltd.

Messrs. Frederick Parker & Sons, Ltd., hereby give notice that they will, for the protection of the public no less than for the maintenance of the reputation of their well-known products, take legal proceedings to prevent the sale, by any person under their name or under any description by which their goods are known, of goods not manufactured by them.

Trouble came with cheap imitations; Parker Knoll went to law.

ABOVE: HM Queen Mary took a look at the product at White City in 1934; George Parker seems more interested in the camera than the Queen! BELOW: HM King Edward VIII told the nation he was 'still that same man' who got to know his subjects as the Prince of Wales. He was broadcasting from Portland Place in 1935, sitting in a PK115.

On Show

Twenty Newman Street is an imposing four-storey building, centrally situated just off the eastern end of Oxford Street. Since 1902 this had provided Parkers with excellent showroom and office facilities in which a selection of their fine upholstery and cabinet goods were displayed. By a simple division of responsibilities between the four directors, all sales matters were controlled in London by TCP and his brother Will, while all production matters were dealt with by Harry at Wycombe, with financial departments the responsibility of Fred, the Company Secretary.

This arrangement worked well, with secretaries in London and Wycombe each responsible for telephoning the other at an appointed time every day. All questions and answers were entered in a book so that they could be relayed at the next telephone call. Failure to report back the same day often brought a heated and dreaded call direct to the offending person from Harry himself. Documents were exchanged mostly by post until 1935, after which a van from Wycombe called daily at Newman Street.

The office and showrooms were managed by W. J. Kindred — always immaculately attired in black jacket, pinstriped trousers and spats — together with a staff of four young men and four typists, Mrs B. who made the tea and dusted all the furniture daily, and Fred Saunders who looked after the back entrance in Newman Passage, receiving all incoming deliveries and parcels. An abiding memory of the showrooms is the concentrated aroma of polished wood, turpentine and beeswax.

Prior to 1936 the tempo at Newman Street must have been quite leisurely but, with the growing success of Parker Knoll, new services were needed to deal with increasing interest from both trade and public. Members of the public were calling at Newman Street to inspect chairs, but there were no proper facilities. Fortunately the ground floor, which had been let, became vacant, facilitating more office accommodation and a whole floor solely to display Parker Knoll.

In March 1936 the author joined the Company direct from school. Through the good offices of the FTBA, T. K. Bowman of Bowmans, Camden Town and G. H. Cooper of Lawrences of Nottingham, he was sent for an interview at Newman Street showrooms, armed with carefully executed scale elevation and perspective drawings of various bookcases and other items of furniture copied onto art paper from *Woodworker Magazine*. They had been heavily woodgrained in soft pencil and were intended to create a good impression. Not surprisingly TCP paid them scant attention. However, at the end of the interview, he did offer the opportunity to start work immediately as a 'pattern matcher' at 20 Newman Street at 17s 6d per week.

On arrival, the junior member of staff was given the task of 'Photograph Books'. Large and heavy ledgers containing photographs and all price and material details of furniture and upholstery made by the Company since 1890 were kept overnight in a basement safe. They had to be extracted first thing every morning and carried upstairs, to be placed during working hours on a wooden rack in the office then on the first floor. The books were used all day for answering queries, calculating prices and making quotations. At the close of business, and not a minute before, the books had to be returned to the safe. By tradition all new male staff members had this responsibility unitl they achieved promotion. Although, by March 1976, when the author had completed forty years' service, the books had gone out of use, he made a point that day of bringing them out of storage at the factory and carrying them all up to the top floor of the Sales Office at Frogmoor. The staff, of course, could not see the point. All fifteen books are now in the Company archives.

The new 'Pattern Matcher' had first to be shown the location of all the textile and trimmings warehouses and showrooms in London. Richard Clibbens, who was promoted to Traveller in the West Country, introduced him to Richardson & Smith, who had a one-room office upstairs in the Linguaphone building in Oxford Street. This part of the job was exciting to a lad just out of school, but much more difficult was understanding the difference between a taffeta and a tapestry or satin, and knowing just which firm was most likely to have the type of material specified. If silk damask was required one did not go to Foxtons, and if high quality uncut moquette, one did not go to Donald Bros or Turnbull and Stockdale. There were both West End and City houses to visit. The search for those in the depressing surroundings of Curtain Road and Great Eastern Street on a wet afternoon was often a miserable and tedious part of the job.

When orders were received in special materials the quantity required was ordered from Newman Street by Charles Johnson, Charles was killed in 1941 when HMS *Chakdina* was sunk.

All such cut lengths of material required by Parkers for specific orders and those sent by customers as 'own cover' arrived at Newman Street and then transferred to Wycombe. These were placed in large wicker skips closed by a drop lid, secured by a bar and padlock. New boys had to beware of being locked in a skip during the late morning, in danger of being sent to Wycombe if they were not released just as the van was driving away. Since the skips stood in the office only a few feet from the Manager's desk, a petrified silence had to be maintained, relying on the general office noises to hide the creaking of the skip at the slightest movement.

The decision to carry a standard range of covering materials for Parker Knoll required a Tapestry Buyer. TCP undertook this initially, as part of the overall marketing policy, but seeing travellers and making selections was only the first stage of the operation, Wycombe submitted a weekly stock list each Monday, which had to be matched to outstanding orders with suppliers, before further orders could be placed. There was constant need to press for delivery as the factory was averse to holding buffer stocks and yet expected never to run out. Certainly 'no cover' meant gaps in production then, just as it does today. Another part of this growing job was to have pattern swatches made of each range of materials for all the retail stockists. This again was an important feature of the marketing of Parker Knoll as it enabled the retailer to offer his customer a choice, allowing them the pleasure of making the final selection, rather than having to buy the chair in the shop.

After a year as pattern matcher, the author was promoted to assist TCP in this work, the chief requirement of which was to operate a 'just in time' policy and still ensure that the factory never ran out of any material. To do so brought retribution from Wycombe and from Harry Parker in person. On one occasion, when stocks of 'Tulip' tapestry ran out TCP said 'I wonder, Bland, if you can do this job?'

At that time all deliveries of covering materials in the stock ranges, many from overseas, were sent to Newman Street, where they were unwrapped from their bales and booked into stock, before being sent to Wycombe on the daily van. Parker's traditional attention to detail meant all materials selected for stock from 1935 were submitted to the Retail Trading Standards Association Laboratory in Oxford Street for testing. In order to offer some chairs to retail at 49s 6d, cover prices had to be keen. The lowest was set at one shilling and ten pence a yard 48″ wide. Additional ranges enabled the customer to purchase higher quality materials at increased cost. The buying prices for these were set at three shillings and six pence and five shillings for the best. It was not difficult to find attractive materials for the lowest range. Mostly these were made in Belgium and it was therefore prudent to establish the quality of the cloth by testing for resistance to abrasion, tensile strength and perhaps most important, colour fastness. Many fabrics had a low resistance to abrasion due to the high proportion of condensor yarns in them and inexpensive dyestuffs of the time were more likely to fade than not. Such quality control was certainly an innovation that most suppliers had not experienced before, but it certainly made sure that Parker Knoll chair covers were all of a standard that made them fit for their purpose. This was a new selling point to bring home to retailers.

Although the office and showrooms did not open until 9 am, travelling to work always involved an early start. It was unforgivable to be late and not waiting on the doorstep when Mr Kindred arrived with the keys punctually at 8.55.

Another new operation, looked after at Newman Street by Philip Alpe, was publicity and advertising. As larger campaigns were mounted, the need arose to supply sales aids and display material apart from descriptive literature. This took the form of leaflets before 1936 but, as the range of models expanded, a more substantial catalogue was needed. The first one, in a cream cover, with a brightly coloured 'Man on the Spring' logo, was produced in 1935, with sixty full-page illustrations of different models, and retail prices on every page. Although Vernons dealt with artwork and general production, Parkers arranged the photography.

To encourage retailers to feature Parker Knoll in local advertising, blocks were supplied free of charge and leaflets overprinted with the retailer's name and address. It was important that all publicity material prominently featured the registred trade mark of 'The Man on the Spring'. Many retailers wished to devote window displays to Parker Knoll and this gave rise to a mechanical version of the logo, to form the centre piece. This was the idea of a stand fitter who was erecting the Company's stand at an exhibition. A number of these were made up, electrically driven, to raise and lower the stylised man onto the tension springs in a sitting motion, at the same time pointing to the Parker Knoll name with his stiff right arm. Although the motors were unreliable when left running for long periods, loan of these units was much sought. All this marketing activity was quite new to Parkers but its collective effect was considerable.

By 1936 it was necessary to increase the number of travellers. The early sales force made up by Messrs Goldie in Scotland, Alan Walsh in Northern England, Maugham in the Midlands and Stettaford in Wales, was increased by young members of staff who had served at Newman Street. Richard Clibbens and Peter Galley were promoted from the office to become representatives in the West Country and the South East. They were equipped with Austin 10 saloons, a great excitement in the days when so few had a motor car.

Although the marketing effort was entirely directed to the domestic market, there was an early spin-off when public authorities, Government Departments and hotels started to show interest in the merits of the new springing system and the strong lightweight chairs which it made possible. Dealing with such orders posed a new problem since, to supply direct breached the strongly held convictions of most retailers that manufacturers should make the furniture and leave selling to them. On the other hand such authorities often bought in quantity, and in excess of retail quantities; they considered they should enjoy some price advantage.

TCP felt that public sector authorities, buying in quantity, could not realistically go through retailers. Discounts were given by retailers to longstanding local customers but these were usually small, and more a favour than an incentive to winning business. Accordingly he decided to supply direct at trade prices when approached. At the same time, under the price maintenance policy, he advised all stockists that hotels, hospitals and local municipal authorities were considered within the retailers' purview, and suggested that, at their discretion, they allow no more than 20% discount.

The increasing interest in Parker-Knoll made the Company realise that distribution and retail stock levels were not consistent with countrywide advertising. If a customer responded and could not find the product, he might buy something else. This suggested a focal point was needed to display the entire range. Retailers in main regional centres could hardly undertake such a facility. One solution was for Parkers to open a showroom for Parker-Knoll. The London showrooms of Frederick Parker & Sons in Newman Street were ready-made and fortunately the ground floor, let for many years, became vacant in 1935. This provided a large, well-lit area in which the complete Parker-Knoll range could be displayed in a variety of covering materials. The showroom was opened in 1936 and had the brightly coloured 'Man on the Spring' device emblazoned on the front window.

TCP told all his customers about these showrooms for the public, stressing the fact that retailers' margins on orders there would be reduced. That did little to dispel the idea that he would sell direct or reassure them that every order would only be executed on confirmation by a retailer. The opportunity was not taken to stress that many potential Parker-Knoll customers would find their own way to the showrooms as a result of advertisements; the opportunity was missed to show retailers they would benefit from orders they had not obtained.

All orders from the public at showrooms or exhibitions, or resulting from a visit to these would be subject to a higher trade price to the retailer than for local orders booked on his premises. The normal trade price was one third below retail, but on showroom orders Parkers would only allow 25%. This policy was justified, because new business would come to many retailers from customers who lived locally but were new to them. Similarly, if a retailer could not suit a customer, he could suggest a visit to the showrooms where any order would be secured for him. To be able to see the whole range of Parker-Knoll furniture, and the best quality cabinet work and upholstery as well, offered serious customers a wider selection than their local shops.

This 'charge for showroom services', as many retailers saw it, was another marketing innovation and hotly contested by them. As TCP commented:

'I never believed in doing something for nothing. A customer rang me up and said "I do not like this showroom service charge." I said "George, you need not send your customers but if you do — by God — I am not going to sell them for nothing," and I heard the telephone drop on the floor. I think this is reasonable enough. Other manufacturers have a way of adding to the prices but that was never the policy of Parker and Sons. We had built up a tremendous name for our integrity. We did not alter prices, nor have special terms for anybody, everybody knew this when they came into our showrooms. The buyers would say "I will have that and that and that." With the retailer's method of bookkeeping a [Showroom] transaction like that showed almost a loss, but if they put it through their Contract Deparment it was a profit'.

There were considerable costs involved in opening the showroom to the public. Two full-time salesmen were employed and later increased to three. Often the showroom was so busy that selling had to be supplemented by office staff, who enjoyed commission. Today, the showroom policy may look archaic, but fifty years ago Parkers were breaking new ground. They felt the retailer should share the costs involved, on orders they received.

With their policy of fixed retail selling prices for Parker-Knoll, and supplies direct to Government departments, Parkers had made some pretty revolutionary decisions for the time, introducing new marketing methods into the furniture trade. The trade was not ready for them until TCP decided to clarify matters by setting the Company's trading policies down clearly in a folder circulated to every customer in 1935 — asking them to acknowledge that they had read it. Since then all new customers have been asked to read and sign the folder at the time their account is first opened. At first there were those who disputed the right of any manufacturer to dictate how they should behave. Although this was quite a departure, most retailers could see the thrust and purpose beind the arguments, designed in their interests.

Throughout, TCP was anxious to keep customers informed and to maintain the Company's policy of never doing anything which it could not justify. He was proud to be able to say that Parker's policies, acceptable or not, were out in the open, and that they applied to everybody.

Company products graced the new *Queen Mary* in 1935.

THE
NEW
SPRINGING
GUARANTEED
for FIVE years
Lift the upholstery of a Parker Knoll easy chair and the secret of overwhelming comfort is revealed. Horizontal coil springs – tension instead of compression. And because you can reach the springs so easily–cleaning is sure and thorough. See the Parker Knoll easy chairs–made in Britain by a famous British firm–for yourself at all the leading furnishing houses.
The Parker-Knoll system of springing and upholstering is jointly covered by British and Foreign Patents.
Parker-Knoll Chairs are priced from £4/10/0 upwards.
PARKER
KNOLL
TENSION SUSPENSION
Write for details to The Managing Director, Fredk. Parker & Sons Ltd., 20 Newman St., London, W.1.
RESERVED
—for a young lady who lives in a bed-sitting room, who must have something for her friends to sit on and must have something to sleep on herself. Since she bought this Parker-Knoll Bed-Settee she almost feels she has a bedroom *and* a sitting room. In the daytime nobody would guess it was anything but the most comfortable settee, but at night—well, it's just a dream. It is sprung on the same clever principle as Parker-Knoll chairs, and made and finished to the same uncompromising standard of craftsmanship. But only when you see it, sit on it, and lie on it, will you realize just how much this means. The price is £12.15.0
PARKER-KNOLL
REGISTERED TRADE MARK
Bed-Settee
There are Parker-Knoll chairs from as little as £2.5.0 up to £15.7.6. See them at your furnishers, write for catalogue or visit showrooms: Frederick Parker & Sons, Ltd., 20 Newman Street, London, W.1.

LEFT: C. Vernon & Sons designed the first advertisement and RIGHT: their 1930s approach selected specific targets within the market.

MATERIAL MASTERS

The hard work and planning to establish the Parker Knoll brand in the home market, were clearly effective by 1936. Company results showed a considerable improvement over the losses of 1931 and 1932, with turnover increasing year by year. Dividends on preference shares, suspended since 1933, were restored, with payment in August 1935 for two previous years. Parker Knoll advertising in 1935 cost £4,736, more than double the previous year. At the same time investment had doubled the value of plant and machinery in use since 1930, with a similar increase in transport. To facilitate extensions to the Temple End factory, the Company bought the Sawmill public house in Dovecot in 1935, for £320. A contract was placed with J. Jarvis & Sons of London EC2 on 17 April 1936 for £14,710 and the new buildings were in use by the end of the year. With this accomplished, the closure of the Cowley factory was completed and all remaining activities transferred to Wycombe.

Parkers' traditional business in fine quality, hand-made cabinet furniture and upholstery continued alongside the Parker Knoll range, albeit on a somewhat reduced scale. Many models, produced over many years, retained an enviable following with leading household furnishers, whose clientele expected and could pay for excellence. Some of Parkers' best upholstery was produced during the thirties, finding its way all over the world, against orders from His Majesty's Office of Works.

The long association with the Cunard shipping company was continued in 1935 with furniture for the new Atlantic liner *Queen Mary*. Known before launch as 'Ship 635', it had been building at John Brown's yard on the Clyde since the early thirties, though work was suspended during the depression. Drawings issued by Cunard for the furnishings were dated June 1930, emphasising the time necessary to bring such a project to completion. Intense competition had developed between the nations to provide the most luxurious accommodation in their trans-Atlantic liners, as well as to capture the fastest crossing. Germany, Italy, France, Holland and America vied with Britain to capture the Blue Riband trophy for the fastest crossing and this involved the introduction of ever larger ships. Cunard, as Britain's leading shipping line on the North Atlantic for almost 100 years, decideed to beat the competition by building and sailing the largest passenger liner. There was intense speculation early in 1935 as to her name. The marriage of the Duke of Kent in 1935 encouraged speculation: perhaps it would be named *Princess Marina* in honour of his bride. It is said that, in talking with a Cunard official, King George mistakenly got the idea that the ship was to be named after the Queen. He was so pleased that he telephoned Queen Mary to tell her. Cunard obliged and the ship was duly christened *Queen Mary*.

Such a vast shipping project provided an attractive opportunity for the best in British furniture and this was supplied by Parkers for the first class staterooms, working to the 1930 Cunard drawings with only small modifications. All chairs for the dining saloons were covered in blue and white hide and fitted with deck chains to anchor them in bad weather. Parker Knoll chairs were also supplied for second class cabins; press advertisements proudly proclaimed 'and of course there are Parker Knolls on the Queen Mary'.

Another shipping job, albeit on a much smaller scale, was the supply of furniture for T. O. M. Sopwith's yacht *Endeavour*. When ready this had to be assembled at the factory, to ensure it would go through the hatches.

The prestige and reputation of the Parker Knoll chair reached the far-flung corners of the Empire. By 1938, agreements had been signed for registration of the trade mark in Australia, New Zealand, India, South Africa, Hong Kong and Singapore. The chairs were soon advertised and sold as 'England's Best selling Chair'. Agreements with Beard Watson in Sydney, Scoullars of Wellington, (later with Hugh J. Eaton), Spencers of Madras, Stuttafords of Cape Town and Robinsons of Singapore, enabled them to manufacture under licence, fitting the springing system supplied from High Wycombe. Substantial business was developed in the few years before the Second World War, and the association was resumed afterwards, until political or business changes brought it to an end. The Singapore connection continues today, and an independent company still manufactures Parker Knoll in South Africa.

The flavour of the daily routine of life at the factory is vividly recalled by Percy Boddington, who joined the Company as a lad and retired almost fifty years later, after running the upholstery shops as foreman and manager at both Wycombe and Chipping Norton, Percy recalls:

'The hours worked were from 7.30 am until 6.30 pm, with a midday break of one hour, and a half-hour break mid-afternoon. There was no need for a large carpark, as the chief mode of transport was 'bus or bicycle, especially from outlying villages.

'There was not really any mass production of furniture, and the machines used in the process were a long way from today's standards.

'The operators then were much more specialists in setting up their machines. There must also have been more than twenty men employed on carving at any one time and it was fascinating to see them at work, and to see them transforming plain pieces of wood into something of a masterpiece.

'[In] the making shop each operator would go to the mill to collect all the rails and other parts needed. He would then work from a drawing and bench [assemble] the frame by hand, as in those days each man was responsible for completing all work necessary on each job himself.

'The polishing shop was run quite differently; again each man completed the work on the job he was handling. Items were stained, coloured in, and then polished, using a rubber made up of cotton wool and calico, altogether a lengthy operation. Large and elaborate pieces could take a whole week. When an antique finish was required, this was done in a small shed in the corner of the yard. This was run by a man called Tom Spalding and he was reluctant to let any in (for) he wanted to keep his trade secrets to himself. I had to go in there as a boy to get hides stained, and remember seeing an assortment of stones, chains and other odd objects which created a distressed finish. The Cromwellian-style chairs were always done in very thick hide; in order to create a despression in the seats, to give a used look, the hide was soaked and, still wet, was suspended over a bucket and weighted to form the dished effect. Because it was so inflexible an "iron hand" was used to stretch it on the job. When finished, the chairs would go to the drying store until completely dried out and then go back to have the whole lot polished, hide included. One of these chairs was brought into Chipping Norton Showrooms a few months ago, by a customer enquiring about a change of cover. I know it must have been in use for over forty years and it was still in as good a condition as when it was made.

'There was also a small painting shop where some very nice pieces of decorated work were done, by John Arnold's mother and Miss Ferry. Upholstery production was split into two shops, one for P.K. which was introduced in 1929, and the other produced all the deep stuffed upholstery. With webbing, springing, fixing cane, stitching up etc one could have a job on the bench for two days or often longer. A settee took a full week to upholster.

'There were about twenty men and boys in the deep stuffing, and the jobs were allocated by the foreman. A work sheet was issued giving details of the model required. With this you obtained your frame and then handed your sheet into General Stores to get issued with all the materials to complete the job. One had to wait while all this was cut, and when it was issued one had to check to make sure it was all there, for Bill Hill, who ran the stores, wasn't the easiest man to convince that he had not given you the right amount.
'There was always a good atmosphere amongst the shop in those days and, although the tempo may not have been quite the same as today, everyone worked hard, (we had no waiting time then, what one didn't earn one didn't get). I think the rate for forty-seven hours was £3 8s 6d, but we were happy and took pride in our work. Payment books had to be made up by eleven o'clock on Friday morning and handed in to Wages for calculating. Wages were paid to the whole factory at six the same day from a small hatch in the main building. Rain or shine, we had to wait in the yard until the flap was raised. You can image the cheer that went up if they were a bit late as they sometimes were. As we were paid numerically, one was fortunate to have a low clock number.
'All apprentices were signed on for five years. They went through all aspects of the trade for the first couple of years, under close supervision most of the time, and then, as they became competent, were gradually allowed to work on their own. There were usually about four or five apprentices in our shop most of the time; the junior had to do a bit of shop work and cleaning. As there were no canteen facilities, one of his duties was to run errands at break times mid-morning and afternoon. In all departments the junior apprentice would do the rounds of the shop and collect orders from the men. Then you would see them all go off down to Frogmoor to collect bottles of milk, cakes, pies etc, until their apron pockets were bulging. It was not unusual for apprentices and learners to make a few pence from these daily skirmishes [from] the bakers and suppliers.
'On return, their next job was to make the tea. It was the recognised thing for each workman to have his own billycan, and bring the little bags of tea and sugar. The shop boys carried a pole with six billy cans on each end and went down to the yard where the hot water tap was kept padlocked. It was opened for only ten minutes at a time.
'It was also common for men from the surrounding villages to bring their dinners with them in a basin. Jim Spicer, who often could not be found, used to sleep on top of the Paxman boiler in the Stokehouse. He would place the dinner basins on top of the boiler to warm up for the twelve o'clock break. Most of the boys got a bit of a perk out of doing these jobs though, for at the end of the week most of the men would give them 3d, or in a good week perhaps 6d.
'The cutting and sewing shops were much the same as today; of course it was all hand cutting then; any fitting required was done by the upholsterer. A group of girls doing slip stitching were always kept busy as all the larger upholstery was finished with braid, fringe or cord. A large quantity of bed heads was done as well and these had many yards of braid worked into all kinds of shapes on the face.
'The packaging and transport side was very different. We had about four lorries, but they did not cover the whole country and a large amount was despatched by rail. This involved packing each piece in straw and canvas. Crates were used for export. All packs (the canvas and any battens) were invoiced and returnable, creating many administrative problems. The claims account with the railway for damage in transit was always an ongoing administrative nightmare. Five packers were kept busy and the straw required was delivered by lorry from Kingston Blount to be stored in a marquee. A horse and cart was still maintained by the Company to deliver despatches to the Station. Drivers for the new motor vans were Stevens, Bennel, Pocock and Jackman. The specially built van body for the daily run to Newman Street was supplied by Davenport Vernons but it was discovered on the first trip that it was too large

to pass through the archway into Newman Passage. This is still there and shows the scrape marks from many vehicles. When modified, the P.K. van went through with literally only inches to spare, requiring extremely exact driving. The Packing Shop foreman, Bert Jemmett, was the factory's cricket enthusiast and ran the packers' team against other factory departments. It is said that they usually won, but probably it is their defeats which have been forgotten.

'As usual, there were a few characters working at the factory. Everyone knew Charlie Farmer; he must have been fired a dozen times, but he was always there the next day. He worked in the yard and when approached by Mr Harry asking why he was still there, he would grin and put on a deaf act. Mr Harry would despair and walk away waving his hands; he could use some strong language too! Another character was Harry Britnell who stood about four foot six, and was a great snuff taker. He used to fit all the castors and do other odd jobs and, whether he had a hammer in his hand or any other tool, there between his thumb and forefinger, was a great pinch of snuff.'

'Cosh' Belson also joined the Company to learn upholstery in the thirties and retired in 1973. He recollects that Joe Bedwell ran the best quality making shop and Percy Harris the top shop where the first Parker Knoll models were made. He would go to the shop in the lunch hour and line up all the completed chair frames. He could detect by eye any that were out of line, marking them with chalk. Belson recalls Harry Parker as a strict disciplinarian and craftsman par excellence. He often wore a grey suit and always a brown trilby. He would often appear inside the swing doors at the end of the shop, with one hand in his jacket pocket, and survey the scene. A frisson would be transmitted round the workmen as Harry walked down the canvas conveyor track in the centre, stopping to inspect the work on the benches on his way. If he changed his glasses he would call the foreman over and emphasise anything that he felt was wrong. He could always demonstrate how a job should be done and it was not unknown for a man whose work was poor to be sacked on the spot. Hours were 7.30 am till 6.30 pm, 6.00 pm on Friday; 48 hours at 1s 6d, making £3 per week, sometimes much less due to short time. Men would call daily at the gate to see if there was any work; otherwise they were sent home without pay. This also applied if a man was finishing a job on his bench and there was no other job following on, perhaps because the chair frame was not ready. In this situation the upholsterer would often take off the outside back of his completed chair and put it on again, as otherwise he would be sent home.

Belson remembers the Caning Shop run by Bill Stevens and Miss Busby, turning out spider-webbed chair-backs and secret caned seats. They spent hours sitting on wooden stools knocking pegs in. Rushing was also done here. Among the upholsterers was George Nash, an old chair bodger from the woods, who was adept at repairing almost anything with linen patches. Hearne was another upholsterer who worked in the far corner of the shop and sported a white waxed moustache. A large order for Parker Knoll in the late thirties was the supply of several hundred PK 326 tub chairs for the House of Commons. All were in hide with the portcullis and crown embossed in gold on the inside backs. These chairs were returned and reconditioned after the war, when a repeat order was placed.

Another long-serving employee was Derek Stewart, who started in 1937 at the age of 16, and describes himself as a late-entry learner to the upholstery trade. Derek rose to become Works Director before retiring in 1986. He came to Wycombe with his father from Sunderland, where he had served almost two years as an apprentice butcher, working an 80 hour week for five shillings plus one pound of sausages and two steak and kidney pies.

Job vacancies were posted at the factory gate and Derek applied. He was interviewed by Mr Richards and was so pleased to get the job that he forgot to ask what the wages were. At 6d an hour he thought they were marvellous compared with those in Sunderland!

Many people were coming to Wycombe from Wales at the time, but incomers were unpopular with local people, especially those prepared to work for lower rates. Parkers were renowned for the high quality of their work and were selective. All craftsmen were on piece work. Those were harsh words in the trade.

Derek spent four years before the War learning all aspects of the upholstery trade. Parkers had good foremen; Bill Richards was one. A skilled upholsterer should be able to cut and sew himself, but many could not. Derek recalls how production was divided into three sections — Frederick Parker's best quality in one, with Parker Knoll divided between the cheapest fireside chairs with polished showwood frames, filled with Kapoc or cotton felt, and the better quality models with more traditional upholstery, often based on original chairs in the antique collection.

After learning the skills of upholstery, Derek started with the better PK models. Standards were so high that he was often made to strip the job and start again. He was not allowed to touch any covers for the first eighteen months, but eventually he was given a chair frame to develop. Every stage was subject to post mortem by the foreman and a constant check.

By 1937 production of the Parker Knoll ranges had reached 800 pieces a week throughout the year and increased in 1938 to 1,000, alongside traditional hand-made furniture. A range of 70 assorted models was catalogued and supplemented by almost another hundred available for normal delivery. Sales focussed chiefly on the least expensive ranges — fireside and small occasional chairs accounted for 40% of sales with the high-back fireside range adding another 17%. However, the more elaborate upholstered wing easy chairs, selling at much higher prices, contributed 25% and this was the most profitable sector. It was this style of chair which the public seemed most to admire, and was undoubtedly the one with which they associated Parker Knoll. Although these designs owed their inspiration to traditional chairs, they were not straight reproductions — the British middle class has had a long and lasting love for the Queen Anne leg. Of these 1930s designs, the Hartley chair, selling about ten a week in the thirties, is still in production today.

The earliest styles with a sprung frame and two loose cushions faded in popularity towards the end of the thirties, as did the adjustable backed variety, usually supplied in brown corduroy. This trend was no doubt as much a reflecton of the widening variety available as changing public tastes. From the British viewpoint a considerable improvement in 1935 was the introduction of spring interior seat cushions. Until then seat cushions had followed Continental preference for firmness, consisting of stitched Kapoc with rolled edges top and bottom. These were extremely durable but short on comfort. Introduction of Elson & Robbins' pocketed spring interiors to all seat cushions harmonised well with the flexibility of the tension spring system and greatly increased seat comfort. Some bordered back cushions were also sprung, but otherwise, upholstered chair backs continued to use a Kapoc-filled tiffany bag, which formed a thin pillow between back spring and cover.

Consistent with their sales promotion policies Parkers had exhibited at international fairs and exhibitions. They won a certificate of merit at the Paris Exhibition in 1925. Closer to home, from 1932, they were regular exhibitors at the British Industries Fair at White City.

Mr F. R. Peacock, Furniture Buyer at William Whiteley of London, commenting on the 1934 exhibition said 'Frederick Parker, whose upholstery has long made them famous, shows, it seems to me, still further progress'. During her visit to the 1938 fair at Earls Court, Queen Elizabeth, now the Queen Mother, paused in the High Wycombe furniture section to inspect exhibits on Frederick Parker's stand.

Parker Knoll was also at the *Daily Mail* Ideal Homes Exhibition. In the thirties the Grand Hall at Olympia was the setting for an up-market display of furnishings and household goods, by the leading London stores and manufacturers. Many were Royal Warrant-holders, and their displays along the Grand Avenue were usually inspected by the King and Queen. Parkers exhibited at Olympia from 1935, seeing it as an extension of their press advertising and taking the opportunity to introduce Parker Knoll to an ever-wider audience. The 1939 exhibition was held for the first time at Earls Court. For some strange reason, the whole Parker Knoll exhibit was covered in the same material. This was a salmon pink 'birdseye weave' tapestry through which ran a gilt thread, anticipating 'Lurex' by many years, but sadly not one of the most successful exhibits.

Parkers had always realised the importance of the covering material. In showroom or shop window, visual appeal was a major factor in obtaining initial interest. Their long experience of handling the most expensive silks, brocades and velvets gave Parkers a keener feel for the right cover for chairs. The policy of providing pattern swatches to retailers, enabling choice, required materials to be purchased in bulk and to remain on offer for long periods. Such arrangements had not previously been necessary. Another important factor for Parkers was exclusivity, to Parker Knoll chairs. The marketing benefits became apparent early on, when customers asked to buy matching lengths for other furniture.

By 1937, they were already using more than 2,000 yards of covering material weekly for Parker Knoll chairs, and needed continuity of supplies. The combined need for exclusivity and TCP's conviction that future demand would involve large quantities plus economies of scale, led him to buy direct from the mills. Such thinking did not suit the Wholesale Textile Association, who had not previously had to face a situation where manufacturers bought outside their members. Manufacturers enjoyed support from many weavers. Continental weavers were not inclined to lose the opportunity, but many British mills did, not realising the large quantities now required by the largest upholsterers. Initially, only a few British mills supplied direct, but Parkers gave them their business whenever possible.

Their first experiment was in 1935 when they embarked on a range of hand-woven tweed covers made in the crofts of the Hebrides. Four special Parker Knoll chairs were developed for these materials and appropriately named Lewis, Skye, Rassay and Barra. Additionally, a separate catalogue was printed with a colour plate to show the materials. There were a number of retailers, notably Heals, Bowmans and Dunns, featuring a new idiom of cabinet and dining room furniture in simple designs, uncluttered with decoration, in light unstained finishes. Many of the Parker Knoll designs were eminently suited to blend with these. The range in hand-woven covers was expected to appeal to customers attracted by this 'Modern' style.

In the event the project was not a success and it is difficult to say why. The covers were of excellent quality and in soft pastel colours, but they were probably 'too modern' for any but the most design-conscious taste. Of the four chairs only the Lewis PK284, selling at £7 2s 6d retail, achieved any real sales. The others and their hand-woven covers faded into oblivion.

Another original idea was the creation of designs for loom-woven fabrics, from original fragments in the antique collection. Over the years a wide assortment of silks and embroideries had been accumulated for their general interest and relation to furnishing styles of the past. Among these is a small piece of fine, early seventeenth century embroidery, adapted by Pastori & Cassonova, an Italian weaving firm, who had a branch factory in Wolverhampton. Their agent was Mr Bianchi of Arighi Bianchi of Macclesfield, retailers who still trade today from their fine shop there. By using a tapestry weave on a pocket cloth the effect of the canvas groundwork and the stitchwork effects of the original were faithfully captured. Special Parker Knoll designs were introduced to combine with the tapestry which became known inevitably as Tulip. Loosely and incorrectly described as Jacobean, the chair and settee were suited to blend with heavy oak furniture and did not enjoy a wide appeal. The Tulip fabric, however, became quite popular and was widely used on other styles. After the War it was recreated by Henry Nathan and in those days of shortage, the cloth enjoyed a second and more successful lease of life.

Another example of needlework from the old records, a second-loom woven design on a tapestry for general use, was created by Brown Vickers of Bradford. Known as Lambeth and worked on a pocket cloth, it again managed to capture the character of the original and was widely used in 1938 and 1939. After restrictions were relaxed in the 1950s Brown Vickers again put the cloth into production and it continued to sell for many years. These first efforts at re-creating the effects of hand embroidery on loom-made cloths added exclusivity and originality to the cover ranges, at a time when most fabrics followed uninteresting stereotypes.

Undeterred by their disappointment over the hand-woven cover experiment, the Company in 1938 produced another special range of chairs. These were no doubt expected to be a certain success for they were faithful reproductions of fourteen original chairs in the antique collection, and something that many of Parker's main customers understood. In period they ranged from a Stuart style at the end of the seventeenth century, through to an Empire style from about 1810. All frames were hand-carved where necessary, inlaid, crossbanded or moulded in the correct timber. Covers in silks, velvets, chintzes and tapestry were carefully chosen for the style and period of the original. A major difference, however, as the advertising explained, was the Parker Knoll springing system, although many of the originals dated from well before springs were invented.

This was a special range of reproduction chairs intended to appeal to those connoisseurs of style and period whose purses did not run to the real thing. A special catalogue was printed showing that retail prices would be between £14 12s 6d and £32 12s 6d which was quite high, but warranted by workmanship and character. As the chairs required so much hand-work and some hand carving, it was necessary to produce chair parts well in advance of the launch date. Unfortunately preparations were not complete when War broke out, after which it was considered inappropriate to sell these rather special models and only a few were made. Some of the chair parts were assembled in 1947, but it was then impossible to find the correct cover and, with purchase tax at 66⅔%, the project was dropped.

The last two years of the decade showed even better results with sales double those of 1930, yielding nett profits six times higher. Parker Knoll had become the predominant brand name in chairs.

Throughout the last years of the thirties, political events both at home and in Europe were beginning to affect public confidence and inevitably depressed retail markets. The abdication of King Edward VIII in 1936 was a great blow, barely relieved by the Coronation the following year. Parkers supplied a large number of small farthingale-style chairs for use in Westminster Abbey. Covered in pale blue velvet and carrying the Royal cipher, many were taken off by invited guests and can still be seen in stately homes. The Ministry of Works issued four passes to Parkers, which admitted the holders to the viewing stand built just across the road from the main entrance.

Appeasement of the European dictatorships from 1935 saw Abyssinia invaded and overwhelmed, Spain invaded by Franco, who gained military support from Germany and Italy. The arrival of Jewish refugees from Germany brought a realisation that something was wrong. The public mood, still conscious of the carnage of the fields of Flanders only twenty years before, reluctantly began to change. Even the Government turned its mind towards re-arming, especially the Air Force.

The halcyon days of peace could not long contine. After the German seizure of Austria in 1938 and the invasion of Prague in 1939, public opinion forced the British Government to a military commitment to defend Poland if attacked, and the stage was set. On 3 September Britain declared war on Germany.

PRIVATE & CONFIDENTIAL

PARKER-KNOLL CHAIRS AND SETTEES may not be retailed at less than the prices quoted in our catalogue—except in the case of contract work (such as hotels, restaurants, clubs, etc.) when the reduction must not exceed 20 per cent. off the catalogue prices.

The full trade discount is 33⅓ per cent. for stock orders and repeats; for non-stockists the discount is 25 per cent. 2½ per cent. is allowed on payments made within 30 days or less. H.M. Office of Works, all Government Departments, County Councils and other Authorities who purchase in quantities are supplied at trade prices.

All orders taken in our showrooms at Newman Street and High Wycombe or at the Ideal Home or other Exhibitions, or resulting from a visit to the above places by prospective customers, are subject to 25 per cent. discount only. (Exception: where contract terms are necessary the full 33⅓ per cent. is always allowed.)

Trade terms are not quoted or accounts opened without our receiving confirmatory acceptance of such terms. No goods are sent on approbation, but all orders are sent carriage paid to the retailer's premises. (Exceptions: for Scotland, 2½ per cent. added to invoice; for Ireland, carriage paid to English port.)

For the convenience of customers who may wish to use Parker-Knoll Tapestries on goods not of our manufacture, we supply the "A" quality at the gross price of 9/9 per yard, the "B" quality at 6/- per yard.

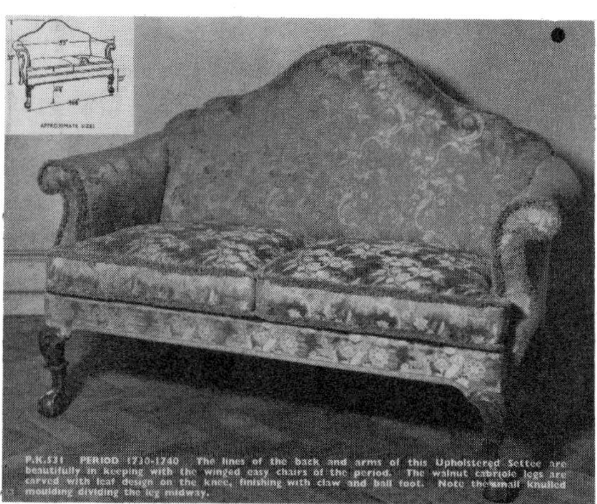

ABOVE: Trade terms were also specific. LEFT: PK518 winged easy chair, based on a 1712-1725 design; CENTRE: PK531 1730-40 style upholstered settee. RIGHT: PK523 1790-95 style tub easy chair.

On the Wings of War

Everyone had their own apprehensions as to what war would mean, the young having no idea at all, and those who had lived through the Great War expecting the whole horror all over again. The fact that the air raid sirens sounded only minutes after the Prime Minister's broadcast lent some reality, although it was a false alarm. The torpedoing of the *Athenia* only hours later created public outrage, but Poland was quickly partitioned between Germany and Russia and life went on more or less undisturbed. The nightly blackout was inconvenient, soon to be followed by food and petrol rationing. Thousands of school children were evacuated to rural areas, the British Expeditionary Force went to France but was not fighting; the Navy scuttled the *Graf Spee* off South America but this was the 'phoney war'.

Trading activity at Parkers also continued with little disturbance. Sales remained strong till August 1940, with turnover and profits only slightly down. However, national measures would bring this to an end. On 5 September 1939 Control of Timber Order No 1 was made under Defence of the Realm Regulations and this was quickly followed by other controls on silk, rayon, leather, wool, cotton, iron and steel aluminium, non-ferrous metals, flax, hemp and jute, all materials used by the furniture industry, although the restriction was not immediately apparent, since many manufacturers had stocks in hand.

Supplies of the special high tensile steel wire required for the manufacture of Parker Knoll springs stopped immediately, but stocks were sufficient to allow production to continue well into 1940. Covering materials from the Continent continued at first, then trickled to a stop, but again there was no immediate shortage as many customers supplied their own covers from stock. Realising that the situation could only get worse, in January 1940 Parkers produced a catalogue of seven new, simple, chairs — 'in spite of the present manufacturing difficulties' — in an attempt to focus resources into a small range which they might maintain. A new price list was issued. Press advertising continued much as before with the copy referring lightly to the trials of wartime life such as 'leaving the sugar ration on the bus'. Initially there were plenty of machined chair parts, and supplies of covering materials for the new range from British makers. TCP's policy of not buying from wholesalers was a great benefit. For the time being, production of the most popular Parker Knoll models continued, although the seats and backs were webbed with jute webbing, customers being informed that these could easily be converted after the War. Quite a lot were! Production of cabinet furniture and upholstery continued for a time but, as the months passed and employees left to join the forces, things gradually ran down.

The sudden German campaigns in May 1940 which resulted in the occupation of Europe and the retret from Dunkirk, swiftly convinced the nation that the War was real. Normal life and commerce ceased for almost everybody. On 10 June 1940 price controls were extended to furniture and furnishings, to be followed in July by complete withdrawal of all timber supplies. 21 October saw the introduction of purchase tax at 33⅓% to reduce consumption as well as to raise revenue. It was argued that many people had surplus income because there was so little to spend it on. The London showrooms remained open until early 1941 and the remaining male staff had to take their turns with the Air Raid Precautions firewatching teams on the roof. The Blitz, which started in earnest on 7 September, involved them in some exciting experiences. The author left to join the RAF early in 1941 as little work remained. There were few visitors to the showrooms. Vivian Card remained until he too joined the RAF but not before spending many nights firewatching on the roof at Newman Street, with London ablaze on all sides.

Although the showrooms were not hit, they had a narrow escape when a parachute mine landed only 100 yards away at Berners Street. It became a matter of honour after the nightly bombing for the staff to get to the office somehow, despite destroyed railways, closed streets and little transport. Getting home again was equally a problem and sometimes refuge had to be taken in a convenient shelter. After a particularly bad night, when the Newman Street showrooms were drenched through all four floors from fire hoses at a nearby incident, the decision was taken to close. All the remaining furniture there was sold to Maples — it included many fine pieces of Parker's cabinet work at much reduced prices.

The showroom closure brought sales operations to an end, allowing TCP, who was then 60, and his brother Will, aged 62, to more or less retire apart from board meetings. Walter Ferry, as Chief Designer, had no further work and retired to start an antique business in Uxbridge. Harry and George at the factory were left to handle the business of negotiating and winning wartime supply contrcts.

By the end of 1940 the Directors realised that the traditional furniture of Frederick Parker & Sons would not be made again.It had depended on craft skills in cabinet making and upholstery, but skilled men were scattered by the war and were unlikely to return; only the younger generation, many of whom had served their apprenticeship at Parkers, did in fact return. The Parker Knoll range had been sufficiently successful to expect a strong market after the War. Proposals were made to the Board in September 1941 to promote a new company to acquire the manufacturing and selling activities of the business, leaving the leasehold and freehold properties undisturbed. Parker Knoll Ltd was created at an extraordinary general meeting on 24 March 1942, in consideration of 39,995 shares of £1. Harry Parker became Chairman, while George Parker, son of William, was made a Director and moved from London to fill the post of Managing Director at the Wycombe factory through the War. Only fourteen days after recording these events, Frederick George, eldest son of the Company's founder, died on 7 April aged 68, having served as Company Secretary since 1902.

Life went on at the factory as it adjusted to the War, seeking contracts for supplies for the War effort. Many employees had gone, or were leaving. Harry Parker, by then 65, assisted his nephew, George, with the day-to-day running and various organisational changes. The first in September 1939 was to make black-out screens for all the windows. The large, glazed, north light windows in the various shop roofs proved a problem as they had to be taken down by day and re-erected at dusk. As the order book contracted and men left, the various production departments were rearranged and concentrated into one building.

Benny Lee was Factory Manager with Charlie Bradley as his assistant. Jack Martin, Bill Richard and Less Fassnidge were foremen of the making and upholstery shops, one best quality and the other pin stuffing. The remaining six or seven upholsterers at the end of 1940 produced the final Parker Knoll orders. The Kapoc store was in the Hermitage, a four-bedroomed house within the factory area, originally Harry Parker's house, and Brenda Busby ran the Tiffany department. Miss Dadd, who had moved to Wycombe from Cowley, looked after slipping, while General Stores was run by the parsimonious Mr Hill. Mrs Nellie Woods, also from Cowley, ran the first factory canteen.

An Admiralty order for easy chairs early in 1940 kept the best quality shop busy working to a high specification, with hand springing, four ties to a spring, cane edges, first and second stuffing, all covered in hide but with rexine outsides. This was quickly followed by orders for a miscellany of items from examination couches, stuffed with black hair and hand stitched with diamond buttoned tops, to a large quantity of stretchers complete with harness, for the RAMC. These were made to a high specification, with the special canvas fixed to side poles by 74 copper nails. A Government inspector had to pass each batch, following a test in which sandbags were dropped onto the open stretcher from a considerable height.

Another job a long way removed from convention involved 'A Frames' to War Office orders and specification. What these were required for in 1941 is difficult to imagine, unless they were for slit trenches or training in trench warfare. Trenches inthe first War had developed a technology of their own, with boarded sides to prevent collapse and a duck-boarded floor to keep out the mud. 'A Frames' were a frame structure built from saplings in the shape of a letter A but with a flat top. These were inverted and inserted at intervals in trenches as frames to which the side boards were fixed. A wide number of furniture manufacturers, including Parkers, received large orders from the War Office in April for two sizes of A Frames which were desperately urgent. Parkers were initially required to deliver 10,000 of each within four weeks, despite the fact that they had first to acquire sufficient suitable timber from the Ministry of Supply. A 25,000 foot run of 4″-5″ diameter poles and 45,000 foot run of 3″-4″ diameter, in six to eight foot lengths, was required and by 27 May only sufficient for 9,000 frames had been collected from local sources. Only larch or fir poles could be used, and delivery was stipulated at the rate of 1,875 of each size a week. Frantic messages were sent to the Ministry of Supply, who had their own difficulty finding suppliers. Eventually they put the Company in touch with the Chestnut Paling Association who found the timber, but it was early August before the first contract was completed. Despite a night shift including Saturday and Sunday, involving 40 men, the whole project was not completed until mid-July. To enable night workers to have tea on shift, the Ministry of Food made a special allowance of 1⅕th ounces of sugar and one ounce of tea per shift. The small frames were charged at 4s each and the large at 5s 10d. All had to be stood for several hours in creosote, which was kept in tanks in the old polishing shop, the stench permeating the whole factory. A repeat order ran into difficulty because the poles supplied by the timber control were too crooked. This resulted in a large part of the second order using nine inch square oak posts, increasing the cost per frame to 7s 10d each, and delaying completion until the end of September.

A string of orders followed for a variety of boxes for all sorts of spares for artillery howitzers, everything to strict specification and subject to inspection. Tent pegs were made in vast unending quantities alongside ditty boxes for merchant seamen and snowshoes for the campaign in Finland. The factory was kept busy with this miscellany of small work through 1941, after which it became increasingly involved with work for the aircraft industry.

Two factors combined to enable aircraft components to be built by the furniture industry — the new techniques in the design and construction of De Havilland Mosquito aircraft and the existence of large factory workshops with skilled woodworkers. The De Havilland Mosquito was unique because it was built in wood rather than alloy and, as a consequence, was much lighter and faster, so that initially it flew as a bomber without defensive armament, relying on speed to get out of trouble. As the aircraft developed, it became one of the major weapons in the RAF armoury. The airframe used a combination of spruce and balsa wood, laminated and bonded into smooth curved shapes for formers, and a skin of formed rigid panels with inner and outer layers of ash plywood.

The Ministry of Aircraft Production took over part of the Parker Knoll factory and appointed Mr Hill Smith to control production of the main wing spar. The ground floor of the mill was the only space wide enough and this was cleared. The main spar was made up in the form of a wooden box girder, thick at the centre, tapering and thinning towards the tips. The main spar was the inner core of the aircraft wing and a vitally important component, 54 feet wide tip to tip. The quick-setting glue used in the laminations was known as 'beetle juice' and each mainspar involved the exact insertion of 4,000 screws and 4,000 panel pins. When finished, each had to be inspected by an Inspector from the Ministry before being collected by a long vehicle known as a 'Queen Mary', and taken to Hatfield for skinning, and assembly into complete aircraft. It took sixteen men to lift the spar out of the workshop. Other Wycombe firms working on the Mosquito were Gommes, and Dancer and Hearne at Penn Street, where they had an impressive laminating shop capable of moulding wood to every conceivable shape. At the end of the War Geoffrey De Havilland visited the factories that had made such a great contribution and gave a flypast salute to the workers who helped to make some of the total of 7,781.

Another aircraft contract in 1943 and 1944 was for the repair and reconditioning of damaged Airspeed Horsa Gliders. Built in wood, using similar techniques to those in the Mosquito, this large and ungainly aircraft was designed to be towed behind a tug aircraft such as a Stirling, Dakota or Halifax. The purpose was to deliver twenty-five fully equipped soldiers to the battlefield and, as it had no engines, it was expendable on arrival. The most memorable battle in which the Horsa took part was the airborne landing at Arnhem in 1944. During 1943 intense traning of airborne forces was under way, and it is probable that the gliders which arrived at Parker Knoll for repair were those which had suffered heavy landing or similar accidents in training. Nine or ten of the long fuselages were laid side by side in the upholstery shop like stranded whales completely filling it. The wings were dealt with separately in another shed where chairmakers replaced damaged ribs. The undercarriage was quite massive and was dismantled and cleaned by by Sid Flanagan. All the electrical circuits had to be replaced, while a squad of twelve girls was required to scrape off all the surplus glue around the fuselage formers. Norman Stewart remembers how pointless this seemed and he thinks that it was merely to give the girls something to do. Norman worked with Nobby Clark and Jack Austin on the lamination press jigs, building new formers to replace damage, and remembers the hours it took to clean off the plywood-covered fuselages. When all structural repairs were complete the wings had to be recovered in canvas, the joins covered in tape with serrated edges. Both wings and fuselage then had to be sprayed with dope and the camouflage then repainted. Jim Aldridge, who had a greengrocer's shop in the High Street, came in on a part-time basis to handle this. Anyone who has been near aircraft dope will know this is a horrible job due to the fumes. Norman Stewart volunteered to move to this work, not least because it paid 2d per hour more plus a pint of milk a day to minimise the effects. Regulations required that ten minutes in every hour was taken in the fresh air. When each airframe was ready it had to be manhandled out of the wide doors at the end of the shop and this took some doing, with the high tail fin perilously close to the roof girders.

Jack Austin worked in the wartime factory, and was always able to supply cigarettes and sweets 'off the ration'. He would walk round the shops with his apron pocket full of Mars bars and Dairy Milk chocolate, dispensing to any who wished to buy. He kept a tally until the end of the week, when he stood at the gate on payday to collect his dues. He often had an attaché case full of butter, chickens and other rationed goods. At most break times he could be found in one of the toilets with a pack of cards which for 1d were cut six times, the highest bidder winning a packet of cigarettes. He also ran the social side by organising outings. Norman Stewart recalls how he was fortunate to be on Jack Austin's firewatching team as he went out to get the fish and chips — another commodity normally in short supply. Cosh Belson and Fred True were the other members of the squad and, as there were never any incidents, they took it in turn to spend the evening in the Palace Cinema. If the siren went they could be back at the factory almost before it had stopped.

During the early 1940s the Ministry of Supply was giving thought to the type of furniture possible under wartime conditions. In February 1941 it announced its range of Standard Emergency Furniture, intended for bombed-out citizens, or 'bombees'. This was pretty basic stuff with 80% plywood. From April 1941 only men over 40 and women were eligible to work in the furniture industry, all others being directed into the war industry. Income tax was raised to 10s in the pound.

In November the Ministry of Supply announced that only twenty specified articles of essential furniture could be made, but did not regulate designs or prices. In May 1942 the Furniture Maximum Prices Order came into force to freeze all prices including those for second-hand furniture, although antiques, described as before 1 January 1900, were excluded. Thus the way was opened to further Government control of the industry.

During the War Parker Knoll Ltd was cut off from all their normal activities. They prototyped a range of six models on which they would base sales and production at the first opportunity. In the summer of 1943 they kept their spirits up by running a small advertising campaign, to keep their name alive, and to assure their public that Parker Knoll would be back.

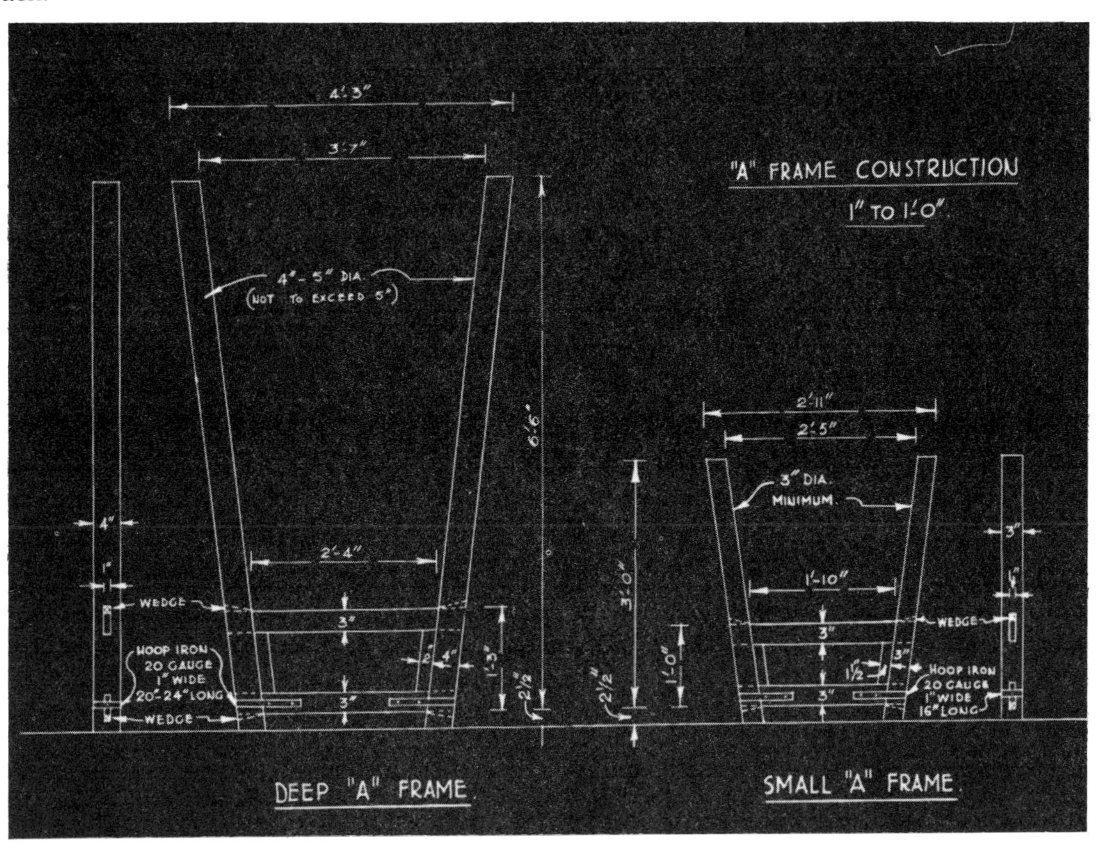

This War Office blueprint of 1939 details the A Frame, thousands of which were made in the early months of the Second World War.

Fredk. Parker & Sons Ltd.
UPHOLSTERERS & CABINET MAKERS.
FACTORIES,
TEMPLE END, HIGH WYCOMBE, BUCKS.
TELEGRAMS. "JOINDERING, RATH, LONDON." TELEPHONE. MUSEUM 0771, 2 & 3.

PARKER-KNOLL
REGISTERED TRADE MARK

20, NEWMAN STREET,
OXFORD STREET,
LONDON, W.1.

January, 1940.

TCP/RS

Dear Sirs,

We have to advise you that as from January 13th there will be a further 10% advance in the price of all our goods including Parker-Knoll, making a total of 15% since the beginning of the war. Much though we regret the necessity for this step it has been forced upon us by the rise in the cost of materials and is fully justified.

However, here is some good news. In order to simplify the difficulty of stocking a full range of Parker-Knoll models in these days we have designed a new series of 7 chairs which we consider meet the requirements and the means of practically all your customers. We are producing this simplified group in much larger quantities than has been our practice in the past, with a consequent saving in production costs which enables us to offer still better value for money.

In looking forward into 1940 we feel safe in predicting a steady demand for Parker-Knoll chairs and hope that you secure your share of the business which we are creating.

With best wishes for the New Year,

We are,

Yours faithfully,

FREDK. PARKER & SONS, LTD.

T. C. P.

P.S. Kindly attach the enclosed price list to existing 4th Edition Catalogue.

The bus was
like a sardine
last evening p
been sold be
had a chance
one. It had
your half-mile
the hill and
your umbrel
office. Your
Knoll is a
need tonight.
Until the war is over there will be no more Parker-Knoll chairs
when they are once more obtainable, they will be as good as ever

LEFT: Part of a long letter advising higher prices and simpler goods in 1940. RIGHT: 'Until the war is over' there were no more chairs — advertising in 1943.

By Design

By the time Frederick Paker retired in 1927 he could look back over fifty-eight years, during which time he had been manufacturing high quality furniture. The business he had created was continued by his sons, and by 1939 Parkers had produced fine furniture for seventy years.

The illustrations give a glimpse of Frederick Parker's achievement. The great furniture designers and makers of the eighteenth century had worked on commissions from wealthy patrons. Records of their contracts provide clear evidence of their achievements, but there was no general market for their skills. Frederick Parker was fortunate for, by the middle of the nineteenth century, more people required and could buy quality furniture. He set out to satisfy this demand. He was able to create and supply on a commercial basis, furniture which acknowledged its debt to the past, yet was adapted to the times.

Parker's furniture was made by the techniques of the old craftsmen, adapted to benefit from improved technology and the introduction of machinery, but always bearing the visible signs of the craftsmen who made it. Parkers were always capable of reproducing the masterpieces of the great makers, and often did so. Regrettably, they did not mark a single piece with their name. Frederick would have said that he had no need to advertise, as the world would find him out if they needed his services. Today we can see all too clearly how such a simple marketing philosophy has been swept away. The relentless introduction of technological ability to continually increase the volume of production has created the need to use the equally relentless growth of mass communication techniques to create, capture and retain markets.

During the life of the Company they had made no less than 5,600 repeatable upholstery models and 2,500 cabinet pieces, which were always available to order. The items illustrated, selected at random from the archives, represent only a small portion of this vast range, but they serve to demonstrate both the wide variety and excellence of that furniture.

During the dark years of 1942 and 1943, the nation was totally engaged in its struggle to survive, recover from the defeat at Dunkirk, and to step up production of guns, tanks, and aircraft.

Hugh Dalton had become President of the Board of Trade on 21 February 1942 and it was under his auspices that thoughts took shape of how, when, and in what form it would be possible for the furniture industry to resume production. Owing to shortages of every type of material, the thinking turned to some sort of standard furniture using minimum quantities. Prices of second-hand furniture were soaring. The Furniture (Maximum Prices) Order of 7 May 1942 froze all prices at the level of 1 May including those for second-hand furniture. In June, making new furniture was prohibited, unless the manufacturer had 'legitimate' supplies of timber from pre-war stocks which had not been commandeered. At the same time it was decided to form a panel of designers to draw up specifications for a range of essential items to be produced only under licence granted by the Board of Trade.

This furniture would only be sold to those who had been issued with 'a certificate of need' and it would be free of purchase tax if the Treasury could be so persuaded. A report by the Central Price Regulation Committee revealed many abuses of the price freeze with gross profiteering. All this reinforced the idea that everything to do with the production and sale of furniture would have to be controlled. Thus the Utility Furniture scheme was born.

The trade was opposed to the whole idea, arguing that only they knew the public taste and that customers would not want the same furniture as their neighbours. An advisory committee on Utility Furniture was appointed and worked to produce designs prototyped and exhibited at the Building Centre. The *Architects' Journal* commented 'very ugly to look at' — but the public were mainly interested in when it would be available. Pricing the designs was a great problem. Figures indicated the cost of furnishing a home was 150% above 1937 levels, but the proposed Utility prices reduced this to £39 14s 5d for a double bed, wardrobe, tallboy, dressing chest, dining table, sideboard, easy chair, three dining chairs, kitchen table and one kitchen chair. This was for oak furniture; in mahogany the cost would be £72 19s 6d. The trade wanted to retain its traditional 50% profit margin rather than the 33⅓% fixed by the BoT, but this was not allowed. Only 32 firms were drawing their quota of timber in December 1942 but 72 firms had applied and been designated to produce Utility furniture, rising to 150 by March 1943. Production of all non-Utility furniture had to be completed by 31 January 1943; it could not be sold after 28 February.

The first firm designated was East Bros of Dundee, with J. W. Hawkins, Smith Bros and Co, Hutchinson & Edmonds Ltd, and B. Cartwright & Son the first firms in High Wycombe, with licence numbers 68 to 70. The first Utility catalogue was issued on 1 January 1943, and offered each model in a choice of oak or mahogany. Only 'bombees' or newly-weds were eligible and had first to obtain an application form for a permit from their local Fuel Office. After scrutiny a permit was issued for sixty coupons (units), valid for three months, each piece of furniture having a different coupon value. These had to be surrendered to the retailer when the order was placed and he was required to send them with his order to the manufacturer. This system prevented the retailer from obtaining any stock to display, so that all choice had to be made from the catalogue. It was not long before retailers were displaying 'Furniture in transit' or bribing customers to defer delivery, allowing them to display it for a time, as demand far outstripped supplies. 18,500 permits were issued in the first six months *ie* 1,110,000 coupons; with production only just starting and few firms designated, only 25,000 coupons' worth had been delivered by the end of February. The larger firms were still committed to War work and aircraft production.

A glance at the contents list of a pamphlet issued by the British Furniture Trade Confederation in April 1945 emphasises to what extent the manufacture and sale of furniture was controlled by Government.

For Parker Knoll, control of all furniture design and production by the Government sapped the vigour of the Company, leaving it without a determined plan for peace and everything was allowed to run down. Despite war work the Company had barely managed to keep its head above water. Profits before tax in 1941 amounted to a mere £16, with £5,822 in 1942 rising in 1943 to £13,453 and £14,243 in 1944. After that they fell away sharply to £6,341 in 1945.

During 1944 Parkers' War contracts tailed off and a grey period developed with less and less work. In early 1945 the Company applied for a licence to make Utility designs, and were designated number 423. This, together with the Utility Mark CC412, had to appear on all furniture produced.

The models confirmed for licence were extremely limited. Much of the woodworking machinery had been out of use for some time and the available labour force was greatly reduced. There was no wish to embark on cabinet production again, the sole objective being to restart production of Parker Knoll chairs as soon as possible. This left only the dining and fireside chairs, which were basic indeed. The first made under the scheme were oak dining chairs Models 3, 3A, and 3C. These had drop-in plywood seats covered in green or brown leathercloth, sold for £1 2s 6d, and cost one coupon each. Starting in October 1945, a total of 42,892 had been delivered by July 1946, yielding a turnover of £42,222 6s 6d. In May, June and July 1945, production started of fireside chairs models 1, 1A, 2, 2A 2B, and the Model 4 and 4A bed settee, but only small quantities were made — 1,027 in three months. No wonder the Company made a loss of £5,582 for the year ending July 1946 on a turnover of only £100,000.

Harry Parker had remained active at the factory throughout the War but was now 69. His brothers William and Tom had been in retirement since 1941 and William had no wish to return. Accordingly George Parker, Managing Director, decided to put the Company up for sale, for £110,000. A prospective purchaser took an option to buy, which was to expire on 31 December 1946. But TCP was not prepared to stand aside and see the family business pass into other hands. He decided to return from retirement in mid-1946, at 65, to retrieve and reinvigorate the business.

With the ending of aircraft contracts Hill-Smith, who had represented the Ministry of Aircraft Production at the factory, left and Alan Walsh, who had been reorganising sales of the small Utility production, also left in 1946. George Parker retired to Canada soon after, so that the business was left without any effective sales or production management. He turned to his two sons-in-law, Geoffrey Alpe, married to his daughter Nancy, and Charles ('Hans') Jourdan, married to his other daughter, Peggy.

Geoffrey Alpe had gained experience of the trade by designing at his father's business in Banbury before the War. Original ideas for unit bedroom furniture with adjustable plinths, which enabled several units to stand together, were developed there. He joined almost immediately, arriving in August 1946. The author was asked to come to High Wycombe as Sales Manager, and started on 6 September.

Hans Jourdan had worked through the War in the milk business, becoming Assistant Plant Manager at the canning factory at Dumfries and then Production Manager in the CWS milk canning factory near Cirencester. In October, he moved to High Wycombe, to oversee production, living in the tiny 17th century cottage at 23 Frogmoor.

TCP appointed both sons-in-law as Joint Managing Directors with himself as Chairman, and set his new team the task of rebuilding the business. In the last months of 1946 it was a question of identifying problems, rather than finding solutions. Shortages meant it was only possible to plan in a limited way.

Charles Jourdan quickly became known in the factory as 'The Old Man' and elsewhere as Hans or by his initials CHJ. He soon found that all the machinery was dilapidated, and appointed Les Hoath as Engineer. Bill Brown of CWS joined the Company as Works Manager and was followed soon after by Albert Billingham, who also became Engineer. The severe winter weather early in 1947 disrupted transport and resulted in a monumental power cut. Most industrial activity had to be suspended for four weeks but Parker Knoll were able to keep working, for Harry had installed two diesel engines and a steam boiler in 1934 for generating electricity. The motors were Ruston & Hornsby 80kw and 35kw respectively and the cylinder head would often glow red hot. Through constant overheating they became warped and cracked. Every weekend they had to be welded and re-fitted and there were also difficulties in sychronising them. Learned engineers were called in only to shake their heads and marvel that the machines ran at all. But they were kept going by careful nursing, even supplying power at times to an adjoining factory as well. Eventually one of Parker Knoll's own men found and corrected the fault. Coal deliveries were erratic making it impossible to heat the factory property: icicles hung from the heating pipes to the floor.

The mill building where all the woodworking machines were located is built over the line of the River Wye which runs down the Hughenden Valley. The stream is culverted under the factory, (and today right through the town centre) and had quietly flowed through the factory site for generations. When the thaw finally arrived, the culvert was overwhelmed. One memorable Monday morning men working in the machine shop quite suddenly found water rising around them until it was ankle deep. Sandbag dams were hastily improvised and production was hardly affected, but many willing 'dam makers' got cold and wet feet.

In Sales the priority was to assess the order book. Business had to be reasonably local as only one van was serviceable and other deliveries had to go by rail and involved complex packing. 40% of all goods sent by rail arrived damaged in transit, requiring return for repair and claims for damage which took months to settle.

There was one area of the market which did offer some scope for new orders. User authorities such as hospitals, hotels, schools, universities and various Government departments had not been allowed to buy new furniture for three years and were anxious to re-equip. The range of Utility seating was inadequate both in style and durability, a fact recognised by the Board of Trade, which allowed special arrangements for them, despite shortages.

In the spring of 1943 Gordon Russell (later Sir Gordon), a member from its inception of the Advisory Committee on Utility Furniture, suggested that a design committee should be formed to determine the type and style of Utility furniture when supplies improved. Its first report was published in August 1946 and proposed that the range should be greatly extended and that supplies should eventually be made to those outside the priority classes. The scheme should not be ended until production was sufficiently high to make price controls unnecessary. Acceptance of this philosophy by the Government resulted in a steady increase in designs and licenses for production during 1946 and 1947, giving Parker Knoll the opportunity to move away from sole dependence on dining chairs. In the year ending July 1947 they delivered 58,054 of the three dining chair models and an additional 8,000 of the new designs 750, 751, and 753, but demand slumped dramatically in 1947, forcing cessation of models 3 and 3C. The Chancellor of the Exchequer had called for general price reductions in his March budget so Parker Knoll cut prices by 10%. This failed to bolster flagging sales.

Of the new and more expensive dining chairs, only the 750 model was in demand. In another attempt to increase sales, Parker Knoll advised retailers they would accept orders for the 750 without coupons as regulations required. This brought in some orders, but also an administrative problem in keeping track of who owed units and how many. It also incurred the wrath of the Board of Trade but they themselves were forced to adopt a similar principle on models 3A, 709, and 711 by issuing what was known as a Q A Licence to certain makers.

A few of the original Utility fireside chairs were made until January 1947 when attention turned to the newly introduced Cotswold three-piece suites. Of several designs introduced, PK opted to make the 11, 11A and 11Ac designs, mostly in wool tapestry or moquette. Brown Vickers of Bradford supplied tapestry, but moquette was unobtainable. Between November 1946 and July 1948, 814 settees and 3,061 chairs were made. In wool tapestry the three pieces sold for £49 11s 9d and 28 unit coupons of the total allowance of 60.

Another upholstered suite based on a metal frame was introduced later in the year, with a three-seater settee. These could not be handled in the factory, so sales were confined to chairs. Metal frames were delivered from South Wales and had compressed paper inserts inside V shaped metal channels round the edges, into which the upholstery was tacked.

In late 1946 the Cotswold range included three new open arm fireside chairs. They were a great improvement over the original Models 1, 1A, 2 and 2A. The new 1450 model had a tightly upholstered seat over a coil spring unit, ash bentwood arms, and was generally similar in style to pre-war PK models. The specified covering was Utility cotton tapestry and the retail price was set at £7 1s 6d with 6 coupon units. Parker Knoll made immediate application for a licence and put the chair into production. Orders arrived in abundance and delivery dates extended. Buying Department, managed by Ron Styles, had to keep their ears close to the ground, to obtain sufficient materials. Hessian was in particularly short supply and necessitated purchase of redundant sandbags which then had to be split apart and re-sewn. 8,697 chairs were delivered between January 1947 and April 1948. This was a well-made chair, but it carried no identification except the Parker Knoll utility number CC41 423. Retailers were quick to emphasise that THIS chair was made by Parker Knoll, selling them as fast as they came in.

The factory had a store of pre-war machined Parker Knoll chair parts with which nothing could be done due to regulations. TCP saw that if these could be made up, they would sell readily as non-Utility furniture, despite 66⅔% purchase tax, to a market starved of good furniture. He pressed the Board of Trade and a licence was finally granted in December 1946. Complete parts were not always available and new ones could not be made, so the factory used its ingenuity in marrying arms, legs and backs with one another to create reasonable chairs using all sorts of unconventional covers. Mostly these were heavy canvas from discarded war contracts, some patterned, most plain, dyed in the most outrageous orange, green or vivid blue. As the word went round, the office was beseiged with customers wanting bulk lots. These were the first freely available Parker Knoll chairs since the War and they sold like hot cakes. 12,911 were delivered by the time the special licence expired on 31 July 1948.

In May 1947 the Board of Trade widened the Utility scheme still further by inviting designs 'for approval by their assessors'.

Sales of the priority Parker Knoll models under special licence for buying authorities showed a useful increase throughout 1947 and 1948, with almost 10,000 supplied. Vivian Card, who joined the London showrooms in 1938, returned from War service in August 1947 as representative in the south.

The success of Parker Knoll 'pre-war' chairs, and increasing demand for the priority chairs, posed problems of how to get high tensile steel wire for Parker Knoll springs. All that was available was then commandeered for renewing winding cables in coal mines. In September 1947 CHJ went to Germany and bought 50 tons of galvanised wire. The pre-war spring making and spring covering machines were also in need of replacement and while there, he found a firm making spring machines. They had brand-new machine tools supplied from America under the Marshall Plan, so he obtained the new machines from them. He also found Kranzlers, who made the spring covering machines, were quoting two year's delivery. CHJ's sister had married into the Kranzler family and he was given priority, enabling the spring-making shop at Wycombe to re-equip. Further suppliers of wire were obtained from Germany until a British firm was able to supply.

LEFT: The PK139 chair was made from 1900 to 1939, covered, lined with loose cover, or in hide, from £10 17s 6d to £15 7s 6d. RIGHT: Chippendale style mahogany chairs 4371, with more modern legs; priced at £13 10s 6d. BELOW: In 1924 this needlework screen cost £120; at today's prices it would go for £3,670 — if you could get it. RIGHT: 1927 — an ash and elm Windsor comb back armchair, to the trade at £5 2s 6d.

LEFT: Saxon oak buffet, 1930, £28 10s. RIGHT: Walnut William and Mary style X-framed armchair of 1929 based on a 1690 original from Furness Abbey, bought for £45 — the reproduction cost 16 guineas. BELOW: A 5 ft walnut commode priced at £90 in 1930. RIGHT: In 1935 this Elizabethan armchair was based on those at Knole House, and supplied to ss *Franconia* 12 years earlier. Price £31 10s.

LEFT: TCP — Tom Parker. RIGHT: Harry Parker (1876-1962). BELOW: The 1930s reaction was stark — away with the ornate with this extending dining table, at £10 12s 6d. RIGHT: This 1928 hand painted leather-headed 3 ft mahogany bedstead cost £16 12s 6d.

The Die is Cast

As soon as the model 1450 Fireside chair was introduced it was obvious the chair could be fitted with springing to bring it up to Parker Knoll standards. Mr Johnson at the Board of Trade was initially guarded but eventually invited a sample for consideration.

While this was going on, another ingenious enterprise was taking shape at High Wycombe and Slough. During 1947 the prospects of an early return to normal production looked bleak. The non-Utility chairs made up under special licence from pre-war parts were limited in quantity, and otherwise only Utility Furniture could be made. TCP and his Board asked themselves if they could produce a chair from materials over which there were no restrictions. Then CHJ suggested die-casting the frame components in alloy. Discussions were soon under way with High Duty Alloys of Slough who had wide experience of quality castings, particularly for the aircraft industry. Exact patterns of each shape were made by the carvers so that moulds could be made. Due to the high cost of moulds the Company had to place a substantial order without seeing the final result. It all took a long time to complete, but in the summer of 1948 the first cast chair parts were available.

By January 1948 CHJ had a standard 1450 chair made up, fitted with angle iron brackets on the inside seat rails. The brackets had drilled holes into which the uncovered tension seat springs were hooked, while the backframe was also fitted with tension springs attached to staples before upholstery. In contrast to the tight upholstered seat on the Utility model, a loose, spring-filled seat cusion was fitted. The sample chair, which was considerably more comfortable than the compression sprung 1450 chair, was put in front of the Board of Trade. They finally reached a decision in February 1948, almost eighteen months after the 1450 chair was introduced, to accept the Parker Knoll design for the Utility range and required working drawings to publish to the industry. It was a tenet of the Utility scheme that any furniture maker could apply for a licence to make any approved Utility model, so the revised 1450 design was likely to be produced widely. TCP had stressed to Mr Johnson all along, that he would fit standard Parker Knoll springing, replacing the angle irons on the sample chair with PK flexible seat webs to anchor the seat springs.

Acceptance of the Parker Knoll design opened the way to produce and market a chair bearing the Company's name. With the original 1450 Utility chair in full production, conversion presented few difficulties. The specified price remained unchanged; £5 8s 3d trade; with a 33⅓% mark-up £7 4s 3d retail and surrender of six coupon units.

The side seat rails were printed with the legend "PARKER KNOLL UTILITY CHAIR, MODEL 1450 P.K.", confirming that the springing system was indeed the famous original. The reversible bordered and piped seat cushion was filled with a coil spring unit wrapped in fibre and cotton wadding which was a vast improvement over the tight seated original. The polished bentwood arms were ash or chestnut which were more suitable for steam bending than oak, while the rest of the frame and the cover was the specified standard Utility fabrics picked out in beige on a plain background in rust, brown or green. To simplify the switch-over to the Parker Knoll chair, outstanding orders for the original utility 1450, totalling over 1,000, were supplied in the new type.

The Company had a head start in spring systems and were able to deliver chairs long before most competitors. First deliveries during the last week of March coincided with the *Daily Mail* Ideal Homes Exhibition at Olympia. Wolfe and Hollander of Tottenham Court Road were among the first retailers to receive the chair, and placed a sample 1450 PK on their stand during the last few days of the show. They immediately booked orders for over 100.

The tempo in Sales and the factory increased dramatically, creating the need for more staff. Two pre-war representatives rejoined the Company after war service, Peter Galley in February, to cover the south east, followed in June by Richard Clibbens who in pre-war days had covered the West of England, and now covered Lancashire and northern England.

Parker Knoll believed it would be sufficient to inform retailers of the new chair, and no photographs of the 1450 PK chair were ever taken. That makes it the only best-selling PK chair that has never received any publicity or any promotion.

In June, shortly after delivery commenced of the 1450 PK, unit coupons were no longer required for Utility furniture.

This decision had been awaited anxiously by the author for, when he returned in 1946 he was handed a wooden box about two cubic feet in size, fitted with an enormous padlock. There was a slot in the top and the key had been lost. He was told 'oh that's the units'. Since Utility production started in 1945 all unit coupons received with orders had simply been 'posted' in the box and forgotten. They covered a whole year's production. When the box was forced open it revealed a mass of coupons, some in large sheets, but mostly in individual pieces about half an inch square. The box should have contained 79,316 coupons, but there was a discrepancy of over 25,000. Although the coupons were sorted, recorded, and returned monthly from then on, demands for a statement and balance seemed inevitable when the scheme came to an end. In the event nobody ever asked!

Reports were received of customers seeing a Parker Knoll van arrive at a shop, literally going in as the chairs were delivered, having the wrappings removed and buying the chairs on the spot. Sales did not have to sell the chair. Astute retailers, realising that they would never have enough chairs in stock unless they placed orders in advance, settled into a routine of ordering a dozen or more each month. Delivery dates lengthened rapidly.

Orders for the 1450 PK chair were soon arriving from all over the country rather than a conveniently limited area in the south east and it was undesirable to despatch larger, upholstered chairs by rail. To allow for delivery by road in either the Company vans or by outside contractors, outstanding orders were filed by region. Orders could then be selected for each separate van-load according to the size of the pool of orders. This system to regulate production has been used with little change until the present day.

Initially there was no regular stock range of cover designs and retailers would merely specify the quantity required in each colour; rust, green or brown. With something approaching 10,000 yards a month, this became a problem. Casse and Harrington, agents for Foulds and Bury, maintained supplies at a difficult time. Parker Knoll were able to buy direct from weaving mills that had felt unable to supply in pre-war days, and put down some long-term orders. By November 1948 it was possible to regulate the covers in use into regular 'A' and 'B' stock repeatable ranges. General Stores were not so lucky and had to turn to ex-War Department sandbags for hessian, kitbags for calico and life jackets for the Kapoc to be stripped out. The pressure for all sorts of alternative materials led to the introduction of coir fibre to replace pigs' and horse hair for stuffing. Rag waste carded into flock replaced Kapoc and Lintafelt while, since cotton thread was unobtainable, a progressive move to the use of translucent nylon thread began.

While all the excitement over the 1450 PK was going on, work at High Duty Alloys on the cast chair parts had continued and preparations were put in hand to market the chair, which became Model PK707 Toledo, registered design number 853391. Due to the long delay, the market situation had changed somewhat; there now was a Parker Knoll chair available, and what is more, it was within the tax-free Utility furniture scheme. The Toledo chair was non-Utility and therefore subject to purchase tax. The trade price was fixed at £12 3s 4d in tapestry covers; with purchase tax at 66⅔%, and a traditional 50% mark-up, a retail price of £18 5s 0d plus £8 10sd 6d — a total of £26 15s 6d. This was a colossal price for a chair, but Geoffrey Alpe had sales literature prepared by Vernons, when the purchase tax was reduced to only 33⅓% and all the literature had to be amended.

The Toledo was an elegant design of traditional Parker Knoll character which hid its unconventional characteristics by its conventional appearance. Only the top back rail and the two arm inserts, to which the arm pads were fixed, were made of wood, often obtained from scrap, and this was not detectable when the chair was finished with paint described as shades of either light oak or walnut. Assembly was straightforward, after which the frame was spray-finished. The Parker Knoll flexible seat webbing, into which the seat spring hooked, was bolted to the rectangular cast seat frame and the back springs, passed through the cast back legs, held in position by metal buttons. The Kapoc-filled back pillow and arm pads were fixed to the wooden inserts and addition of a spring-filled seat cushion completed the chair. Non- Utility covering materials made it considerably more colourful than the market had been accustomed to, and its comfort was assured by Parker Knoll springing in seat and back. First orders were received in the middle of October and first deliveries went out the following week, after which the chair took its place as a steady seller until early 1950, at around 50 chairs a week, when the whole quantity originally ordered from Slough had been sold. A small programme of advertising for the Toledo in national papers made it known that a Parker Knoll chair was again available after all the restrictions of recent times. The chair was heavy due to its metal construction and the bottoms of the tapered legs were hard on carpets but perhaps, as a chairframe, the Toledo is the nearest to indestructible that it is possible to achieve.

As production of Model 1450 PK got into its stride it was soon apparent that more upholsterers were needed, but none could be recruited. The woodworking mill was able to put through larger batches of chair parts and the chairmakers were able to send a strong flow of chairframes forward for polishing. CHJ decided to break down the whole upholstery operation into ten separate sequences, each of which could be executed by dexterous but unskilled men with no upholstery experience. A large horse-shoe shaped table was built at which the men could work, and all necessary materials and frames were fed to it by labourers. Each chair passed from man to man until it arrived at the last, who was a fully qualified upholsterer. This revolutionary procedure not surprisingly met with opposition from the Union, who objected to unskilled men, known as 'improvers' to the Company and 'Dilutees' to the men, in their workshop.

The upholsterers expressed their fears of 'cheap labour' and 'lack of quality'. When Geoffrey Alpe joined he Company in 1946, one of the first things he had done was to pay a production bonus on every piece produced. The bonus was paid on a shop basis, and CHJ said he would pay the same on production from the horseshoe table, and agreed with the upholsterers that the 'dilutees' would not be taken into the shop until they could earn as much as the upholsterers. Neither they nor CHJ expected the 'dilutees' to become proficient for a long time, but he underestimated them, and the effect of breaking the job down. Their output rose steadily, driving the bonus higher and higher until it was only a few pence below that of the main shop. As a result the upholsterers took the hint and started working faster themselves, increasing production and bonus at the same time. The men in the Machine and Making Shops, seeing what was happening, also worked faster. Output went up and up and shop bonus rose above 100%, resulting in Parker Knoll paying the highest local rates, making recruitment much easier.

Acceptance of the Parker Knoll designed chair within the authorised range of Utility designs brought a mass of other chairs with cable-spring seats and backs. Not all the springs were metal; some were of rubber and these undoubtedly infringed the Utility specifications.

After a few months the Board of Trade notified the Company that they were breaking the Utility regulations on the 1450 PK chair because their chair was different. In truth the Parker Knoll chair was of higher quality, but the Board of Trade required conformity to Government Standards. They claimed that approval had only been given for a chair with uncovered seat springs fixed by metal angle brackets between spring and frame, but TCP was insistent that Mr Johnson had agreed Parker Knoll could fit their standard system. Mr Johnson had departed to Canada and the Board of Trade wanted to take legal action against the Company, for contravening the Utility regulations, but were advised by their Legal Department that they did not have a strong enough case. In June 1948 several relaxations were announced, and CHJ claimed the variations on the PK chair were similar to those already permitted, but it was still some time before this was eventually accepted.

Demand was increasing for non-Utility Parker Knoll chairs for authorities and a leaflet was published. Customers included many large hospitals. Towards the end of 1948, the National Health Service was created and this led to discussion on how hospital customers could buy direct at trade prices. There were also increasing enquiries for renovation of pre-war chairs. It was evident that many chairs sold in the 1930s, particularly those in public buildings, were in need of recovering. A separate renovation workshop was opened.

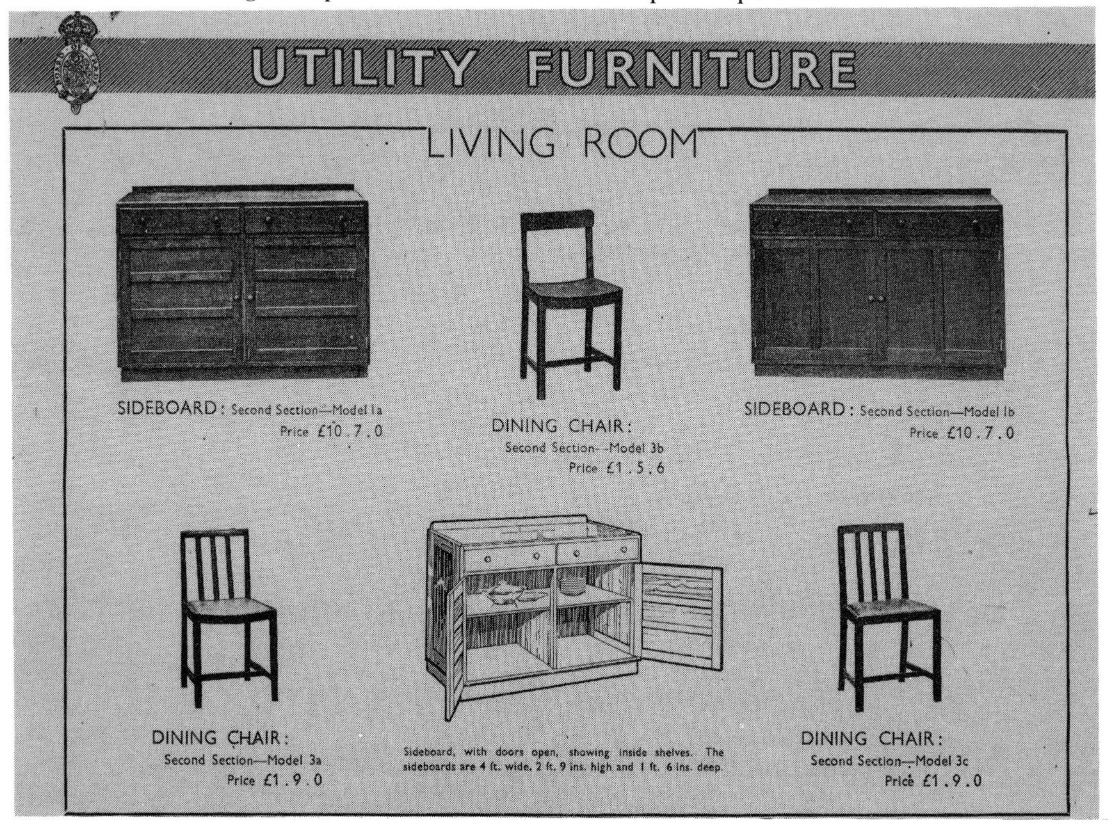

ABOVE, OPPOSITE: Pages from the first Utility catalogue. In 1945 and '46 the Company was making dining chairs 3a and c and models, 1, 1a, 2 and 2a.

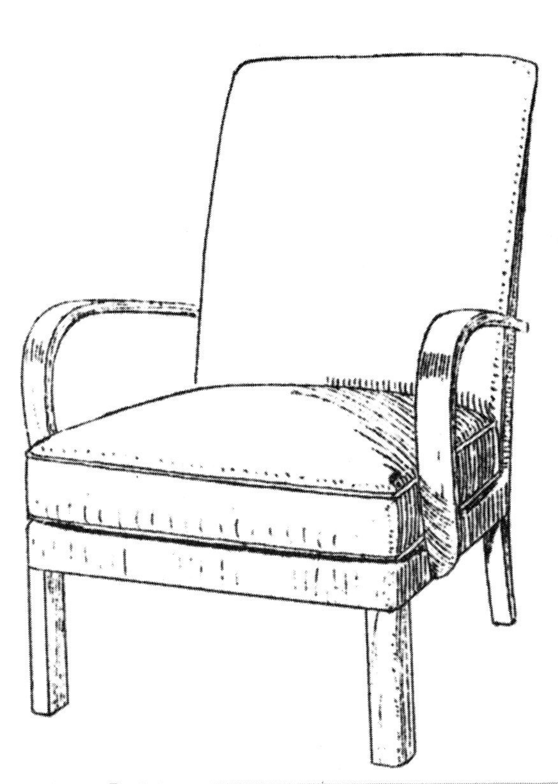

The 'Toledo' Chair, covered in the smartest available furnishing fabrics, is supplied with a choice of two finishes—Light Oak or Walnut.

UTILITY FURNITURE

MISCELLANEOUS

ADJUSTABLE FIRESIDE CHAIR:
Fifth Section—Model 1
Price £3 . 1 . 6

This chair has an adjustable seat and back. The 3-inch cushion seat is filled with flock and the back is stuffed with cotton felt.

Position 1

This model is 3 ft. high and 2 ft. 6 ins. wide. The three shelves are 8 ins., 9 ins. and 10 ins. deep.

SHELVES:
Fifth Section—Model 6
Price £2 . 4 . 0

FIRESIDE CHAIR:
Fifth Section—
Model 1a
Price £2 . 19 . 0

This chair has a fixed sprung seat and back padded with cotton felt.

This model has stuffed arms and an upholstered seat, with double-coil springs. The lower part of the back is also spring-upholstered.

This model is similar to Model 1a, but has an upholstered seat with single-coil springs.

FIRESIDE CHAIR:
Model 1 Position 2

EASY CHAIR:
Fifth Section—Model 2a
Price £5 . 19 . 0

OPEN-ARM EASY CHAIR:
Fifth Section—Model 2 Price £3 . 16 . 0

Page 10

LEFT: The famous PK1450 chair — never photographed or publicised, altogether 47,584 were delivered between April 1948 and May 1949.
RIGHT: The PK707 Toledo retailed at £26 15s 6d.

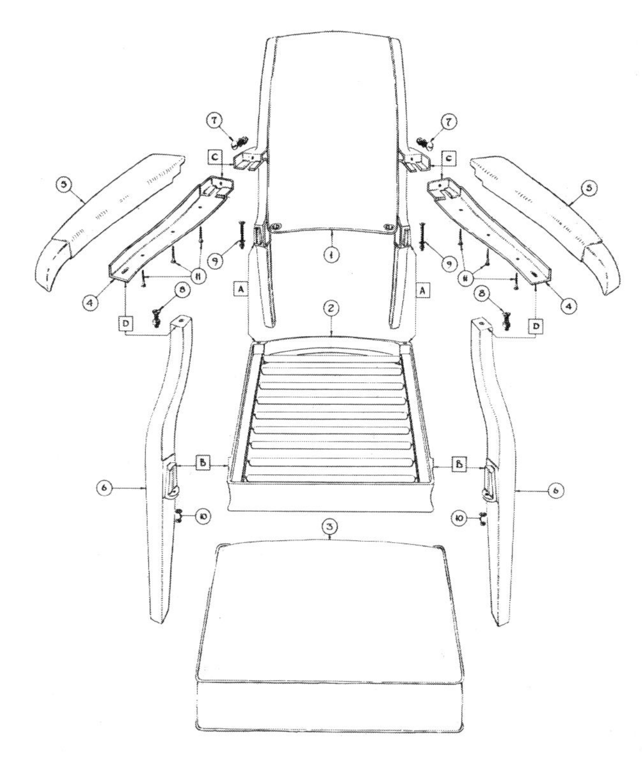

ASSEMBLY DIAGRAM FOR PARKER-KNOLL 'TOLEDO' CHAIR.

Punch October 12, 1949

Some visitors never know when to go. And you've heard that story of the visit to Dinard so often before. But at last the place is your own once more, and as you sink to rest in the arms of your recaptured favourite chair, you murmur "I really must get another Parker-Knoll."

The ROMSEY Model

Ask to see it at your local furnishers. To be sure you get the genuine article, see that the salesman writes the name "Parker-Knoll" on your receipt.

Parker-Knoll

PARKER-KNOLL LIMITED · TEMPLE END · HIGH WYCOMBE · BUCKS

November 29th 1948.

PARKER-KNOLL
REGD TRADE MARK

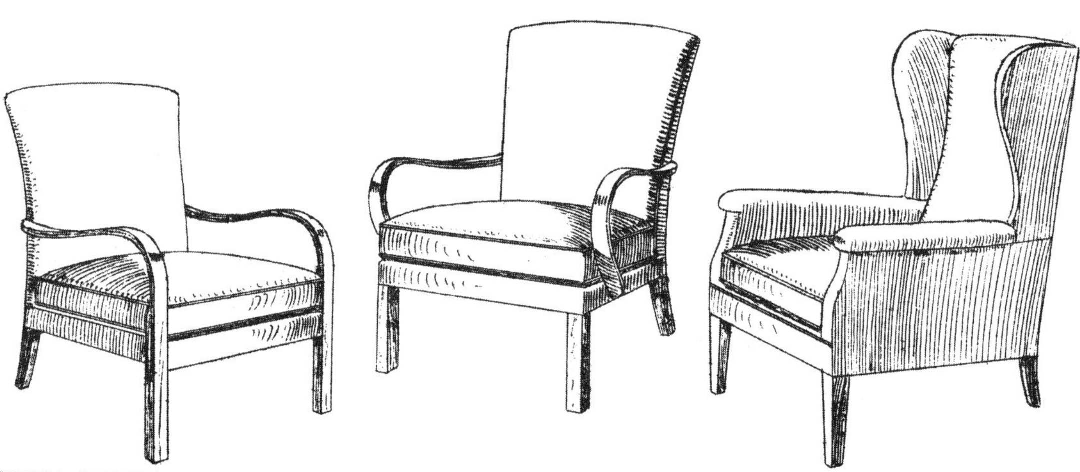

P.K:704. PARKER-KNOLL CHAIR.
(Utility) in B. Tap.
RETAIL £7. 13. 6d.
Circ.G.187.

P.K:708. PARKER-KNOLL CHAIR.
(Utility) in B. Tap.
RETAIL £8. 8. 0.

P.K:709. PARKER-KNOLL CHAIR.
(Utility) in A. Tap.
RETAIL £16. 16. 0.
Prices subject to confirmation.

LEFT: The assembly diagram for the Toledo. RIGHT: Readers of the 12 October 1949 *Punch* saw this advertisement for the Romsey. BELOW: Before that, on 28 November 1949, a broadsheet was circulated, when design controls were relaxed.

TOWARDS FREEDOM

It began to look as if manufacturers would be allowed to make their own designs, providing they conformed to specific dimensions and controlled prices. Work was still to be subject to inspection by the Board of Trade and all furniture must still carry the Utility mark, as a guarantee of minimum standards and confirming exemption from purchase tax.

This was good news and what the whole furniture industry had been waiting for. Reg Gomme, the Company's Designer, under guidance from Geoffrey Alpe and TCP, had developed prototypes of three chairs in readiness. Of the two open-arm chairs with bentwood arms, one (the PK 704 Cambridge) was a replica of the pre-war best-seller, and the other, (the PK 708 Romsey) was less upright and of more generous proportions. The third chair (the PK 709 Campden) although plain in style, continued the tradition for comfortable wing easy chairs for which the Company was so renowned.

Once it became clear that the Board of Trade announcement would not be long delayed, and although the dimensions and price levels were not then known, Sales Office prepared for action. So swiftly did they place details of their new models in customers' hands, that many said afterwards that they must have had inside knowledge. This was not so.

A mailing was prepared and the information arrived giving the vital details on sizes and prices. The two open-arm easy chairs were within the dimensions laid down and could be sold for the specified price — £17 13s 6d retail for PK 704 and £8 8s 0d for PK 708. There was a problem with the upholstered wing easy chair, which had to be a minimum of 31 inches wide overall to qualify for a trade selling price of £12 12s 0d. The prototype chair conformed in all other respects, but was only 28 inches wide and consequently would have had to sell at the unacceptable lower price of £9 15s 0d. The simple solution was to widen the arms on the production chair (PK 709) by 1½ inches each side. 3,000 mail shots went out that night.

The *Cabinet Maker* is published every Friday and carried news and details of the new Utility scheme in its 29 November edition, but many buyers learnt about the new scheme from the circular. The impact was astonishing. By Tuesday the first orders started to arrive and by Friday the value of orders for the three new models was £32,560 7s 0d from a total of £34,853. Total order intake for all three models in previous weeks had been running at about £3,000 to £4,000. In the following week, orders for the three models totalled £67,638 13s 0d, from a total for the whole range of £69,478 9s 5d. At today's values that is around £1.5 million.

More orders for the three new chairs arrived during December, so that by the end of the year a total of 7,351 PK 704, 8,173 PK 708 and 3,147 PK 709 had been received with a total value of £129,921.

This radically transformed situation came close to that envisaged in 1932 by TCP when he wondered if it were possible to produce a small group of chairs in large quantities and sell them at extremely keen prices. Pent-up demand had built up during the War years for good furniture. Utility Furniture was tax free and the price was controlled by Government and by keeping the retailer's margin down to 33⅓% on cost.

Working drawings of the three new Parker Knoll Utility chairs were submitted to the Board of Trade and approved, while Sales had to radically assess factory requirements for covering materials. The Trade's enthusiasm for the new chairs created just the right conditions in which the woodworking side of the factory could operate to the greatest advantage. Parts for the chairs on order by the end of December totalled 179,742 machine parts, 31,408 bentwood arms, 75,404 corner blocks and 6,294 solid wings!

The factory rose to the challenge, delivered 258 wing chairs by the end of December, only four weeks after the relaxation. Increasing deliveries during January brought in repeat orders at between 400 and 500 a week. First deliveries of PK 704 and PK 708 models were made in March 1949 (at least three months after orders were placed) and had the same effect, keeping the whole organisation running flat-out. The textile industry was trying to recover from a long period of restriction, with clothing rationed until early 1949. Weavers of upholstery fabrics were not always able to obtain the yarns required for this heavier cloth and, throughout the Utility period, covering materials lacked colour. Brown Vickers of Bradford reintroduced several cotton cloths and designs made for Parker Knoll before the War, which lent the chairs an attractive appearance. Henry Nathan was soon asked to supply useful quantities of fabrics woven exclusively for the Company.

By the time delivery of the three models commenced, the order book contained 11,580 PK 704, 12,650 PK 708, and 6,925 PK 709 wing chairs. With this foundation, CHJ started to reorganise the factory. Although a small battery of drying kilns had been built before the War, they were out date and had not been used since. The Company had little ground on the site at Temple End for timber storage and used a field in Hughenden Valley for bulk stocks valued at £100,000. Apart from the capital tied up, this was inconvenient and increased handling, as it was two miles away. A battery of modern kilns were built at Temple End. These cost £30,000 and, by allowing timber to be kiln-dried immediately following delivery, made it possible to reduce the bulk stock to £10,000, paid for as delivered. There were other benefits. A new Conversion Shop facilitated rearrangement of the machinery in the Mill, on the ground floor of the four-storey building built in the 1930s, thus releasing the first floor for assembly of chairframes.

Towards the end of 1948 the Company sent four antique chairs on loan to Canada, where they were exhibited to help George Parker introduce and manufacture Parker Knoll chairs in North America. This was an independent enterprise, George Parker having obtained permission to use the Parker Knoll trade mark in Canada and the US. Unfortunately, the project failed.

THE PARKER - KNOLL "CAMPDEN" WING CHAIR.

MODEL PK. 711.

Hardwood Frame.

COVER.	"S" Quality Tapestry.
FINISH.	Medium Walnut, Light Beech.
CUSHION.	"Parkertex" Latex Foam Interior.
PRICE	£17 - 17 - 0.

MODEL PK. 711 N.

Model as above but covered in "A" Quality Printed Linen.

PRICE £16 - 16 - 0.

SIZES.	Height overall 38ins.	Depth of Seat 20ins.
	Width overall 30¾ins.	Width of Seat 20ins.
	Depth overall 32½ins.	Height of Seat 17ins.

Prices include delivery in England, Scotland and Wales.
Carriage paid to English Coast only, for Northern Ireland, Isle of Man and Channel Isles.
Prices charged will be those ruling at time of delivery.

RETAIL LIST,
January, 1950.

PARKER - KNOLL LIMITED, HIGH WYCOMBE.

THE PARKER - KNOLL "CROMFORD" EASY CHAIR.

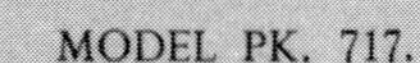

MODEL PK. 717.

FINISH.	Natural Oak, Brown Oak.
COVER.	"A" or "B" Tapestry.
CUSHION.	"Parkertex" Latex Foam Interior.
PRICE	£10 - 10 - 0.

MODEL PK. 717N.

Model as above but covered in "N" Quality Printed Linen.

PRICE £9 - 18 - 6.

SIZES. (Approx).	Height overall 34½ins.	Seat Depth 20½ins.
	Width overall 26½ins.	Seat Height 16½ins.
	Depth overall 32½ins.	Seat Width 22ins.

We reserve the right to revise prices without previous notice.

RETAIL LIST,
16th October, 1950.

PARKER - KNOLL LIMITED, HIGH WYCOMBE.

There were no immediate post-war catalogues, but these broadsheets did the same job in 1950.

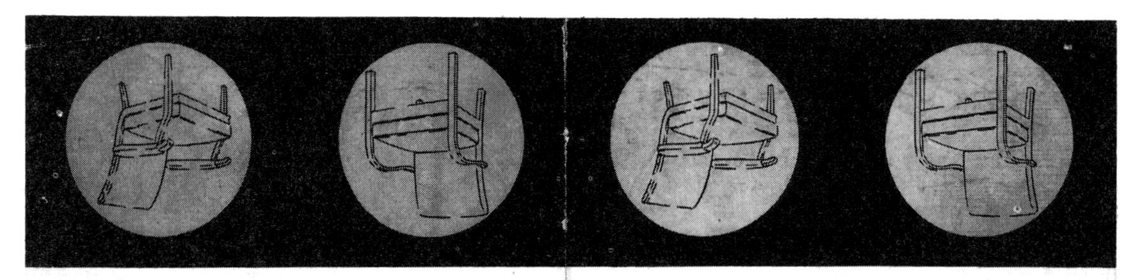

Antidote for Austerity

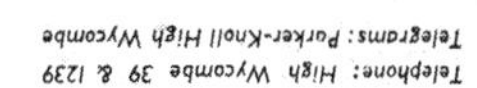

PARKER-KNOLL
LIMITED
TEMPLE END HIGH WYCOMBE BUCKS
Telephone: High Wycombe 39 & 1239
Telegrams: Parker-Knoll High Wycombe

Parker-Knoll

FOR THE BENEFIT OF THOSE who had not the good fortune to know Parker-Knoll before the war, let us explain that it is a brand of chairs which employs a transverse system of fabric-covered tension springs. Now, what that means in terms of comfort is a matter for a small experiment. Just sit in a Parker-Knoll chair. Then, when you are persuaded reluctantly to rise from it, you will be convinced that at last you have found a new quality in ease which surpasses all that you had thought before to be superlative.

is here again

In 1947 and '48 the literature was improving.

Companions in Comfort

On 31 January 1949 the Board agreed to form a new company to be known as Parker Knoll Textiles Ltd, operating as a separate entity. Partly due to pre-war difficulties persuading British weavers to supply Parker Knoll direct, and the continuous orders from retailers for short, matching lengths of fabric for Parker Knoll chairs sold by them, TCP had intended to form a textile subsidiary in 1939, but war prevented that. A new company could produce its own ranges of exclusive soft furnishing fabrics with textile manufacturers in both the United Kingdom and on the Continent, supplying retail trade, manufacturing upholsterers and Parker Knoll. In addition, they would act on Parker Knoll's behalf, buying whatever was required, and provide a warehousing function. The new private company was incorporated on 31 May 1949 with TCP as Chairman and CHJ and Geoffrey Alpe as Directors. Trading stared in July 1950 when Douglas Kitching, who had worked before the War with Sir Ernest Goodale at Warners, was brought in to manage the new venture.

In March, the first waste-heat boiler was installed. Before, burnt shavings and wood offcuts had not been used for heating because the original boiler would not raise steam. The new equipment had a capacity of 2,500 lbs of steam per hour. In August the directors discussed the possibility of adding another floor to the mill building, but planning permission could not be obtained. To make more use of available space an extensive conveyor system was introduced in several departments, linking them and eliminating awkward manual movements. This was one of the first comprehensive conveyor systems in the furniture industry.

As the volume of incoming new orders grew, it overwhelmed factory capacity and delivery dates extended relentlessly, eventually reaching nine months on the PK wing chair. Sales department was inevitably under constant pressure from retailers and the small force of representatives was calling on customers who had orders outstanding and were more interested in delivery than further orders. A better information system was needed.

The author created what was to become known as the 'shuttle card' system, a record card for every customer, with a unique internal order number, intended despatch date and other relevant information. The representatives had the same up to date information. As the cards went backwards and forwards between Sales Office and Representative they became known as 'shuttle cards'.

Discussion had taken place before the War with the Dunlop Rubber Company concerning the possibility of fitting Dunlopillo latex foam seat cushions in Parker Knoll chairs. Dunlop approached the Company again in 1949, wanting to display a Parker Knoll chair fitted with a Dunlopillo cushion at an exhibition. This was arranged and, when CHJ tried out the chair, the seat cushion collapsed so that he hit his back on the upholstery tacking rail glued to the inside of the back seat rail. With the customary firmer spring-interior cushion this could not occur. This made sure the position of the glueing was altered. It was decided to use a Latex seat cushion with a three inch front border in the PK709 wing chair. To cover the specification change, the chair was renumbered PK711. The cushion was moulded in two halves which, when sealed together face to face, had a domed centre, providing both firm support and yielding softness in combination with the Parker Knoll tension springing system. A method of fixing the front border of the cushion case to the cushion interior prevented it winding round during use and ensured that the appearance of the cushion remained neat and square.

In view of the large order book for the original PK709 chair, the changeover occurred as soon as Latex cushions were available, and took place in mid-October 1949 with invoices quoting the new model number PK711, and no increase in cost. Very soon the Company were taking 450 cushions a week, the total Dunlop production, but it was not long before the Board of Trade inspectors heard about the change and arrived to say that this type of cushion was not allowed under the terms of the Utility scheme. It transpired that the background specifications for cushion fillings under the 'freedom of design' were not well drafted, but wide and unspecific. When CHJ pointed this out it was accepted and when he suggested that to regulate the matter they could issue a Variation Certificate this was accepted too. Other manufacturers then asked for certificates and the Board of Trade adopted the PK cushion as a standard.

The Company was wary of acknowledging the Dunlopillo branded product name as part of their own, as it might inhibit future developments and restrict the use of cushions from other makers. To avoid this, they used the name 'Parkertex' for all latex foam cushions, overlooking the confusion this would cause later with the abbreviated form of Parker Knoll Textiles. The first sales literature since the War was printed about this time in the form of single sheets for each model. The seat cushion for the PK711 was described as 'Parkertex Latex Foam Interior'.

Dunlop had already objected to this description and wanted their own name used. Just as relations were becoming strained, a lady in Holland rejected delivery of a Dunlopillo mattress insisting that she wanted a Parkertex mattress instead. Dunlop gave instructions that all Parker Knoll's cushion requirements must be met. This opened the way for other models to be converted as soon as moulds could be made, with the PK708 renumbered PK713 and delivered from 11 February 1950. The PK704 model was not converted but discontinued in December 1949 for newer designs, all fitted with Latexfoam seat cushions; a total of 20,505 had been sold during the eleven months of its life.

Demand for cushions grew and Dunlop sent all they could make. It is said that the launch of the Austin A40 Somerset saloon was delayed six months because Dunlop could not supply the latex foam seat squabs until they enlarged capacity.

John Black was recruited in May 1949 to represent the company in Scotland and north of England, and two young trainees were also recruited to work in the office, initially to familiarise them with the business before they went out on the road. Jeff Chandler was one and went onto represent the Company in the West of England until his death in 1987.

Geoffrey Alpe had artistic flair, which he devoted to the development and introduction of additional chairs and more attractive covering materials. Customers such as hospitals, buying for their own equipment, and previously restricted to priority licences, were not overlooked. As early as April 1949 a higher seated occasional chair, PK710 Harvey was introduced, allowing them to partially escape the licensing proceedure. By November it was possible to supply this chair with a Latex seat cushion when it was renumbered PK715. In November another much more elegant chair, the PK712 Chatsworth, was added to the general range together with the PK714 Newark occasional chair. The two halves of each cushion had the PK model number embossed, making these cushion interiors exclusive to Parker Knoll.

There followed innovations in covering materials. Walsh & Mcrae of Halifax had supplied multi-coloured wool weft tapestries before the War and now resumed supplies. These were in great demand because of their superiority in style and colour. The Company had extra designs made and Henry Nathan also supplied fabrics woven to Geoffrey Alpe's ideas, when elsewhere fabrics still followd pre-war ideas towards durability rather than design and colour.

The Company turned to heavy-weight printed linens, which were quite freely available and offered an escape from drab tweeds. Warners Minster linen, a pre-war design, was allied with the PK711 wing chair in November 1949. It was an immediate success, partly because the price was lower, and led to the use of printed linen on several other models. Hunting up fragments of needlework from the Parker Knoll antique collection, Geoffrey Alpe had these translated into printed designs, one of which was based on the Tulip tapestry of pre-war days, and another, excellently flamboyant Jacobean design.

At the end of 1949 Vernons were commissioned to produce the first post-war leaflets for retailers and to book space in the national press, quoting the message 'Antidote for Austerity'.

Meanwhile a dispute broke out in the upholstery shop over the time allowed for upholstering the new PK712 Chatsworth chair. This was a straightforward job, but CHJ consulted the Confederation of British Industries for an independent time-study; it was July 1950 before this was finally settled. More than 25,000 chairs were sold.

Harry Parker resigned as Chairman of the Company on 20 September 1949, his place taken by his brother TCP. A month later, in October 1949 CHJ visited the USA *en route* for New Zealand and Australia, to make the first post-war visit to the Parker Knoll licensees, Beard Watson of Sydney and Hugh J. Eaton in Auckland. On his return journey he called on Robinsons of Singapore and Spencers in Madras, who were also manufacturing Parker Knoll.

In 1949 sales functions were separated by engaging a Sales Office Manager, Leonard (Dane) Baskerville on 23 November.

During December 1949 while CHJ was away, and on a day when all the other Directors were out, Board of Trade inspectors arrived unannounced and demanded to see various models in production, claiming they were investigating the Company for breaking regulations. Norman Stewart recalled looking up from his bench in the Upholstery Shop to see 'a man in a trilby hat and a military trench coat walk into the shop through the end door, look around, and then move over to a PK711 wing chair where he produced a knife and ripped up the inside back. Pulling out the Kapoc bag which formed the filling, he also slit open the cushion cover. The same operation was carried out on several other chairs without anybody challenging the man, who then without a word to anybody, walked out'. When TCP heard about this 'raid' he was furious and demanded instant explanations. When the Inspectors returned they were met by TCP and Geoffrey Alpe who were informed 'that anything they said would be taken down and could be used in evidence against them'. It emerged that regulations for the category into which the PK711 wing chair had been classified, required the inclusion of a hair pad at the bottom of the inside back, whereas the chair was being produced with only the standard Parker Knoll Kapoc pillow. This, said the Inspectors, meant that it was breaking regulations and was not a Utility chair. As such it was subject to purchase tax which amounted to over £100,000 for the chairs by then delivered. TCP's immediate answer was that the drawing had been submitted to the Board of Trade and approved — the mistake was obviously with the Board.

When CHJ returned from abroad, he took the drawings to the Board of Trade in January 1950. It appeared that complaints had been made by competitors that PK were breaking the specification. The smaller size of chair under the 'freedom of design' categories did not specify a hair pad in the back whereas the larger one did. When Parker Knoll adjusted the overall width of their chair for inclusion in the larger higher priced category, they did not realise that a hair pad was required. The revised drawings of the chair had been properly submitted and signed by an official who had also overlooked the requirement. It was agreed that the Company has not been at fault and to insert a hair pad in all future chairs. A total of over 55,000 PK711 chairs were sold by April 1951 when it was replaced by a chair which was destined to become a classic of its time.

LEFT: TCP conducted HRH the Duchess of Kent round the factory in February 1951 — behind, in the centre was CHJ. RIGHT: The 1953 national press advertisement for the outstandingly successful Penshurst chair. BELOW: The Museum set up by TCP in 1946 to display some of the antique collection.

Post-War Promise

By the beginning of the 1950s Parker Knoll had shaken itself free of lethargy and recovered its pre-war prominence. Expansion brought the appointment of extra managers and staff, many of them recently demobilised, creating a team which worked until retirement. Among this group was John Arnold, one of TCP's grandsons, who joined in October 1950 as a junior trainee.

Willi Knoll, accompanied by Dr Combie from Stuttgart, paid a visit to High Wycombe early in 1950, and came again in August to discuss future co-operation. Knoll felt that he had a right to participate in the success enjoyed by Parker Knoll. He suggested that he should become a Director and have a seat on the Board. TCP said that in that case, an English member should be appointed to the Board of the German company. The matter was never raised again but Michael Knoll recently recorded that PK had sent a cheque to Germany for royalties accrued under the original agreement since 1939.

CHJ also made a trip to France with Mr White, the Parker Knoll Timber Buyer, to secure supplies of beech. Timber was still in short supply in the United Kingdom and, although the French timber was expensive, it was essential to bring in supplies.

To preserve the fine antique chairs in the company collection, which had been stored since their removal from Newman Street in 1941, a small space in the factory was allocated to displaying a cross section on a rotating basis. By use of supplementary carving, tapestries and relics, TCP created 'The Museum'.

Parker Knoll Textiles started trading in the middle of 1950. They were forced to use makeshift premises. Douglas Kitching and his assistant, Miss Moss, worked in cramped conditions in the seventeenth century cottage at 23 Frogmoor, while the warehouse was two miles away on the edge of town.

The Korean War broke out in 1950, resulting in the Company sewing up heavy parachute harnesses for supply dropping. This facility also produced bayonet frogs in their thousands. On a happier note, during a tour of the High Wycombe area, HRH the Duchess of Kent, (Princess Marina) paid a visit to the factory in February 1951.

Echoing the Company's earlier opening in Berlin in 1913, a company was set up in Paris jointly with Maples et Cie (Paris) Ltd — Parker Knoll France SARL — using some empty factory space in their own Paris location. Maples subscribed 500 shares at 5,000 francs each and Parker Knoll 1,500, with the objective of manufacturing and selling the Company's chairs and settees throughout Europe. The timing was not good for it coincided with many economic crises in France and severe restrictions on all imports. The whole operation shut down for three months at one stage, but the Company persevered. Due to agreements with Knoll, already selling under his own name in Europe, the world Knoll could not be used by the French company, which operated under the title 'Sieges Parker'.

The Directors assigned Derek Stewart to commission the new factory and, during the three months he spent there, he established the production layout and engaged and trained the necessary labour. Initially the required frames, springs etc were assembled in two metal staining tanks and delivered to France by a Parker Knoll van. Most orders came from Maples and it was soon obvious that the standard designs had little appeal in France. Derek handed over a production facility, somewhat bereft of orders, to Monsieur Moulet.

Next, the Board considered death duties and that it was necessary to form a public company to mitigate these and preserve the future. During 1951 the share capital of the Company was reorganised by resolution; 50,000 unissued Ordinary shares of £1 each were issued, credited as fully paid up, to the then Ordinary shareholders by capitalisation of reserves. By special resolution the 40,000 5% Redeemable Cumulative Preference shares of £1 each ceased to be entitled to a fixed dividend and were converted into Ordinary shares from 30 June, then consolidated with the existing 90,000 Ordinaries of £1 into a single class of 130,000 Ordinary shares of £1. Each share was then sub-divided into four Ordinary shares of 5s each, the authorised Capital being increased by the creation of a further 280,000 Ordinary shares of 5s. This was accomplished on 23 June 1951 when 150,000 Ordinary Shares of 5s each were offered for sale at 10s per share, bringing the authorised share capital to £200,000.

It was anticipated that profits for the year ending July 1951 would exceed £140,000, although attention was drawn to the effects of increasing costs of raw materials.

By the end of 1949, Geoffrey Alpe had realised that Sales required more suitable office space. There was just one small room inside the main entrance to the administration building used by visitors and often already occupied. It was about 10 feet square and panelled from floor to ceiling in maroon Morrocco leather and antique brass nails. Many trade buyers recalled being ushered into this stuffy room and left to wait. One of the many regular visitors to the 'Padded Cell' was a well known principal of a North Wales retailer, who always arrived by taxi from London, to visit all his suppliers in High Wycombe, usually arriving after a more than convivial lunch. The taxi ensured that he got safely back to London.

The old Frogmoor factory had been leased since it was vacated by Frederick Parker & Sons in the 1930s and was then occupied by furniture makers Hall Edwards & Youens Ltd. These old Company buildings, on three floors, were suitable after considerable renovation, as headquarters for the whole Sales Administration and offered limited showroom space as well. The lessees agreed to find a suitable site and the buildings became vacant in early 1950. Geoffrey Alpe immediately set to work on a conversion, contracted to Y. J. Lovell & Son Ltd on 28 July for £7,688. The work was completed early in 1951, allowing Geoffrey Alpe as Sales Director to move his complete staff. Space was also found for Parker Knoll Textiles to bring their warehouse to the Courtyard, occupying what is today's canteen. The Sales Offices are still located at the Courtyard, some forty-two years later.

The PK711 had been designed under strict limitations of timber and materials which had now ceased. In pre-war days the name of Parker Knoll was synonymous with a wide selection of wing easy chairs, all of which had some characteristic period flavour; now the Design Office started to create another such chair. This developed into the elegant PK720 Penshurst, designed to embody the greatest possible comfort for modern living, while still, with its cabriole legs and scroll arms, reflecting the styles of the past.

When it was launched in April 1951 at a retail price of £23 10s 0d, the Penshurst benefitted from all the years of Parker's chair-making experience and was designed for quantity production. An all-time classic, it has continued in production ever since, and is still a best seller. There can be no other chair which has continued in production for virtually four decades during which a total of over 360,000 were made and sold. It is a sobering thought that around 15,500 good sized beech trees have gone into making them and looms have woven around 900 miles of material in which to cover them.

The Company employed its first Personnel Officer in 1951, necessitated by the number of employees, which had risen from 300 to 650 in five years. Further expansion of overseas licensees took place in 1951 when Richard King, a furniture man from Norwich, decided to move to Rhodesia and set up a plant to make Parker Knoll chairs. He worked for three months in the Wycombe factory learning all the techniques, before setting out for Salisbury. He encountered local labour problems, however, and was subsequently bought out by Ponters.

After expanding steadily since 1949, the furniture trade suffered its first post-war recession. Consumer expenditure on furniture and floor coverings rose from £254m in 1950 to £276m in 1951, only to fall back to £250m in 1952. This lack of growth continued for the rest of the decade, with industry profits dropping as low as £14m in 1958. By contrast, motor vehicles rose from £111m in 1952 to £586m in 1960, and radio and electrical goods from £212m to £400m.

In early 1952, all production employees were asked to accept a cut of 10% in bonus earnings. All except the upholsterers agreed, and they went out on strike on 28 April. This stopped the factory, Derek Stewart as Upholstery foreman, visited the Red Cross Knight, where the Strike Committee had its headquarters, to persuade them to return to work. Yet not a single order was cancelled during the strike, which lasted for six weeks. The Union challenged the legality of the proposed cut and took the Company to court, but this went against them, and eventually the other departments demanded a vote as a factory, rather than a single shop. By this time many upholsterers were ready to return and the strike ended with the 10% reduction taking effect.

When sitting discussing their problems in the Upholstery shop, Derek Stewart and Les Fessnidge often used the nearest unupholstered chair frame, throwing a Kapoc bag over the springs to make it more comfortable. This gave Derek the idea of producing a chair with a biscuit-thin seat cushion and back pillow, which could be attached to the polished chair frame with only a minimum of work. Once the principle was established, Design Office were asked to produce a suitable frame. Designed by Roy Asplin, it was an ingenious solution to creating an attractive wood arm chair with maximum comfort and minimum upholstery. The lightweight frame was of normal construction and all polished show-wood. The seat and back were sprung with Parker Knoll tension springs which carried a thin Parkertex latex foam seat cushion and a Kapoc filled back pillow, both anchored to the chair by passing the front and rearmost springs through pockets sewn into the cushions, so that the chair did not need to pass through any of the normal upholstery operations. The back pillow was attached at the top by press studs.

This chair, the Perth PK725, was extraordinarily comfortable, and, at a retail price of 8½ guineas, it was immediately popular. It has often been suggested that the chair was conceived as a strike breaker, but this is not so. Although the Perth was delayed by the strike, it was a resounding success and 26,000 were delivered in the first year.

Almost all new furniture made since the end of controls on design in 1948 enjoyed being classed as 'Utility' and thus free of Purchase Tax. This was at the rate of 25% on all other goods, and inevitably, when the Utility scheme came to an end, the exemption would have to end too. To avoid a sudden and dramatic increase in prices, the 'D' scheme was devised, whereby tax was introduced gradually.

Parker Knoll saw the 'D' scheme as an opportunity to improve profit margins for their loyal retail customers, and calculated their retail prices to give the retailer a mark-up of 40% on cost, improving the return to 28.57% with purchase tax added as applicable. At the same time, the opportunity was taken to restore normal settlement terms and allow 2½% discount discount for prompt payment.

Ironically it was the Perth chair which led to another fracas with the Board of Trade. The seat cushion at 1½ inches was thinner than usual and was anchored to the frame by a fly under the cushion case, giving the impression of greater depth. This design feature gave the front of the seat a fully sprung edge rather than a hard rail under the knees. Some time after deliveries started, a Board of Trade inspector arrived at the factory to say that complaints had been received that the Company was again breaking the Utility regulations. The inspector pronounced that the thin seat cushion infringed the licence which specified cushions of no less than three inches. CHJ showed the variation certificate issued when the rubber cushion had been installed into the PK711, which made no mention whatever of any dimensions or thickness, but merely authorised 'use of Latex Foam cushions'. The Company then received a letter insisting that the regulations were being infringed and threatening to withdraw its licence to make Utility furniture. This was serious, and could force the Company into bankruptcy.

It seems that when the Board of Trade received applications for variation certificates in 1949 from other manufacturers, they looked at the cushion Parker Knoll were using and, finding it was three inches thick, wrote this into the certificates. The original one issued to Parker Knoll made no such stipulation.

The matter dragged on for weeks with the Board of Trade unwilling to accept their mistake and persisting with their threat. After taking legal advice CHJ wrote to say their attitude amounted to persecution of the subject and was against the principles laid down in Magna Carta. He was then summoned to a meeting in London, but he day before, he was told a statement would be made in the House of Commons the next day, bringing the Utility Furniture scheme to an end. No further action was taken. For a long time afterwards the bureaucrats felt that Parker Knoll had been instrumental in wrecking the Utility furniture scheme.

Revocation Orders for the marking and supply of Utility Furniture came into operation on 15 December 1952, the Labour opposition forced a debate on the matter, but on 21 January 1953 the cause was lost by thirty-seven votes. The Utility furniture scheme was finally at an end.

In 1952, the Company reopened its London showroom at 13, Henrietta Place, Cavendish Square. It displayed the full range in production and provided Parker Knoll Textiles with a small office. Allan Barnett joined the Company from Dunns of Bromley to manage it.

The Perth chair with its 1½ inch seat cushion had cotton-covered back springs and the first use of the 'look for the name tape' message.

AN IMPORTANT ANNOUNCEMENT TO P-K RETAILERS

MODELS AND MARGINS

The D Scheme for Furniture enables us to introduce plans already prepared for improved retail margins and a settlement discount. Under today's more competitive retailing conditions we have appreciated your need for the best possible mark-up.

The new retail prices for Parker-Knoll Chairs and Settees will allow for a **mark-up of 40% on our wholesale prices.** *The purchase tax will be shown separately as an extra charge where applicable.*

In addition we shall re-introduce **a prompt settlement discount of 2½%** *for settlement on or before the 20th of the month following delivery. This will apply to all future orders at adjusted prices, but your outstanding orders will be completed at the prices as booked on a net cash basis. We shall be obliged to add purchase tax where chargeable. A new price list with full details is now being printed. This will be sent to you in the course of the next twenty-four hours.*

PARKER-KNOLL LIMITED

ABOVE: Improved profit margins for shops were announced in March 1952. BELOW: Robin Howland and Roy Asplin worked in the drawing office in the 1950s.

ABOVE: At the FTBA annual dinner, Grosvenor House, 19 February 1953, left to right were J. Marshall, Geoffrey Alpe, Hans Jourdan, Tom Parker and Stephen Bland. BELOW: In the fifties, senior staff held a Christmas lunch; here, left to right, were designers Reg Gomm and Robin Howland; transport manager Len Cox, Dianne Saunders (the Chairman's secretary), timber yard manager Jack True; purchasing manager Ron Styles, C. H. Jourdan and Company secretary E. T. Down.

Ways and Means

By 1953 the volume of chairs to be delivered the length and breadth of the country had increased and with it the fleet of vans and drivers. Len Cox was appointed Despatch Manager to administer the whole delivery organisation including the Packing Department and Despatch Office.

In 1953, a budgetary control sysem was introduced throughout the Company. The foundation of this was the annual Sales Forecast, made in April, for the year from August until July the following year.

Harry Parker, who had courageously postponed his retirement during the War and then continued to assist the Company, finally took his well-earned retirement, aged 76, after 60 years' service.

Strong evidence of the strength of the Parker Knoll brand and the Company's already considerable capacity were revealed by figures published by the Board of Trade for the year to the end of 1951. As a percentage of total output of fireside and wing easy chairs for the United Kingdom Parker Knoll accounted for 9.6% in Quarter 1, 11.2% in Quarter 2, 10.4% in Quarter 3 and 7.5% in Quarter 4.

Expansion was continuous through the early years of the 1950s resulting in several new management appointments, among which were E. T. Downs ACIS, as Company Secretary, Robin Howland from the Royal College of Art as Chief Designer, W. 'Bill' Brown as Works Engineer, and L. G. Cox, who previously ran the Tapestry Store, as Despatch Manager. In recognition of the success and potential of Parker Knoll Textiles, Douglas Kitching, who had managed the Company since its inception, was appointed to the Parker Knoll board.

C. J. 'Jack' True was Timber Yard Manager in 1851, and then Parts Production Manager. Jack recalls how the Company's first fork lift truck was introduced when the Hughenden Valley timber store was in use. This was driven by 'Tubby' Stevens who joined the Company as a lad in 1936, driving the daily van to Newman Street.

In the early 1950s manufacturers of woodworking machinery only made standard machines, mostly for the building industry. Parker Knoll needed to develop new machines so they turned to making their own. This was made possible by the skills and inventiveness of Arthur Travers, an engineer working in the Maintenance Shop, and George Lewis, foreman in the Mill. Typical was the machine developed and made internally to simplify the job of making corner braces for chair frames. Each chair uses four braces, or corner brackets, to reinforce the seat frame at the corners. The angles of the seat rails are certain to be different at front and back on anything except a square seat. Although insignificant in appearance, the brackets have to fit the angles of the seat rails exactly and had always been a problem to make in the vast quantity required, keeping two men fully employed. Arthur Travers produced a machine which cut the angles of brackets correctly and then bored and countersunk the screw holes for fixing, rejecting any faulty items before counting those accepted. 'Wally' Bedwell who operated the new machine for only four hours a day, was able to supply all the corner brackets required. This was the start of automating production on many machines and impressively, the method has not been improved upon and is still in use.

Arthur Travers also evolved new machines which greatly improved production in the Spring Making Shop. Originally the hooked ends on the Parker Knoll seat spring were formed by inserting each spring end individually into the machine which formed them. This was a slow and tedious process, which was abolished by Arthur Traver's hopper fed machine which formed hooks at both ends simultaneously. This again remains in use today. Another difficult operation was the insertion of the eyelet holes into the flexible tape which anchored the Parker Knoll seat springs to the chair frame. Spacing for these eyelets varied for each different chair and a stick rule was originally used to mark the positions on the tape before inserting the eyelets with a foot operated punch. Following this, a wide top tape into which the Parker Knoll name was woven, had to be sewn onto the eyeleted tape. In an endeavour to improve and simplify this string of labour intensive operations, visits were made to Germany but nothing suitable could be found. Visits were also made to a corset manufacturer, but it was found that their equipment was not capable of coping with the requirements of variable spacing. Using great ingenuity, a machine which did the complete job was finally built at the factory. By using a combination of pneumatics and timing solenoids, the machine not only inserted the eyelets at the correct spacing into a continuus roll of the special Parker Knoll webbing, but then cut it to the required length and then fed the eyeletted webbing to a sewing machine which attached the top tape, all in one operation.

More technical innovations were made by working closely with manufacturers of woodworking machinery. In Wycombe, the first automatic shaping machine was developed in conjunction with the Company by Rye Engineering. Again this made it possible for one operator to process large batches of shaped chair parts by leaving the machine to do the work while he loaded the sawn blanks and unloaded the finished shapes without moving. This was made possible by a rotating turntable and jigs, designed and made in a special shop.

Use of such sophisticated machinery led to creation of a Tool Room to service the sets of cutters where previously each wood machinist had been responsible for sharpening the tools on his own machine.

Mr A. G. Tomkins, General Secretary of the Furniture Operatives Union, advised against calling it a Tool Room as this might mean having AEU members to run it. If that Union went on strike the whole machine shop would be brought to a standstill, so it became known as the Jig Shop. Changes were made in Upholstery as well, such as the installation in the mid-1950s of the first conveyor.

Another change was the abolition of tacking upholstery to the chair frame, with a handful of tacks in the mouth and a magnetic hammer. Development of the pneumatic staple gun abolished tacks, but met with hostility and prolonged negotiations with the Upholstery Committee. When finally the principle was accepted Senco staplers were chosen and the ring circuit air main and swivel attachments were made and fitted to each upholstery bench by maintenance staff. That finally broke down the long-standing traditions and mysteries of the Upholsterer's craft.

On upholstered chairs another traditional method involved hand-sewn slip-stiching to finish the cover where it met on all outside edges. Derek Stewart discovered in Cologne a new concept of upholstery closure known as 'Palty Puntstrip' in use by the Dutch. This fitted round the outside contours of a chair in the form of a flexible toothed metal strip into which the covering material on outside edges can be folded to give a perfectly smooth finish without any sewing. It dispensed with the slipstitching operation. Initially, thousands of metres of this strip were purchased in Holland and yet again detailed negotiations took place over new upholstery job times. Eventually the spacings and number of teeth on the strip were modified and Jack True was given the job of developing a suitable flypress with an automatic feed to manufacture the strip required, with twin spaced holes in the flange plate to facilitate attachment to the chair frame by staple gun.

At its peak the Upholstery Shop numbered a full complement of 112 personnel, half a dozen of whom were blind, plus some 15 to 20 apprentices.

Many other new production methods were introduced throughout the 1950s and Parker Knoll became the most up-to-date large-capacity chair plant in the country.

The division of Sales Department duties was initially sufficient to cope, but eventually, increasing pressure led to further delegation. Arthur Newell joined the Sales Office in 1952 and was appointed Cover Buyer in 1964. Aubrey Saunders joined the Company from Dancer and Hearne in 1954 and took over all retailer services such as distribution of pattern books, advertising blocks, literature and display material. John Arnold was appointed in 1956 as Assistant to the Sales Manager. This team successfully ran Sales under Geoffrey Alpe, until further developments brought change in the early 1960s.

Almost by definition it was accepted in the furniture trade that Parker Knoll furniture was an up-market product. Initially Parker Knoll captured a large part of the market because they were equipped, while other makers had to start from scratch. There had been only a few lower priced imitations in pre-war days, but as the 1950s advanced there was a steady proliferation of chairs with cable sprung seats. Invariably they were at much lower prices and quality, but to the layman, the plastic covered springs were similar to the original Parker Knoll and this led to confusion. Many of these chairs would have been sold under the description 'Parker Knoll type'.

Legal action was taken in several cases to protect the trade mark and given prominence in the trade press. At the same time, Parker Knoll chairs carried the trade mark and chair model number imprinted on the side seat rails and, on a wide tape, the name Parker Knoll was woven in red. This message was extensively featured in advertisements under the heading 'PARKER KNOLL have comfort taped — LOOK before you BUY!!'.

To provide direct support to provincial retailerss, in addition to advertisements in the national daily press, a campaign of Parker Knoll advertisements also appeared regularly in most of the leading provincial papers. Many retailers frequently staged window displays — devoted entirely to the Parker Knoll range.

By 1953 the author had written a Sales Training Manual of some 100 pages, which fully covered Product, Sales Policy, and Sales Administration. The Sales Manual became the standard reference book and, much elaborated and with different emphases, continues in use. In addition all new representatives attended a three week induction course during which they spent one week in the factory. In 1955 the Company made a short film of the production sequence. Bob Debenham, who worked in the production office, was a keen amateur film maker. He approached the Directors with the suggestion and the Company invested in the necessary Bolex camera, projector and accessories. The shortcomings of the first film soon became apparent and led to a new shooting script for a second and more detailed film entitled *Comfort Created*. When complete the film ran for thirty minutes and had a voice-over by Michael Aspel. It was given its première at Colour Film Services Theatre in Portman Square in mid-1961 before an invited audience of trade buyers.

Other films made 'in house' were *Cover Counts* to show in detail the creation and weaving of all types of upholstery fabrics; *Screen Block and Roller* for Parker Knoll Textiles showing the processes involved in creating printed soft furnishing fabrics and *The Chiltern Bodgers* recalling the way in which legs and underframes for Windsor chairs were made in the woods around High Wycombe during the last century. All these films were produced for a few hundred pounds.

Need by retail salesmen for product information was provided in information sheets called 'Parkerknolledge'. Representatives were equipped with small trolleys and provided with a sample chair to carry in their cars.

LEFT: This automatic shaping machine was the first to be installed in Wycombe. RIGHT: H. A. Freeth painted wood machinist Walter Bedwell, who joined the firm in 1916 and served 32 years; his brother Joe joined in 1907 for 53, and another brother Tom in 1907 — he became foreman chairmaker. Walter's daughter, Joyce, managed the Contract Sales Office and her sister worked in Buying for six years until 1955. BELOW: The chair parts store, Bob Soamer (left) and Alf Stone.

ABOVE: The chair frame assembly shop at Temple End in the 1950s.
BELOW: Upholstery shop at Temple End, with overhead and floor conveyors, 1950s; Bert Belcher on the left.

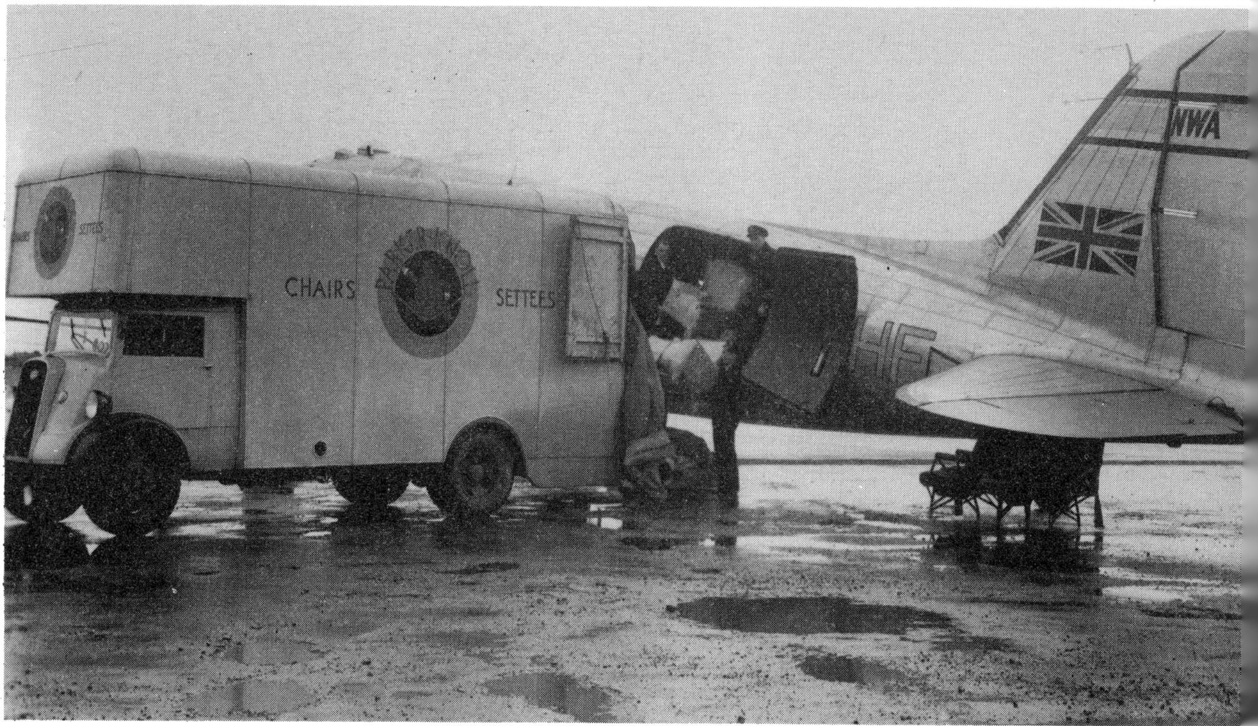

ABOVE: The sales team, January 1954 — back: John Pryce, Bernard Sharpe, Frank Ashwood, Jeffrey Chandler, Vivian Card, Richard Clibbens, Alan Palmer; front: John Black, Fred Bryant, Dane Baskerville (Sales Office manager), Steve Bland (Sales manager), Arthur Newell (tapestry buyer), Les Robson and Jimmy Greensides. BELOW: An urgent delivery was despatched by North West Airlines DC3 in 1950.

A WARNING

The attention of Messrs. Parker-Knoll Limited, the manufacturers of the well-known "Parker-Knoll" Chairs, has been drawn to an occasion on which a firm of Auctioneers recently advertised for sale chairs described as "Parker-Knoll" Chairs which were not in fact manufactured by Messrs. Parker-Knoll Limited.

THE WORDS "PARKER-KNOLL" ARE A REGISTERED TRADE MARK

The Auctioneers in question have given an Undertaking not in the future conduct of their business to sell, offer or expose for sale or cause to be sold, offered or exposed for sale any Chair, Settee or other article not manufactured by Messrs. Parker-Knoll Limited under the name of "Parker-Knoll" or any other name or by any other description such as to lead to the belief that the Chairs, Settees or other articles so sold were manufactured and sold by Messrs. Parker-Knoll Limited.

Messrs. Parker-Knoll Limited hereby give notice that they will, for the protection of the public no less than for the maintenance of the reputation of their well-known products, take legal proceedings to prevent the sale by any person under their name or under any description by which their goods are known of goods not manufactured by them.

The cost of this advertisement has been paid by the Auctioneers in question.

PARKER-KNOLL

Tension Suspension

PARKER-KNOLL LIMITED

Temple End, HIGH WYCOMBE, Bucks

PARKER-KNOLL
There is a saying that "In the night, all cats are grey". It would not be true to say that "In the showroom, all chairs are Parker-Knolls". None the less, a great many of them look as if they might be. The subtle refinements in design, workmanship and construction that distinguish a genuine Parker-Knoll are only obvious to an expert eye. But there is one infallible way of making sure that you are buying the real thing. Simply raise the cushion seat and look for the Parker-Knoll name tape. This is your guarantee of deep, luxurious comfort in your leisure hours.
These and other chairs are shown in the Parker-Knoll catalogue—available from Parker-Knoll Ltd., The Courtyard, Frogmoor, High Wycombe, Bucks. You can meet them personally at your favourite furnishers or at any of Parker-Knoll's showrooms—13, Henrietta Place, Cavendish Square, London, W.1, 3 Barton Square, St. Ann's Square, Manchester, and 43 Temple St., Birmingham.

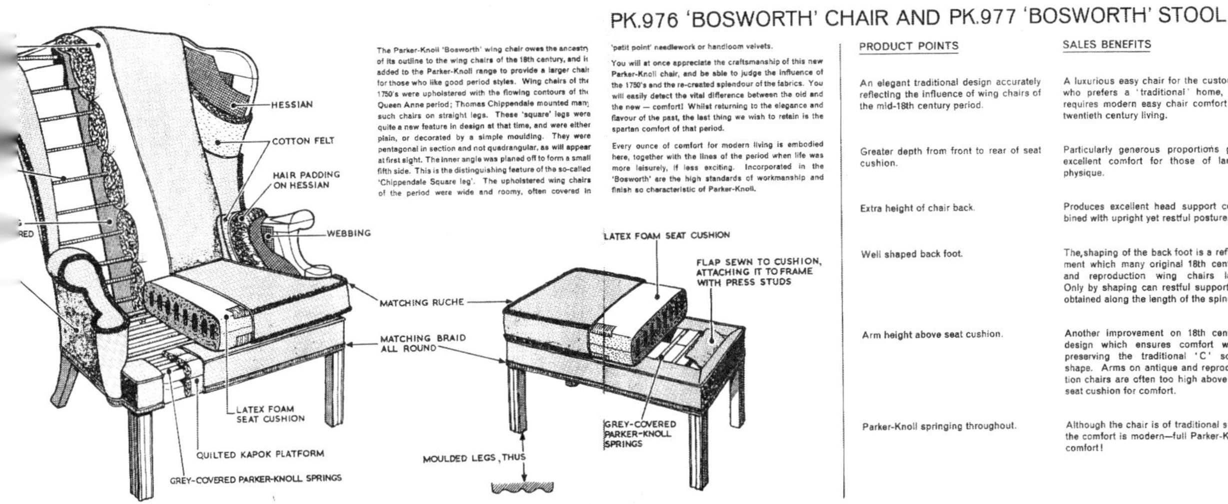

PK.976 'BOSWORTH' CHAIR AND PK.977 'BOSWORTH' STOOL
The Parker-Knoll 'Bosworth' wing chair owes the ancestry of its outline to the wing chairs of the 18th century, and is added to the Parker-Knoll range to provide a larger chair for those who like good period styles. Wing chairs of the 1750's were upholstered with the flowing contours of the Queen Anne period; Thomas Chippendale mounted many such chairs on straight legs. These 'square' legs were quite a new feature in design at that time, and were either plain, or decorated by a simple moulding. They were pentagonal in section and not quadrangular, as will appear at first sight. The inner angle was planed off to form a small fifth side. This is the distinguishing feature of the so-called 'Chippendale Square leg'. The upholstered wing chairs of the period were wide and roomy, often covered in 'petit point' needlework or handloom velvets.
You will at once appreciate the craftsmanship of this new Parker-Knoll chair, and be able to judge the influence of the 1750's and the re-created splendour of the fabrics. You will easily detect the vital difference between the old and the new — comfort! Whilst returning to the elegance and flavour of the past, the last thing we wish to retain is the spartan comfort of that period.
Every ounce of comfort for modern living is embodied here, together with the lines of the period when life was more leisurely, if less exciting. Incorporated in the 'Bosworth' are the high standards of workmanship and finish so characteristic of Parker-Knoll.
PRODUCT POINTS
SALES BENEFITS
An elegant traditional design accurately reflecting the influence of wing chairs of the mid-18th century period.
A luxurious easy chair for the customer who prefers a 'traditional' home, but requires modern easy chair comfort for twentieth century living.
Greater depth from front to rear of seat cushion.
Particularly generous proportions give excellent comfort for those of larger physique.
Extra height of chair back.
Produces excellent head support combined with upright yet restful posture.
Well shaped back foot.
The, shaping of the back foot is a refinement which many original 18th century and reproduction wing chairs lack. Only by shaping can restful support be obtained along the length of the spine.
Arm height above seat cushion.
Another improvement on 18th century design which ensures comfort while preserving the traditional 'C' scroll shape. Arms on antique and reproduction chairs are often too high above the seat cushion for comfort.
Parker-Knoll springing throughout.
Although the chair is of traditional style, the comfort is modern—full Parker-Knoll comfort!
HESSIAN
COTTON FELT
HAIR PADDING ON HESSIAN
WEBBING
MATCHING RUCHE
MATCHING BRAID ALL ROUND
LATEX FOAM SEAT CUSHION
QUILTED KAPOK PLATFORM
GREY-COVERED PARKER-KNOLL SPRINGS
LATEX FOAM SEAT CUSHION
FLAP SEWN TO CUSHION, ATTACHING IT TO FRAME WITH PRESS STUDS
GREY-COVERED PARKER-KNOLL SPRINGS
MOULDED LEGS, THUS

LEFT: Once again, Parker Knoll makes its legal point and RIGHT: reinforces it on the product and in the literature. BELOW: The Bosworth is extolled in trade promotion.

PARKER-KNOLL

have comfort *taped*

To the casual glance, there are many chairs that look as if they *might* be Parker-Knolls. So before you buy, delve a little deeper. Raise the cushion seat and look for the Parker-Knoll name-tape. This is your guarantee of first-class design and workmanship. Wing chairs and other types can be seen at your local furnishers.

P.K.740 "LINGFIELD"
In tapestry 'A' £14.14.0
In moquette or tapestry 'S' £15.15.0
In moquette or tapestry 'P' £16.16.0

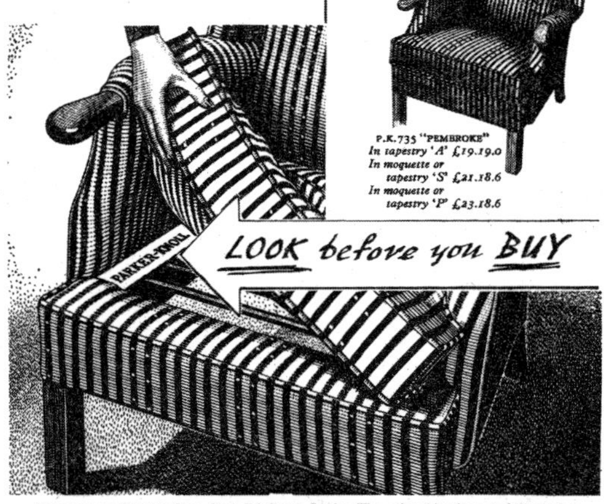

P.K.735 "PEMBROKE"
In tapestry 'A' £19.19.0
In moquette or tapestry 'S' £21.18.6
In moquette or tapestry 'P' £23.18.6
LOOK before you BUY

Showrooms: 13 Henrietta Place, Cavendish Square, London, W.1. Also: Manchester and Birmingham
For fully illustrated catalogue write to: THE COURTYARD, FROGMOOR, HIGH WYCOMBE, BUCKS

YOU CAN'T GO SHOPPING WITH A PENKNIFE

to see what's underneath when buying upholstery.

There is a saying that "In the night, all cats are grey."

It would not be true to say that "In the showrooms, all chairs are Parker-Knoll."

Nevertheless, a good many look as if they might be. A chair is not a thing to buy in a hurry—you will need to live with it.

So choose carefully.

The infallible way of making sure you are buying the genuine article is simply to raise the seat cushion and look for the Parker-Knoll name tape. This is your guarantee of deep, luxurious comfort in your leisure hours.

THE PERTH PK725
A Parkertex Foam Model

PARKER-KNOLL

have comfort taped

Ask to see them at your favourite furnishers.

Registered Licenses and Distributors to the trade in the Auckland Province.
HUGH J. EATON LIMITED,
336-342 DOMINION ROAD, AUCKLAND.

LEFT: National advertising emphasised the genuine article, to highlight cheaper imitations. RIGHT: Overseas licensees enthused — Hugh J. Eaton of Auckland, NZ was one. BELOW: Douglas and John Kitching.

Under Cover

During the 1950s upholstery covering materials were developed to improve the quality and value of Parker Knoll chairs.

The key to offering the customer a choice of materials in quality and price, colour and style, lay in comprehensive pattern books. To provide these across all price ranges to several thousand customers, and keep them up-to-date, was a big operation. To cope with this a special Pattern Book Department, run by Bill West, was set up. Here they made hundreds of thousands of patterns with oversewn edges, each one ticketed, collated into ranges and fixed into a cardboard swatch heading. Eventually, pressure on factory space closed the Pattern Room and the work sent to outside suppliers.

One upholstery material which offered long life and hard wear was wool pile 'Uncut Moquette', which became the workhorse for the industry throughout the 1950s and early 1960s.

Assisted by Douglas Kitching at Parker Knoll Textiles a close working relationship was formed with T. F. Firth of Heckmondwike, one of the largest British moquette weavers, who had the capacity to deliver large quantities of several designs and colours weekly. At one time demand was so strong that over 50% of all yardage used weekly was coming from Firths. In the six years from 1954, Parker Knoll used sufficient material woven at Heckmondwike to drive from High Wycombe and back again on a carpet of Firth's cloth; 367 miles.

The PK720 Penshurst wing chair immediately became popular, but there was a severe shortage of traditional fabrics of suitable colour and design. The only way to obtain what was required was to get something made specially; a formidable job. Geoffrey Alpe secured from the old records in the Parker Knoll antique collection fragments of hand embroidery and needlework from which he believed designs for a heavy duty upholstery tapestry could be created. Only a large weaving mill had the resources to tackle the intricacies of weaving adequate supplies on a continuous basis. Listers of Bradford were probably the only completely integrated firm who could tackle the job. Listers were keen to assist. They submitted a design which closely reflected the character of the original needlework and said that they could obtain all the yarns required and set up a loom as soon as an order was received. In this way 'Bodiam' tapestry was created, which was used for many years to cover countless Penshurst and other Parker Knoll models. Following this success the Company went on to work closely with Listers to create other tapestries such as 'Cornucopia' and 'Norwich'.

A final extension of high quality and style for the Penshurst chair was the use of hand embroidered Crewelwork panels from Arthur H. Lee of Birkenhead. They had long supplied the trade with beautiful wool materials of the highest quality in traditionally embroidered patterns.

As more modern styles of chair were added to the range in the late 1950s, there was usually an extra special make-up available for them in an ultra smart high quality fabric.

'Arizona', a memorable heavy weave in sulphur and red from Edinburgh Weavers was one of these and it was not surprising that it had far more appeal for retailers specialising in modern design, such as Heals, Dunns of Bromley and Elders of Glasgow, that the standard range fabrics of the time.

The use by the trade of the term 'contract' to describe the supply of furniture direct to end users has always been a puzzle, as not every order supplied is the subject of one. It dates back to pre-war days when large retail houses had a separate department dealing with non-domestic customers. Since the war, the term has been adopted by manufacturers to define a department which handles all sales made other than to retailers, mostly at trade prices.

Following the introduction of Parker Knoll furniture into the market in 1930, it was not long before interest was shown by a variety of end users who expected to be supplied at preferential prices.

Frederick Parker had supplied Government departments through the Office of Works for many years and as a result his products were to be found in embassies and residencies through the British Empire; Parker Knoll chairs were supplied on the same basis.

During the Utility Furniture era between 1943 and 1945 all pre-war connections with these customers were broken. In May 1945, all sorts of authorities and organisations were anxious to otain new furniture, and the Company received many approaches.

Alan Walsh, who represented the Company before the War in Yorkshire and the north east, returned in 1945 to canvas this business. He was able to offer a few pre-war Parker Knoll models as non-Utility, together with five simple, newly designed Parker Knoll models which could be made from the strictly limited supplies of timber allowed. These chairs were only available to priority groups who could obtain a special licence. Walsh had laid some ground work and booked some orders, but by the summer of 1946 only a few deliveries had been made, and he left.

During 1946 it became possible to establish much more clearly who could be supplied with what, providing a licence could be obtained. Customers themselves had to undertake the rigmarole of applying for a licence which involved long delays. The much delayed first orders were finally delivered in October 1946, after which the demand, although slow at first, built up. In the ten months ending July 1947 a total of 4,619 non-Utility Priority Parker Knoll chairs were delivered.

The key facor was the timber licence on form TC3/8/CPL and the author went to London each Friday with the week's accumulation, and toured the offices of the various issuing authorities; Ministry of Health for hospitals, doctors and dentists; Ministry of Food for hotels (who were allowed dining chairs only), Ministry of Education for schools and universities, and Ministry of Transport for shipping. All that was required to validate the form was the department's rubber stamp. Once validated, this form was given to the Company's timber buyer for issue to his suppliers.

Joyce Bedwell, who joined the Company in 1946 after service in the ATS, at first looked after all correspondence, but gradually became more involved with Contracts, until eventually, she acquired the specialist expertise and dealt with it exclusively. Fred Bryant was recruited in 1951, to start an organised canvass of contract authorities and deal with special visits as necessary.

The canvassing and winning of orders from user customers was treated as a separate part of the Sales Organisation and built up slowly into a Contract Department. In 1954 George Moss for the northern half of the country, and Jimmy Baker for the south, were engaged as Contract Representatives to methodically search out and establish connections with every hospital and county council supplies officer.

From the outset the Company objective was to win the business without becoming involved in making special models for Contract users. The benefits of flow production of a small range of chairs which had been set up to meet the demand from the domestic market, made it possible to supply the Contract user with his requirements without difficulty or delay. The open arm style of Fireside chair so popular with the domestic market at the time was eminently suitable for many Contract situations, and these were sold without modification.

Further publicity was given to contract availability of Parker Knoll by exhibiting at the Hotel and Catering Exhibition. It provided a useful platform for the display of the Parker Knoll range and also for new contacts with a wide circle of interested users.

From these beginnings, Contracts business developed and grew steadily year by year, contributing an increasingly important share of total sales. Later, without making them exclusively for Contracts purposes, chair models which took account of special needs of hospitals, homes for old people and for use in universities were designed and added to the range. These often were of interest to domestic users, helping elderly and disabled people to find more comfortable seating than was generally available.

During the year August 1950-July 1951 140,945 chairs were sold yielding a profit before tax of £179,553. The six week strike by the upholsterers in April and May 1952 was a severe blow from which it took several years to recover. This coincided with a time when the whole industry was suffering from depresed trading due to credit restrictions imposed by a Government trying to curb spending and the extension of credit. As a result of the strike only 67,686 chairs were delivered in the year ending August 1952, and profits slumped to only £27,468. It was the year ending August 1955 before profits recovered to £103,268, but they dropped again to £83,164 before tax in 1967/8 due to difficult trading conditions, after which they increased steadily for the next four years, reaching a record £232,898 before tax in 1961/2.

As incomes in all sectors increased steadily during the 1960s, a newly affluent middle class was able to exercise choice with many new and exciting products, such as washing machines and labour-saving devices for the home, television, and above all motor cars. The attraction of these proved stronger for many than new furniture and furniture began to lose the battle for a large share of consumer spending.

Furniture purchases have always been of a capital nature and credit trading facilities have always been important. Multiple shops in 1960 transacted 88% of their business on credit. This did not greatly affect Parker Knoll, as the majority of their business was with independent furniture shops and department stores, where the proportion of credit business was much less at 28%. Prices rose by 13% between 1954 and 1960, and bank rate rose too in 1957 to 7%. Government controls on hire purchase credit, from 1956 to September 1958 required a 20% cash deposit on any transaction, with only two years to repay, effectively retarding many sales. All these restrictions were removed in September 1958 and not surprisingly resulted in a surge in consumer spending on furniture. The boom was short-lived. In April 1960, credit restrictions were reimposed for furniture, requiring a 10% deposit on hire purchase transactions, and a maximum of two years in which to repay. In April 1962, purchase tax on furniture was doubled to 10% and in June the deposit on other durables was cut to 10% with no adjustment on furniture. Later in the year, purchase tax on motor cars was cut from 45% to 25% and cuts were made in purchase tax on other durables. Furniture sales fell substantially between 1960, when the 1958 boom from the removal of hire purchase restrictions was exhausted, and 1963. Despite all this, Parker Knoll managed to sustain its market image and rebuilt its profitablity.

Looks
and
Comfort
Good looks are not everything—neither is comfort. But in choosing a chair one wants both. In choosing a Parker-Knoll one *gets* both.
If you want to LOOK FIRST, write for our illustrated folder, to Dept. X, Parker-Knoll Ltd., High Wycombe. If you want to SIT FIRST—visit your local furniture store or come to our London Showrooms at 13 Henrietta Place, Cavendish Square and sit to your heart's content.
PK 732
'LINCOLN'
from
£10.15.0
according to cover
PARKER-KNOLL
CVS-86

ABOVE: A 1950s view of Frogmoor offices. LEFT: Penshurst enjoyed a variety of coverings, including this Tulip tapestry pelmet from a Jacobean original. RIGHT: The Lincoln.

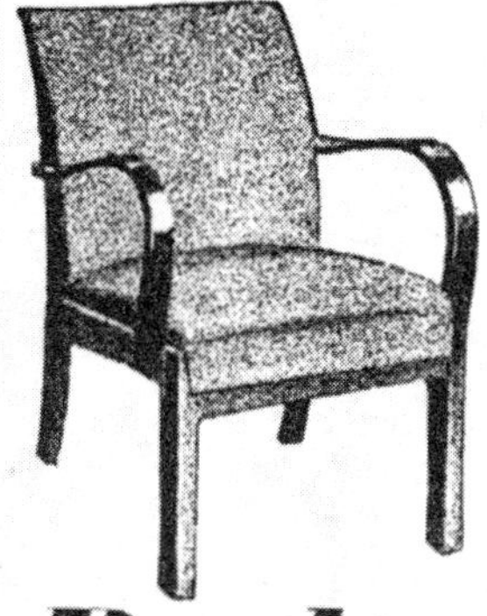

ABOVE: In 1947, advertising concentrated on privileged users — the start of the Contracts division. BELOW: In 1956 HM Queen Elizabeth (now the Queen Mother) visited Olympia for the Hotel and Catering Exhibition.

LICENSEES

AFRICA

West Africa

Construction & Furniture Co. (W.A.) Ltd..
P.O. Box 282, Ring Road, Accra, GHANA.

Construction & Furniture Co. (W.A.) Ltd.,
P.O. Box 42, Mushin, Lagos, Nigeria.

Construction & Furniture Co. (W.A.) Ltd.,
27 Garrison Street, Freetown, Sierra Leone,
British West Africa.

Rhodesian Federation

Ponter Chairs Associates (Pvt) Limited
Box 800, Salisbury, Southern Rhodesia.

Branch Factories in:—Ndola, and Bulawayo.

Union of South Africa

Rand Upholsterers (Pty) Limited

P.O. Box 4317, Johannesburg.

ASIA

Hong Kong Lane Crawford & Company
P.O. Box 83, Hong Kong.

India Spencer & Co. Limited,
Mount Road, Madras,

Malaya Robinson & Company
Raffles Place, Singapore.

AUSTRALASIA

Australia

Beard Watson & Co. Limited
359/363 George Street, Sydney, New South Wales.

Hoopers Furnishers Limited
41 Hindley Street, Adelaide, South Australia.

Tritton (Pty) Limited
254/262 George Street, Brisbane, Queensland.

The Myer Emporium Limited,
Melbourne, Victoria.

Boans Limited,
Wellington & Murray Street, Perth, Western Australia.

New Zealand

Scoullar Co. Limited,
88/90 Lambton Quay, Wellington.

Hugh J. Eaton Limited
336–342 Dominion Road, Auckland.

Also by Parker-Knoll's subsidiary company in France,
PARKER-KNOLL FRANCE S.a.r.l.,
29 RUE DE LA JONQUIERE,
PARIS 17, FRANCE

Parker Knoll supplied the Empire — and France.

OUT OF EMPIRE

While every effort was bent on rebuilding the Company, TCP was also anxious to re-establish contact with overseas licensees.

As early as 1934, PK was approached by Mr Kibblewhite of Beard Watsons of Sydney, for an arrangement to sell the Parker Knoll chair in Australia. Other approaches led to similar agreements with Scoullars of Auckland, New Zealand, Robinsons of Singapore, Stuttafords of Cape Town and Spencers of Madras, allowing them to either import Parker Knoll chairs or to have them made locally, for sale through their department stores.

They were appointed as licensees permitted to use the Parker Knoll trade mark on chairs manufactured to PK specifications and designs. Their managers visited High Wycombe to gain technical knowledge and information. Mostly they stuck to successful models from the home market, but some ventured into designing their own, on lines which they found simpler to make within the limits of their own production resources. All the necessary Parker Knoll springs and fittings were supplied from High Wycombe, and the chairs were advertised under the Parker Knoll brand.

Early in the 1950s several manufacturers from the African continent approached the Company for licences to manufacture and market Parker Knoll. It was said that in Singapore wood was planed by hand while the Chinese operatives held each piece between their feet. Faced with such local customs, to ensure that products met the quality standards, four trips were made by polishers and upholsterers to train operatives and adapt local resources.

Construction and Furniture Co run by Bill Read, with plants in Accra Ghana, Lagos Nigeria, and Freetown, Sierra Leone British West Africa, were first in the field, followed by Richard King who emigrated from Norwich to Salisbury Rhodesia. He eventually sold out to Springmaster Corporation who have plants in Bulawayo and Ndola in what used to be Northern Rhodesia. The Rand Upholstery Ltd from Johannesburg became licensees for South Africa, establishing an association which continues today. By the end of the 1950s a wide network of manufacture and distribution had been established across Africa.

During their visits to African countries members of the Royal family often found that locally made Parker Knoll chairs were provided for their use. On one occasion, when it was pointed out to Her Majesty that the chairs in the Royal train had been made in Africa, she is said to have replied 'Yes, Parker Knoll. We have them at home too'.

In March 1956, Parker Knoll chairs had been selected to furnish the officers' quarters aboard the new oil tanker *Spyros Niarchos*. At the time she was the largest tanker in the world. Chairs selected were PK735, PK717, PK748, and PK749.

Closer to home, chairs were being exported to many European retailers in Holland, Belgium and Germany. To broaden the market, a subsidiary company, Frederick Parker GMBH was set up in Bonn. Dane Dew, who had been Contracts Manager for several years, was appointed resident Manager. However, selling in Europe proved to be much more difficult than expected and, after struggling for three years to obtain worthwhile results, the operation was closed down in 1972. Throughout this period the factory opened in conjunction with Maples in Paris was struggling to run profitably.

Martin Jourdan, eldest son of CHJ (and now the Group Chairman) in his younger days spent ten months in 1961 in Paris attempting to overcome Gallic sales resistance to Sieges Parker. With a year's hands-on experience of all High Wycombe factory departments, and a year in the retail trade at Heals, he arrived in Paris full of enthusiasm. He became a well-known figure in Paris streets, for his bowler hat and rolled umbrella. Despite this brave effort by 'Monsieur L'Anglais', success was limited. Martin returned to High Wycombe in April 1962 to take up management of the Chairmaking and Polishing Shops. The French experiment lost money for a number of years, until John Ross, who managed the French factory, was appointed as European Manager operating from Brussels. He developed a range of models better suited to French and Continental tastes, enabling the business to become profitable.

The whole operation continued on a knife edge until towards the end of the 1960s when the production facility had to vacate premises shared with Maples and move to the outskirts of Paris. The increased costs proved impossible to absorb at the existing sales volume. It became plain that sales were unlikely to improve and in 1969 the business was abandoned. The intention had been to develop the whole European market from the French factory as a centre for chairs imported from England and at the same time to make a range there for France and North Africa. This was well in advance of present ideas in the European Community and sadly too far in advance to have been successful.

Over the years other efforts were made to win business in both Europe and the Middle East with chairs from the standard British ranges. Exhibition space was taken at the Cologne Furniture Fair in conjunction with export efforts by the BFM but it was clear that each country had its own special requirements and most of these were met by their own industry. The market for 'English' chairs as novelty items was not worth the investment of time and money and these efforts were also finally abandoned. The licensees in Australia and New Zealand continued successfully until takeovers of their business brought an end to the arrangments. The operation in Madras succumbed to the new situation created by Indian independence. In the same way, the terrific effort made the African licensees succumbed to the crumbling of the British Emire and different ideas followed independence. Of all the licensees during the 1950s only two still sell Parker Knoll today — Messrs Lane Crawford in Hong Kong and Robinsons in Singapore.

Add new pleasure to an old habit

P-K No. 12, a delightful chair with sprung seat, comfortable padded arms and reeded legs. Priced from **£24/8/10**

P-K No. 7, suitable for modern or traditional schemes. Luxuriously comfortable with deep spring unit seat cushion. Priced from **£21/11/3**

P-K No. 44, the latest English model with shaped r u b b e r seat cushion, padded back. Priced from **£25/16/4**

the evening paper . . . and a

PARKER-KNOLL

. . . and you'll find that the man who was so dogmatic is now such an old dear. The man who always argued now agrees. The tired man isn't tiresome any more. And, the secret . . . the world-famous English Parker-Knoll coil springs, of course. They soothe the muscles, settle the mind, smooth the brow. Come in and experience the sheer comfort of a Parker-Knoll and you will realise why so many people are so enthusiastic about them. You have the choice of 21 different models (some with matching settees) . . . cedar, walnut or natural maple colour . . . and a magnificent selection of coverings. An illustrated leaflet will be sent to you on request.

P-K No. 38, a beautiful "Queen Anne" boudoir chair featuring elegant gooseneck arms. Priced from . . **£32/4/-**

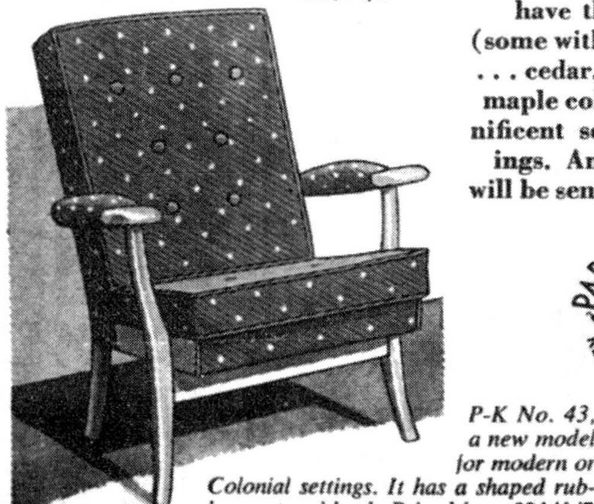

P-K No. 43, a new model for modern or Colonial settings. It has a shaped rubber seat and back. Priced from **£31/1/7**

P-K chairs are made and sold only by

Beard Watson's

GEORGE AND YORK STS. (NEAR KING ST.). PHONE BX3281

In Australia, Beard Watson's waxed eloquent about their Parker Knoll range.

LEFT: In 1954 the Wings for Winter campaign promoted the variety of wing easy styles. RIGHT: The Kirn advertisement of 1955 unleashed a storm of public protest over coarse language, pet abuse and the corruption of Shakespeare's text! BELOW: Opening the Bristol showrooms — G. H. Alpe, T. C. Parker, W. S. Warry, director and buyer for Newberry & Spindler, and C. H. Jourdan. Mr Warry always wrote 'Thank you' under all his orders.

Moving Markets

Frederick Parker had always pursued a policy of absolute integrity in his dealings with both customers and employees and the same ideals were continued by his sons and grandsons. Integrity of both product and service have always defined Company objectives and these attitudes have permeated the whole organisation. Known and respected for the quality of their products, Parkers were also known by their staff not to be among the highest payers, but nevertheless there was always a well developed loyalty to the Company, reflected by the many long service employees both in production and administrative positions. It was a good firm to work for.

To prepare the way for TCP's retirement, CHJ was appointed Deputy Chairman in 1954 and became Chairman in December 1955. He also became one of the founder-members of the Furniture Makers' Guild. TCP continued as a Director until he retired on 1 November 1959, having served the Company for sixty years. During this time he had seen vast changes in the furniture industry and had introduced Parker Knoll springing, which is seen by many as the most significant development in upholstery since the coil compression spring was introduced in Victorian times. Even more important was his determination, by returning from retirement in 1946, to rescue the Company from probable oblivion.

TCP before he retired saw a small book published illustrating some of the interesting items from the Parker Knoll collection of antique chairs. The foreword by Cecil Turner CBE, past President of the Antique Dealers' Association, gives fulsome praise to the achievements of the Company.

In November 1955 a meeting of manufacturers interested in the marketing of branded furniture was called by Geoffrey Gomme of E. Gomme Ltd. This was to discuss pressure from retailers for an increase in profit margins and to exchange information of mutual interest. CHJ attended this initial meeting which led to the formation of the Branded Furniture Society, providing a focus for the trade's leading and largest manufacturers.

Modernisation went ahead steadily in many small ways and one major alteration to the machine shop was made early in 1957. Under the new scheme the shop was split up into separate groups for bonus, as an incentive to increased output. The organisation of the change over was placed in the hands of consultants, Urwick Orr and Partners.

Sales momentum was maintained throughout the 1950s by special promotions and increased press advertising. One notable success was the 'Wings for Winter' campaign in the autumn of 1955. The slogan was an echo of the not long past 'Wings for Victory' campaigns during the war, when towns collected money for the purchase of a Spitfire or Lancaster which carried the town name into battle. A window display competition was held for the best display in each region and advertisements were run in national and local papers throughout the autumn. Sales of wing chairs increased dramatically and the campaign was considered to be so successful that it was repeated the following year.

Douglas Kitching became a Director and joined the Board of Parker Knoll in 1953. Under his guidance Parker Knoll Textiles had grown swiftly and was badly in need of space. From the outset they had set themselves the objective to provide a by return delivery service, but could only do this if they had a large warehouse. In 1956 they acquired the old Goodearl chair factory in West End Road which, after alteration, was ideal for the purpose. To complement this advance, they opened a showroom and design studio at Maidstone House, Berners Street, which placed them among the West End showrooms of other leading soft furnishing companies, enabling them to display their ever-increasing ranges of soft furnishings to interior decorators and others unlikely to make the trip to High Wycombe.

The Parker Knoll showrooms in London provided a useful link with members of the public responding to press advertising or unable to see the full range of chairs and covers at local shops. They were also a useful base at which to meet trade customers in London.

During 1954 showrooms were opened in the provinces; first at Barton Square in Manchester, and then at Temple Street, Birmingham. A third showroom was opened in 1956 at Park Street, Bristol. These moves came as some surprise to local retailers who did not think that a showroom would help to increase Parker Knoll sales.

The London showrooms moved in 1956 from Henrietta Place to 234 Tottenham Court Road. This showroom, though small, was adequate to display the chair range of that time and was kept busy by the increasing numbers of visiting public. Geoffrey Alpe, anxious to avoid reflection problems with the display window, decided to have non-reflecting concave glass fitted similar to those which had become famous at Heals since the 1930s, but it was soon discovered that dust from traffic made it difficult to keep clean.

Many designs inspired by Geoffrey Alpe and introduced in the mid-1960s were extraordinarily successful. Three of these, the Langford PK733, Froxfield PK749, and Frith PK750 chairs, require no better testimonial than that they are still popular and selling well today. The style of the Froxfield and Frith chairs is derived from a chair in the antique collection. Many other models from this era ran for many years and when eventually replaced with 'something more modern', sales often were disappointing. Geoffrey Alpe was confident in his own design ideas which he brought in with the aid of the Company's design team led by Robin Howland.

A particularly successful chair was the Wingfield wing chair, in a modern style, introduced with a matching two-seater settee in 1957. This was also offered with an open-padded arm version but it was the upholstered chair and settee which took the public eye. Firths of Heckmondwike had produced a new moquette with a mixed cut and uncut pile dyed in bright primary colours. This cloth had 20% nylon spun into the wool yarn and proved extremely hard wearing, without the customary harsh feel of usual moquette. This cloth, known as Monmouth, was exactly right for the new chairs and gave Parker Knoll another best-seller.

One design idea which the general style and construction of the Parker Knoll chair made possible, was the production of several different chairs built around the same basic chair frame. The addition of a few extra rails, wings and panels made three or four different styles of chair without greatly adding to the variety of chair parts. Families of chairs were first built and successfully marketed in this way by developing the PK740 Lingfield wing chair and the PK739 Litchfield high back chair from the basic PK732 Lincoln chair. The matching style of the different models in the group appealed to Contract customers who were able to mix different models in a large room.

Conscious that average price for an open arm easy chair was between half and two thirds the Parker Knoll price, Geoffrey Alpe spurred the design team to come up with quality models. The first chair was the Kirn PK753, introduced in early 1956 at £10 19s 6d.

The chair was a resounding success, selling 20,000 in its first year. To build onto this success, another less elaborate chair, the PK773 Arran was introduced in January 1958. This was larger than the Kirn without the padded arm, but otherwise a complete Parker Knoll chair, selling retail at £8 18s 6d. The frame was made in epepe, a West African timber not previously used in the United Kingdom. The chair sold 50,000 in the first year, in both retail and contract markets, where its size, strength and price particularly appealed to hospitals.

The interest in modern styles became something of a vogue in the late 1950s, spurred on by the home interest magazines, and the import of Scandinavian cabinet furniture. This was an opportunity for Parker Knoll to develop chair designs in Limited Editions, which would enhance the Parker Knoll image as *avant garde*.

To meet this objective, a design by Walter Knoll was introduced in 1957 as the Menton PK768 and was accompanied by a Robin Howland design, PK769 Meriden. It was accepted that as these two smart and comfortable designs would sell only through retailers specialising in the best modern furniture, they would be made in a special workshop, with a minimum of machine work, being virtually hand-made. Prices at £33 15s 0d for the Menton and £36 15s 0d for the Meriden compared favourably with such established models as the PK720 Penshurst wing chair at £32 10s 0d, while the use of what had by then become exotic timbers, gave the chairs a cachet lost in any but the hand-made upholstery market.

Both chairs were warmly applauded by design-conscious journals such as the *Architectural Review* and by the Council for Industrial Design, as well as design-conscious retailers such as Bowmans of Camden Town and Heals. Almost before the chair was launched, it was specified by the architect furnishing the new Skyways Hotel at Heathrow. Universities too became interested. A three-seater settee to match the Meriden was made to special order, providing a stylish and comfortable suite at a retail price of £163 5s 0d. Of the two designs, the Menton was the most popular, so that the limited production resources were overrun. The chair had to be redesigned (PK940) to allow it to go through the main factory. As happens in the furniture trade, competitors swiftly produced an accurate copy which they sold for far less, but it lacked the quality. The Meriden chair continued as a Limited Edition for three years when it gave way to another new design based upon a completely different concept.

This took shape as new materials and the techniques for using them were developed in 1959, when Robin Howland created his first chair with a moulded glass-fibre shell, replacing the conventional frame construction. This was the PK938 Malton chair with smooth sculpted lines, quite different from any so far achieved by traditional chairmaking methods. With showood legs in either rosewood or English walnut and price between £34 15s 0d and £38 15s 0d, according to cover quality, the chair was widely noticed and sold strongly, keeping the special workshop which made it working to absolute capacity for several years. Additionally, the Malton chair, following the earlier Menton and Meriden models, made clear to those interested in modern furniture that Parker Knoll was in the vanguard of modern design and interested in breaking new ground. The creative design aspects of Malton received an accolade when the Furniture Makers Guild awarded one of their rare Guild Marks for craftsmanship and design.

New materials required ingenuity to turn them into viable furniture products. At Parker Knoll a great contribution in this field was made by Reg Hopkins, who initially managed the Drawing Office and was then given responsibility for all Research and Development, as well as all Design and Production Prototyping.

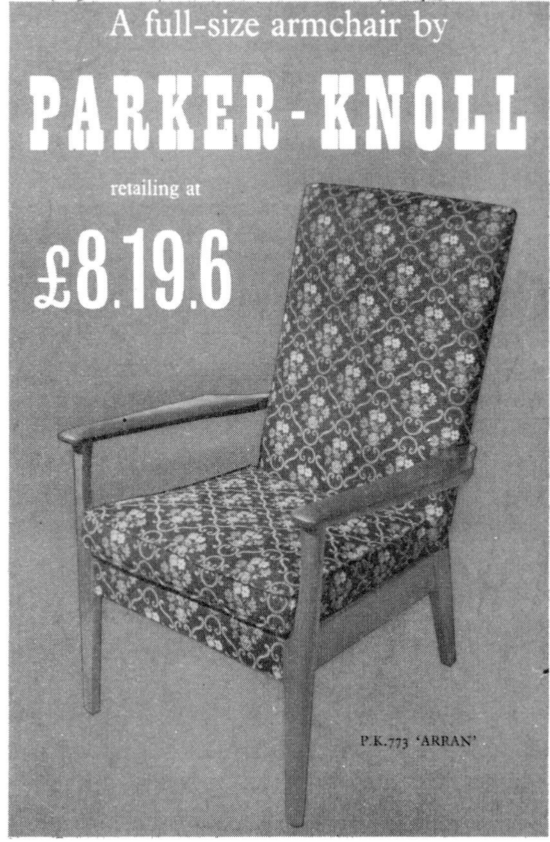

A full-size armchair by
PARKER-KNOLL
retailing at
£8.19.6
P.K.773 'ARRAN'

ABOVE: Bristol, 1956 — Steve Bland, Graham Dean, showroom manager, Jeffrey Chandler, West of England representative and Dane Baskerville. LEFT: The Arran and RIGHT: the Meriden.

Family Friends

CHJ had been the author and inspiration of the changes in production departments during the 1950s, and at the same time provided for future management. Carefully chosen young management trainees were recruited to start at the bottom, and learn the structure of the business, through every department in factory and sales, over several years. The trainee was next given the responsibility for a single department, then moved to another, until finally being appointed to a management position.

The first trainee under the scheme was John Arnold, great-grandson of Frederick Parker. John joined the company from school in 1950 and, after an extensive period in factory departments, took up office duties in 1956 as assistant to the Sales Manager. This involved clerical jobs and eventually, in 1958, he assumed responsibility as Field Sales Manager for the growing force of Contract Representatives. In 1960 he was able to spend six months with Kroehlers, one of the largest upholstery manufacturers in the States. When he returned from America he became General Sales Manager, while Dane Baskerville became Assistant Sales Manager. His position was filled by Simon Young Jamieson, who joined the Company from Van de Burghs. The author became Marketing Manager with a specific brief for research, product acceptance, and the effectiveness of the company's sales efforts.

Geoffrey Alpe as Managing Director retained his long established responsibilities for new model design and all advertising. The Company had previously not concerned itself with measuring markets and performance, or indeed paying much attention to statistics which defined their nature. There was therefore a lot to be done.

A second management trainee, Michael Harvey, joined the Company in 1955 and was from the outset trained in and destined for all aspects of production and factory management. After working his way through all the departments from Timber Yard to Upholstery, he was appointed acting Manager of the Wycombe mill in 1958, and in 1959 took up Production Manager in the Chair-making and Polishing Departments.

In 1956 Jack True was given more responsibilities in the Mill and Derek Stewart was appointed Manager of all polishing and upholstery operations plus all upholstery engineering in the special shop and prototype departments. He first visited Sweden to study methods in the Dux organisation at Trelleborg and Malmo, and later made several study visits with other managers to factories in America.

Bill Brown joined the Company as Works Engineer in 1946 having previously worked with CHJ and was appointed Works Manager in 1954 but left due to ill-health at the end of 1957. Edna Cooper, who had joined in 1948 as Supervisor in the Despatch Department, became increasingly involved with factory matters, and was appointed Planning Controller in the Production Office in November 1951. Edna was an energetic and strong-minded maiden lady who said what she thought and was used to getting things done. In an otherwise totally male factory environment, her popularity suffered but she was completely committed and frequently clashed with other strong personalities such as Dane Baskerville. Her success led to her appointment in 1953 as Personal Assistant to CHJ. When Bill Brown left, Edna Cooper and CHJ fulfilled the duties of Works Manager between them, while CHJ as Joint Managing Director became Chairman of the Company as well. He also became increasingly involved in the Branded Furniture Society. Edna Cooper came to represent CHJ at many meetings and policy-making discussions.

In 1958 the new Works Manager was Hugh Cartwright. Captain Cartwright RN had been, prior to leaving the Service, Captain of the Royal Naval Rhine Squadron. He answered an advertisement for Works Manager although he had none of the required qualifications. 'Jock' Stewart, the Personnel Officer, made his views clear, when CHJ suggeted that he be interviewed, that it would be a complete waste of time. However, Captain Cartwright got the job and, with his service background, 'no. nonsense' attitudes and absolutely no pre-conceptions about the furniture trade, brought a completely new approach to the Company and its problems. Strongly supported by TCP and CHJ he was left to do the job on his own and make whatever changes he felt necessary.

As EHC, as he came to be known throughout the organisation, recalled his first few weeks in High Wycombe it is clear that he assessed the situation carefully. It is difficult to resist the impression that he saw the factory as a new command of which he was the captain, with CHJ as his Admiral and his department Managers as officers who ran the ship by organising and maintaining discipline among the other ranks on the shop floor. This analogy is apparent from his summing up after retirement, of his 'Ward Room' as it existed when he took over as Works Manager:

'Upholstery Manager:	A good leader, but not easy to manage.
Making Shop Manager:	Technically Efficient.
Drawing Office Manager:	A clever Technician. Very good at jigs.
Timber Buyer:	Quiet and Knowledgeable.
General Stores Buyer:	Conscious of keenest prices.
Despatch Manager:	Great ability but has a low opinion of Naval Officers. Not an easy character.
Engineer:	Excellent man though old fashioned. A very hard worker.
Works Study Manager:	Not right for the job. Replace.
Personnel Manager:	Hard worker popular with the men. Gives me full support.'

EHC found that the men on the shop floor often went direct to Personnel when they had problems, and not through their line managers. He saw this as a breakdown of the chain of command and insisted that the managers should in future be responsible for managing their own men in every way, consulting Personnel themselves when necessary.

His early impressions found production and manufacturing techniques to be good and CHJ a good leader. Sales was 'efficient in its way' but could be considerably improved. He was surprised that Sales and Production were controlled by Joint Managing Directors who had become virtually polarised within their own areas of responsibility.

EHC soon concluded that his factory managers 'did not really pull together', and that he needed to get Sales into a closer working relationship with the factory. He set about unifying the factory managers and by a policy of total openness and divulging information, he soon succeeded.

The Unions were powerful within the Company and in the Upholstery Shop held the Company to ransom as far as job prices were concerned. He resolved to do something about it. This resulted in many battles, a classic instance being when the shop floor imposed a limit on production in the belief that it would keep their wages up. It did not take long for EHC's authority to be accepted.

It was not long before there was a clash between the equally strong personalities of EHC and Edna Cooper, who he said 'had become a power in the land and unofficial Works

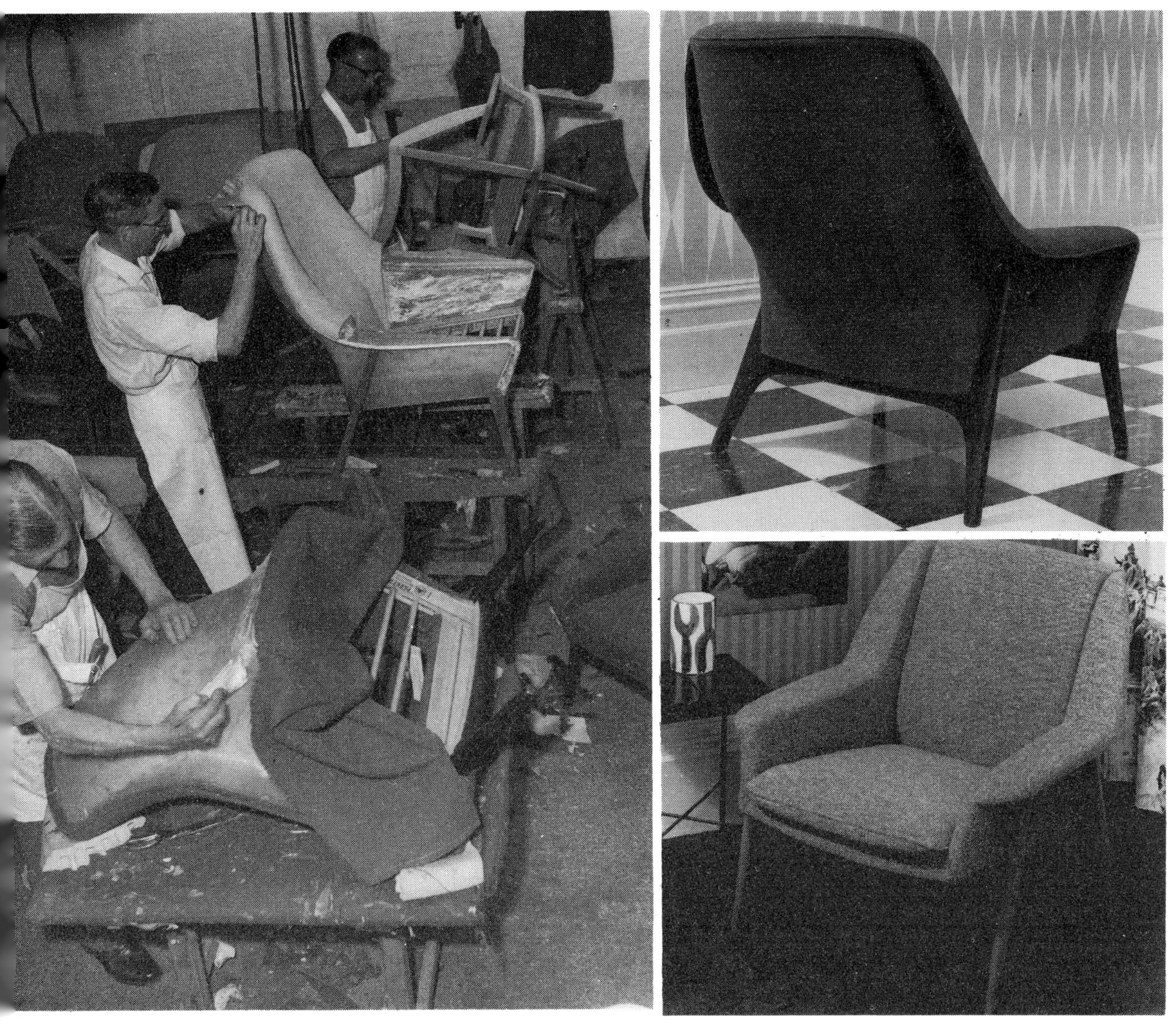

LEFT: Moulded glass fibre shells for Malton chairs being upholstered; behind, a conventional Meriden is being sprung. RIGHT: This chair was designed and produced in Germany by Walter Knoll. At Wycombe it became the Menton, to show the firm's aptitude for advanced design.

Manager. She was an astonishing girl and very able, but with no tact whatever'. Although still working as CJH's Personal Assistant, the friction between them could not be resolved and Miss Cooper eventually left after eleven years with the Company.

As the '50s came to a close, more potential for the future management of the business arrived in the form of CHJ's eldest son, Martin Jourdan. He came straight from Mill Hill school in 1959 as a management trainee, and as another great-grandson of Frederick Parker imbued with the family tradition. His father made sure that he started at the bottom and was shown no favours.

In 1962 Tom Jourdan, CHJ's second son, also commenced his training in engineering, obtaining a BSc Honours degree at City University, London preparatory to joining the business in 1968. In this way the groundwork was laid for continuity of well-trained management. With the benefit of hindsight how fortunate was the appointment of Hugh Cartwright in 1958 and the effect it was to have on the survival of the business.

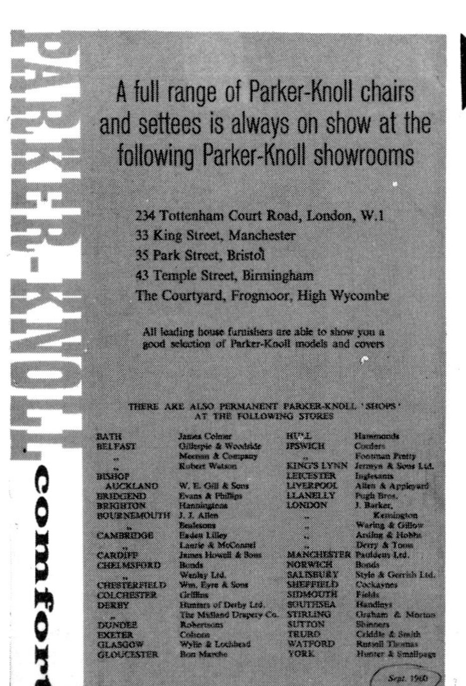

DOES IT PAY TO SELL HIGH QUALITY?

Yes, we at Parker-Knoll think so. And so that our retailer friends can be in no possible doubt about it, we have carried out a thorough examination of our price structure in order that the mark-up on practically every Parker-Knoll that you sell from December 27, 1961 onwards will be 50%. This has inevitably meant some change in retail prices, but we have left most of the prices quoted in our national advertisements undisturbed, reducing trade prices as necessary.

It is no secret that demand for Parker-Knoll is very satisfactory, and retail turnover on Parker-Knoll sales is correspondingly buoyant. On the other hand we know that selling expenses have risen too, particularly for the class of retailer where the public expect to find Parker-Knoll. High standards of display and service mean high costs, and we ourselves know only too well what has been happening to rents, rates and wages.

We hope that our new price structure, which will apply to all orders booked after Christmas, will produce even better and more enjoyable Parker-Knoll business for us all.

There are just two 'B' cover exceptions to the 50% mark-up plan. These are the low priced PK773 Arran and PK927 Dunster *only when sold in 'B' covers.* All other covers will carry the new 50%.

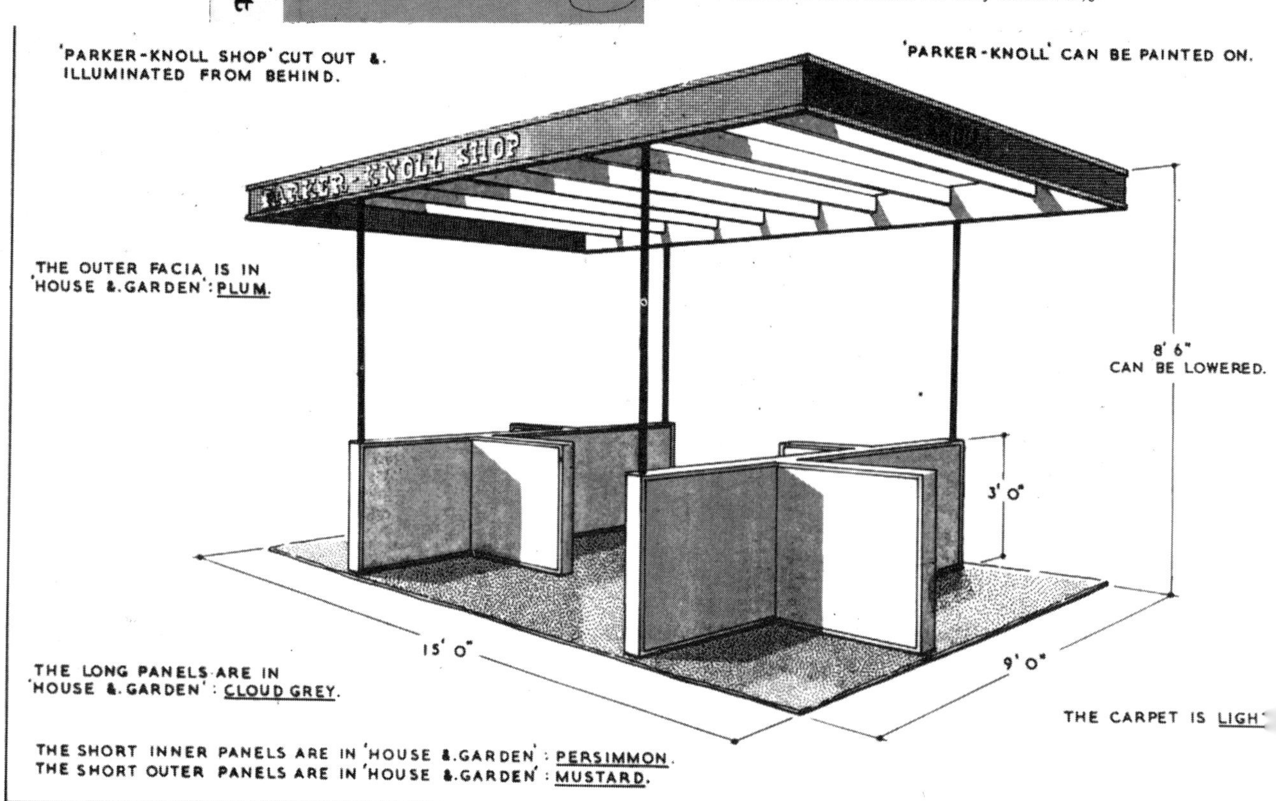

'PARKER-KNOLL SHOP' CUT OUT &. ILLUMINATED FROM BEHIND.
'PARKER-KNOLL' CAN BE PAINTED ON.
PARKER-KNOLL SHOP
THE OUTER FACIA IS IN 'HOUSE &. GARDEN': PLUM.
8' 6" CAN BE LOWERED.
3' 0"
15' 0"
9' 0"
THE LONG PANELS ARE IN 'HOUSE &. GARDEN': CLOUD GREY.
THE CARPET IS LIGH
THE SHORT INNER PANELS ARE IN 'HOUSE &.GARDEN': PERSIMMON.
THE SHORT OUTER PANELS ARE IN 'HOUSE &.GARDEN': MUSTARD.

LEFT: The range of major stockists in 1960. RIGHT: The incentives to sell that range. BELOW: The 1965 Parker Knoll 'shop' which displayed twelve leading models, chosen by the Company, in seventy stores.

LAW AND PROFITS

'Never go to law Parker' — this sage advice was given to TCP one day by the leading barrister of the time, Marshall Hall, over lunch in the Strand; it lodged in TCP's mind as wry paradox, coming as it did from one of the most eminent practitioners.

Despite any misgivings this left, the Directors were faced in 1957 with going to law, to protect the Parker Knoll brand and name. An American furniture company, Knoll International of New York, selling furniture and textiles, intended to extend their activities to the United Kingdom and sell furniture here under their company name.

The American company had evolved from family links with Willi Knoll, when his nephew Hans Knoll went to America and started his own company. This made modern, high-quality office and architectural furniture and also sold suitable modern chairs such as those designed by Eames and Bertoia. Hans Knoll was tragically killed when a tanker lorry overturned onto his car. His widow, architect Florence Knoll, continued the business, developed and expanded it successfully, to become recognised in America at least, as pre-eminent in its field.

When Parker Knoll were so advised, they immediately saw there would be confusion between trading names using the word Knoll. The fact that each company supplied a totally different range of furniture was irrelevant. The Parker Knoll brand name had been steadily built up in the United Kingdon and British Empire ever since the agreement with Willi in 1930. This had been achieved by continuous advertising of the brand name, exhibitions, and strong support by leading house furnishers over twenty-eight years. As a result it had become sysnonymous with high quality upholstered chairs and settees.

Knoll International were advised that, should they commence trading in the United Kingdom, Parker Knoll would take steps through the courts to protect their trade mark. Undeterred, Knoll went ahead and opened a London office from which they started selling under the Knoll International name. It was not long before evidence of the effect appeared. Both by correspondence and telephone, enquiries were received at High Wycombe and showrooms for details of desks and other Knoll furniture in press editorials and magazines. Although the Knoll range was of no interest to and not offered to most retailers, many were confused and thought that Parker Knoll had started a new division without telling them. When they realised the position many retailers offered to support the Company's case by swearing affidavits and volunteering to give evidence. Parker Knoll applied for and won an injunction on 11 July 1958 pending trial of the action, restraining Knoll International from using the word Knoll on any furniture sold by them in the United Kingdom. And so began protracted litigation, during which Knoll labeled their product as 'Design International'.

It was not until 1960 that the action between the two parties took place in the Chancery Division of the High Court, where judgement favourable to Parker Knoll was given on all counts. The defendants decided to appeal and the case was heard by the Appeal Court on 9 February 1961. Meantime, instances of confusion between the two companies and their products still occurred, notably by the BBC during a broadcast all of which was avidly collected and passed on as evidence for the Company's case. The Appeal Court confirmed the findings in the Chancery Division, but the defendents were not satisfied and appealed to the House of Lords. In due course their Lordships held in favour of Parker Knoll, but the Company considered that, while these judgements were awaited, the activities of the American company had been in breach of the injunction and started another action. A decision on this, favourable to the Company, was given by the Chancery Division but the defendants again sought leave to appeal. Again the original finding was upheld. However, still unwilling to accept the findings, the American company once again sought leave to appeal to the House of Lords. It was not until 1963 that the matter finally ended, when the House of Lords decided that they could not try another appeal, since the previous actions had clearly established the position in favour of Parker Knoll.

The whole sequence had taken five years to resolve, and finally determine, in the form of a permanent injunction, that the American company could not use the word Knoll, when selling furniture in the United Kingdom. At the same time it was an ample illustration of the protection afforded by law to any registered trade mark.

It was during these protracted legal battles that TCP died on 29 October 1961, aged 80, followed by his brother Harry on 8 April 1962 at the age of 86. Both had been actively involved in the business for over sixty years. As the last of Frederick Parker's sons active in the business, they were the remaining link with their father's original business. William Parker, their younger brother, although remaining a Director, had not been actively involved since he retired at the outbreak of War and continued in retirement until he died in 1969 aged 90.

Both Harry and Tom Parker were concerned to protect the Parker Knoll trade mark. Sadly, neither lived to see the issue resolved in the House of Lords. Had they done so, Tom Parker may have felt that going to law had its good points after all.

During 1959, relieved of his more immediate responsiblities at the factory, CHJ made a second tour of all the Eastern, Australian and New Zealand licensees, once again returning via the United States and visiting several factories there. In many cases High Wycombe methods were more effective, although there is no doubt that productivity per employee was often much higher in America.

The Company Secretary, E. T. Down, resigned at the beginning of 1949 and was succeeded during the summer by Peter Bolding.

On 2 July 1959, a serious fire occurred at the factory. This started in an old wooden building known as the 'Pneumonia shed' due to its lack of heating. It adjoined the main manufacturing block and was used as a store for machinery not in use, old patterns and a quantity of wood and veneers. Prompt action by the Fire Brigade prevented the blaze from spreading to the main production block, but the store was totally destroyed. Sad to say it contained the majority of the remaining full-sized drawings for the Frederick Parker best quality models. They were drawn, as was the custon, on large sheets of plywood, which made them much more durable than paper, but they were completely destroyed. The estimated damage was put at £12,800 and finally settled by the insurance company at £13,463. The space occupied by the old shed, adjacent to the boiler house, was then used to store the mountain of wood offcuts which often intrigues visitors to the factory and still feeds the furnace today.

The number of representatives calling upon retailers had, by the end of 1959, increased to ten. As early as 1959, steps were taken to work more closely with retailers, encouraging them to broaden their stocks and derive the maximum possible benefit from larger advertisements.

Departing from TCP's rigidly applied principle of 'the same price for every customer large or small and no discounts', the first steps were taken in 1959 to increase orders from retailers by introducing special promotional offers. These gave the retailers the opportunity to buy a parcel of chairs at the basic price, but covered in higher quality covers from the more expensive ranges. This was a form of price reduction on specified products, and avoided any suggestion of discounts as an inducement. At the same time the consumer received better value for money.

The PK753 Kirn chair was offered in a good quality moquette from the middle cover range, normally £12 10s 0d retail, at a new lower price of £9 19s 6d. 3,000 extra chairs were sold in ten days. As trading conditions became increasingly difficult in the 1960s, this promotional technique was extensively employed.

Sales of the Penshurst PK720 chair had decliend in 1959 and fewer retailers were now stocking it. To reverse this trend, several covers in the high quality ranges were reclassified into the basic price range, making them available on the Penshurst at a price reduction from £26 15s 0d to £24 15s 0d. Several other chairs were included. These price reductions were achieved by the Company reducing its normal margins.

Such merchandising allowed the Chairman to report substantially increased profits at £229,173 in 1961, and a marginal increase of £3,725 to £232,898 in 1962, an all-time record.

John Arnold as General Sales Manager was soon applying some of the ideas obtained during his sojurn in America. He developed and extended the recently introduced policy of market promotion by increasing the number and scope of 'special offers'. But trade conditions were to worsen still further. In October 1964, when a Labour Government came to power, the balance of payments deficit was £700 millions. A 15% surcharge was immediately imposed on all imports and bank rate again raised from 5 to 7%. Minimum deposits required on all hire purchase transactions for furniture and bedding were increased from 15% in 1965 to 25% in February 1966 and to 33.3% in July 1966, while the corresponding repayment period was cut from 36 months to 30 and then to 24 months. With almost 40% of all furniture sold on hire purchase, this severely depressed sales.

Profits reduced to £123,079 in the year to July 1963 compared badly with the all-time record achieved the previous year. Yet the success of the marketing and merchandising policies under John Arnold reversed the decline and results for the year ending July 1964, lifted to a new high of £243,462. Turnover again increased in 1965, but margins were tighter, giving a slightly decreased profit of £237,100.

Another component was the introduction of Parker Knoll shops within department stores and larger retailers. One of the difficulties faced by the increasing number of branded furniture manufacturers was to obtain sufficient retail floor space. The majority of smaller shops did not do much to display their stock, and often kept it lined up in rows with the minimum of space. Only the departmental stores and shops with more than average space could afford to do anything better, and not all did.

Parker Knoll first experimented with portable screens placed in the furniture department at Inglesants of Leicester. These formed bays in which groups of Parker Knoll chairs would be displayed together but, although more shops were equipped with screens, it was generally agreed that they were not really effective, or sufficiently attractive. What they did was to create an awful lot of extra work of a type for which the Company was not equipped. Initially Allan Barnett, Showroom Supervisor, had his duties extended to administer the installation of displays and then the task of originating and designing them to fit into specific retail locations. Although the first efforts were not right, the concept was welcomed. Alan Barnett was appointed Manager, Interior Planning Department in December 1964.

Inevitably, the necessary decor for an attractive display came to involve outside contractors to build the fittings and eventually install them. By the mid-1960s it was necessary to review what the displays had accomplished against the expenditure they entailed. Problems were revealed; chairs were sold 'off the floor', a practice discouraged by Parker Knoll, but impossible to stop when a sale was at stake. When the retailer could not replace the chair from stock, the long delivery time sometimes resulted in other makes filling empty spaces, which was quite unacceptable. The portable equipment could, if a retailer lost interest, be too easily moved to some inaccessible corner. It was decided to dispense with portable screens and instead, to concentrate on installation of a less moveable structure, which gave more prominence to the Parker Knoll name.

This was the 'Parker Knoll Shop' which was installed over a blue 9 x 15 foot carpet and displayed twelve chairs in bays, illuminated by spotlights mounted on the top canopy, which carried the Parker Knoll name on all sides. This was offered to selected leading retailers in larger towns across the country, on the basis that the display would remain in place for a minimum of one year, and the display chairs, although paid for by the retailer, would not be sold from the display. Furthermore, the covers on the display chairs were to be selected by Parker Knoll, with the purpose of showing the chairs in the most attractive materials regardless of price. This was a difficult condition for retailers to accept, but was seen by Parker Knoll as essential. Chairs could be ordered and made up expressly for customers as an alternative to selecting from stock on the shop floor. As each chair was available at four different prices according to the cover grade, many retailers always carried their stock in the lowest grades, leaving the customer who wanted a higher grade to select from the pattern books and place a 'special order'.

By installing the shops in agreement with seventy carefully selected retailers, Parker Knoll sought to establish permanent centres where they could exert more influence than was normally possible, over what was displayed. There was an average increase by shops with displays, of from 15-20%, but these figures take no account of increased sales from stock.

Difficulties arose when the time came to change the chairs. Selling off the old ones was dealt with by making an allowance to the retailer, but when it came to Parker Knoll wishing to decide on models and covers for the replacements, several retailers objected that the previous display had been unsuitable. Rightly or wrongly, Parker Knoll gave way, and in doing so blunted the edge of the presentation. Finally, objections were raised by several retailers, especially department stores, that the Parker Knoll shop limited their freedom to move things around and resulted in the place looking as if it never changed. Some shops were moved to less prominent positions, some were moved out completely and, after three years, the whole operation began to decline. Much of the experience gained was later put to good use in formulating marketing polilcies to meet the changes dictated by the Resale Price Maintenance Act.

Improvements were still continuing at the factory to cope with increased sales. To enlarge storage capacity for machined chair parts prior to assembly, in 1960 a new building was erected, across the road from the factory site at Belfield Road. A new factory boiler was installed in 1960. The Special Shop was made independent by equipping it with its own machinery.

CHJ could see that the Wycombe factory was approaching the ceiling of its capacity. The buidings were designed in 1928 and, although every opportunity had been taken to introduce conveyors for all movements of work from assembly of chair frames, through polishing and then across into another building for upholstery and then to despatch, the buildings themselves were limiting further developments. Until now, production had been almost totally confined to chairs and Sales believed that the Company should move into the market for three-piece suites, a new market sector, which offered prospects for expansion. The openings in the walls of the old buildings through which the conveyors carried frames from one deparment to another, were only large enough to permit chair frames though and no further improvements were possible. The Board knew that they would have to acquire a new factory.

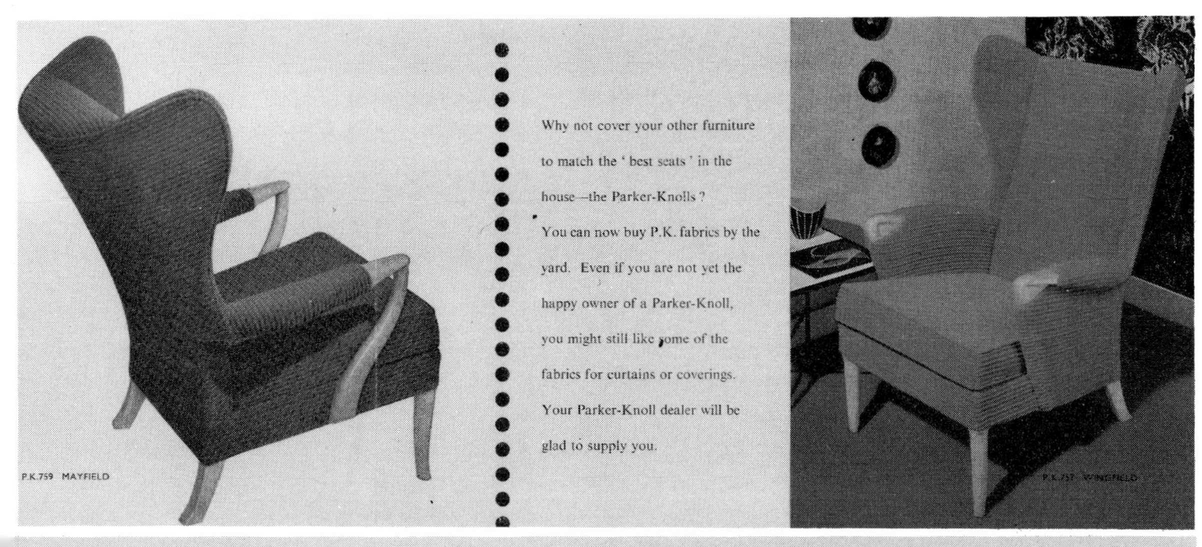

Why not cover your other furniture to match the 'best seats' in the house—the Parker-Knolls?
You can now buy P.K. fabrics by the yard. Even if you are not yet the happy owner of a Parker-Knoll, you might still like some of the fabrics for curtains or coverings. Your Parker-Knoll dealer will be glad to supply you.
P.K.759 MAYFIELD

VE: Covering every contingency — from curtains to coverings. BELOW: Retail and Contracts Sales force at the Rye, High
ombe, in Spring 1964, for a car exchange — Jock Black, Bill Morris, Alan Barnett, John Pryce, Harold Brown, Fred Kitson,
obson, Richard Thackeray, Haydn Gabb, Mark Hudson, Dane Dew, Ian Brewster, George Wilson, Bernard Sharpe, Steve
d, Dickie Clibbens, Alan Palmer, Vic Card, Dougy Pipe, Arthur Rose, Ralph Fisher, Raymond Billington, George Moss,
Jimmy Baker, Alan Taylor, Arthur Newell, Simon Young-Jamieson, Dane Baskerville and John Arnold.

LEFT: The Tirano had a glass fibre shell and a stove-enamelled base — it won the Furniture Makers' Guild certificate for good design and craftsmanship. RIGHT: Family groups extended the range. BELOW: In August 1962 the Gavotte was the first three piece suite.

Pace and Style

In January 1960, CHJ reported that 10,000 more chairs had been sold in the past six months, but the profits had been absorbed by extra costs. This was partly due to the price reductions on covers for the 'special offers'.

Buyers soon realised that the representatives always had something 'special' to tell them about when he called and refrained from their usual practice of ordering what they required to maintain their general stock. They bought the 'special offers' and little else, which resulted in declinig sales of a wide number of best-selling chairs which were no longer in stock, which was full of 'specials'. Eventually the decline in general business became so serious that 'special offers' had to be stopped and Sales then faced the diffcult task of restocking the shops with the normal range of chairs without the inducement of bargains.

About twelve years after the end of the War, a change in preferred styles for sitting rooms began to emerge. Hitherto, popular choice had been for two or perhaps more chairs usually of the open-armed type with polished showwood. Gradually this began to change, prompted to a large degree by the home furnishing and women's interest magazines. All new ideas in fabrics, soft furnishings and furniture were constantly written up, often illustrated in colour. This trend was welcomed by Parker Knoll.

Following their success with the Malton chair, built on a moulded glass-fibre shell, Parker Knoll won acclaim among the design cognoscenti when they introduced a second shell chair in November 1960. This was the Tirano PK939, desinged in Germany by Walter Knoll. The outside back of the shell presented a smooth surface of neutral grey, contrasting pleasantly with the texture and colour of the covering fabric, while the seat revolved on a rigid, stove-enamelled metal base. Retailing at prices between £32 10s 0d and £33 15s 0d this chair appealed to specialist furnishers and architects filling modern interiors. The Tirano was awarded a certificate for good design and craftsmanship from the Furniture Makers Guild and did much to project the Parker Knoll image for up to date styles and production techniques.

Parker Knoll had concentrated almost entirely on producing individual chairs for the better quality market and consequently, by 1960, held a considerable market share. For chairs selling at above £12 Parker Knoll accounted for 12-15%, with a correspondingly higher share of the higher priced market. Chairs with more upholstery were now required and the Company set about the necessary design work, without attempting to enter the large market for fully fledged three-piece suites.

Retailers were telling representatives that they wanted to see Parker Knoll make a three-piece suite. Despite the difficulty of handling it in the factory, a two-seater settee to stand with the Penshurst wing chair had been available since 1956, but was there more to complement the chair.

In 1957 two more two-seater settees were added to match the successful Wingfield chair and its 'cousin' the Mayfield. These models were displayed more widely as suites and successfully sold.

Retailers were not aware and could not appreciate the limitations within the factory which prevented the handling of such bulky items. Going as far as it was possible, the Rowstock and Merrow designs was introduced in 1969. These had good clean, modern lines and did quite well in a critical market. The following year, another group of different models, but with the same design theme, was introduced. The Nutley group incorporated both high back winged chair and matching two-seater settee as well as low-backed versions of the same design. Based on the mix and match principle and described as 'Family Groups', they suggested how rooms might be furnished with a selection of different chairs in the same style. This range was not at all successful, probably because of the cantilever design, and seemed to be striving for a modernity which it did not achieve. The group was discontinued after only eighteen months.

The first serious attempt to market a carefully designed three-piece suite was made in May 1960, when the Gavotte was launched. This had a three-seater settee for the first time and was designed to have an elegant long, low look. Criticised in some quarters because it was 'still on legs' and in others because 'it lacked a full headrest back', the Gavotte suite was a great success and widely stocked by Parker Knoll retailers. Aware of their lack of success in selling suites, Parker Knoll offered it in a new uncut wool mixture moquette from T. F. Firth and Sons, in the lowest price range, instead of at its true higher level. This allowed the suite to be sold in this special cover at £10 less than its true price. This was the first time such a launching offer had been used to tempt reluctant retailers and was one of the marketing techniques learnt by John Arnold in America. As always the key to the success of any new model is to obtain the widest possible initial distribution to stockists, which is then followed by an extensive advertising campaign to inform the public. Both objectives were achieved with the Gavotte.

One area in which the Company had long taken an interest was the provision of high-seated chairs suitable for the older customer. It is extremely difficult for many people to rise unaided from a soft chair with a low seat too near the floor. After studying the ergonomic needs in seating of a wide selection of people, chairs were made up and submitted to various hospitals to obtain their advice. From further trials and study it was possible to finalise a version which could be produced in quantity. Trial batches were put into mental homes and geriatric departments where exceptional demands are made.

Strength of construction was a prime feature of the chair frame as anyone who has seen a nurse drag a patient in a chair the length of a ward will know. Special attention was given to the stability of the chair to prevent tipping forward or back when the sitter flopped into it. Arms were fixed to the front legs by means of a through tenon which was wedged to ensure maximum possible strength. Special density cushion and back fillings were chosen to allow the chair to remain comfortable to the user for long periods despite the upright posture. Another important feature was the seat height of 20¾ inches, far higher than usually comfortable or required, allowing great flexibility in reducing the seat height to the patient's own measurement by cutting down the legs. It is of course impossible to supply a standard chair with longer legs. The chair which emerged onto the market from all this testing and study was the Highworth PK928, destined to enjoy a production run of over 30 years, becoming a boon to many elderly and incapacitated users. It became a particularly important chair in the hospital world where many thousands can still be found. Later versions were supplied with padded arms and wings while, at the suggestion of institutional users, a sturdy clip-on tray was developed.

Attention was given to a completely different aspect of the business at the end of 1961 when retailers were advised that the mark-up on Parker Knoll trade prices would be restored to the pre-war and customary level of 50%. In those days resale price maintenance still allowed a manufacturer to fix his prices, basing them at a level giving a fair return on cost, and to enforce them if they were broken. Other manufacturers of branded furniture had returned to the higher mark-up some time previously.

Go-ahead firms who wished to have their own or intended markets examined for them could always commission their own surveys, but this had never been necessary in the furniture trade; they had always formed their own judgements and did not need to spend money on having outsiders 'blind them with science'. Consequently there was little hard information, a lot of outdated pre-conceptions and no finance available for employing somebody at great expense to present in esoteric detail what you thought you knew already.

It was often said in those days that people preferred to furnish their sitting rooms with individual chairs which gave more flexibility without the bulk of a suite. This attitude was disposed of by Urwick Orr and Partners, who were asked by the Company in 1960 to carry out a survey to examine the nature of the three-piece suite market. They concluded that this was substantial. Their main findings stated:

'It has been widely suggested that the three-piece suite is on its way out. To quote just one example, a survey of "Furniture 1950-1960" in the *Architects Journal* of 11th February 1960 stated: "As professional designers get to work, the sanctity of the suite was challenged and it has now been replaced by a series of pieces which allow people to cater for their own individual requirements and the rooms in which they live. . . ." This suggestion has not been borne out by our survey; in fact we have found that in the opinion of the retailers we have interviewed, the reverse is true in all regions, types of shops and classes or market. The three-piece suite is still the most popular item for furnishing the living room . . . The two-seater is losing ground to the three-seater and there is a tendency towards four-seaters. The impact of television together with the decline of the parlour and the use of the "through room" seem to be the major causes for the desire to provide additional seating accommodation. . . ."

The author carried out his own survey of the market for three-piece suites at the beginning of 1962, interviewing retailers with different classes of trade and covering the length and breadth of the country. The results clearly showed that retail furnishers believed that an upholstered three-piece suite was the firm choice of 62% of the public, with 21% choosing a suite which included a convertible sofa. The proportion of the public choosing fireside or easy chairs was unchanged from the 1960 level of 15%.

Retailers selling to the AB class markets made 40% of suite sales in 1961 at prices between £90 and £120 retail and 15% between £120 and £140 retail.

Price	*Style*	*Best seller with % of retailers*
£90-£120	Modern down to floor	39%
	Traditional down to floor	38%
	Modern on legs	15%
£120-140	Traditional down to floor	51%
	Modern down to floor	26%
	Traditional with 4-seater	10%
£140 plus	Traditional down to floor	48%
	Traditional with 4-seater	21%
	Modern down to floor	17%

The market for suites above £140 accounted for 3% of 1961 sales and represented about 6,000 suites a year. The market at prices between £120-£140 secured 8% of the 1961 sales and totalled about 20,000 suites a year The market at prices between £90-£120 secured 24% of the 1961 sales and totalled about 66,000 suites a year The market at prices between £60-£90 secured 38% of 1961 sales and totalled about 93,000 suites a year.

These guidelines as to the parameters of the three-piece suite market indicated at which price and style any suite made in a new factory might be aimed.

The search for a new factory site commenced.

ABOVE: The new factory takes shape at Chipping Norton. BELOW: Moulded shells for the Novella, Cornwell Norton's first product.

Pastures New

The decision to search for a site, on which a new factory could be built, posed several immediate problems. The intention was to produce upholstered three-piece suites there and bring Parker Knoll into a new market sector. However, this projected production could not be supplied with the machined chair parts by the Wycombe factory, which was now working to maximum capacity, and it was unlikely that the necessary wood machining skills would exist and be readily available far from Wycombe.

Robin Howland became Design Director in 1960 and continued investigating materials and methods by which chairs could be built inexpensively and in quantity, without using the conventional wooden chair frame. Study suggested that, if a suitable material could be found, a moulding process could produce contoured shells of great strength, whereas these could never be made using normal wood part construction, because of the complexity of the woodwork required to produce a sufficiently rigid structure. With the mood of the time for 'furnishing to become more modern', the public was interested in upholstery with softer lines, but anything different from conventional shapes was expensive and beyond middle market prices. The two experimental Parker Knoll chairs, Malton and Tirano, built on glass-fibre shells, had been warmly received and had created wide interest. Their originality and flowing lines were seen as a welcome departure from shapes which had long been conventional. Although this indication of market interest was encouraging, the method employed, of laying up the glass-fibre by hand in the mould, was too slow and thus too expensive to sell at a price which would create a larger volume market. For success, a simpler, cheaper and quicker method was needed.

The development work in this direction was coming to completion by 1961, coinciding nicely with the decision to build a new factory, as well as to enter the three-piece suite market. During a visit to an exhibition Reg Hopkins and Derek Stewart had discovered Novacore, a new sheet material with potential for moulding. After a lot of research and testing Reg Hopkins was convinced that, with assistance from Robbie Howland, he could handle this technology and, with the design and factory development teams, evolve a manufacturing method. The sheet material impregnated with thermo-setting phenolic resin could be laid around a mould and then cured in a vacuum by intense heat to form rigid contoured shapes ideal for upholstery. This facilitated fullsized three-piece suite production at a separate location from Wycombe, where new methods could be introduced more easily, and meant that almost no woodwork from Wycombe would be required — apart from four stumpy teak legs screwed into the base of the moulding. It also meant that the new factory would not be seriously affected by any work stoppage at Wycombe.

The search for a new factory site was governed by the planners' attitude to expansion, which precluded a Wycombe site. At the same time, Parker Knoll did not relish a large administrative machine away from Wycombe. With the assistance of the Board of Trade, two sites within a radius of forty miles were found and considered, one at Watlington and the other at Chipping Norton. The Clerk of the Chipping Norton Council was of great assistance, and the Town Council co-operative, enabling CHJ, on 20 February 1962, to show Harry Parker a level, eight-acre site on the edge of the town. The 45 miles from Wycombe was well served by road, by-passing Oxford. Although only 15,000 square feet was immediately necessary, the site was large enough to allow for expansion. By incorporating de-mountable wall panels in the first building, successive units could be added swiftly as the need arose. Today the factory covers the whole site.

The land was swiftly purchasd and Hugh Cartwright as Works Manager at Wycombe took on the intricate job of organising and planning the whole operation. Drawing deeply on the expertise of his Departmental Managers at Wycombe, he formed a planning team to cover every phase, using Critical Path Analysis to keep the operation on schedule. Derek Stewart was made Group Upholstery Manager to advise and oversee the many aspects of starting a completely new operation with a completely new product, in a completely new place, involving most departments in the Company in one way or another. For instance, there was no pool of trained labour in the Chipping Norton area, which was largely agricultural. This meant that Personnel had to find and recruit a labour force of about 30, who were then trained on site by people from Wycombe. Many of these had previously been postmen, cowmen, drivers and simply housewives.

The Novacore moulding sequence was developed by Reg Hopkins in conjunction with the material suppler, Turner & Newell, the Parker Knoll Production Engineering departments and the Designer, Robin Howland. The factory was equipped with the necessary moulds for the chair shells and plates which formed the inside arms. Another mould formed the centre section of the settee to which the right and left hand halves of a chair shell were eventually assembled. The resin impregnated sheet was cut into shapes and laid onto the mould, building up extra thickness at positions which required extra strength. The edges of the moulds were sealed with grease, covered with a form-fitting rubber cover which was clamped round the edges to obtain an airtight seal. The moulds were then connected to an air pump which extracted all the air until a vacuum was created. The moulds were then loaded into a rack and pushed into the intense heat of a 69 KW oven for twenty minutes. After cooling and removal from the mould the resulting shells were quite rigid and only needed the edges cleaning up to be ready for upholstery.

The knowledge Derek Stewart had accumulated on breakdown upholstery techniques was now put to use. Cutting and sewing of the covers, springing, fillings and cushion filling all followed normal procedures, but the upholstery operations were all devleoped by departing from normal upholstery traditions and breaking each job down into several separate operations. It then became possible to train each new operative to specialise in one particular function. By further training as production increased from the first beginnings, it was then possible to expand the skills of each operative to cover more operations, gradually making the organisation more and more flexible.

There were problems on the Sales side. If products from the new factory were sold under the established Parker Knoll brand, difficulties could arrive in shipping parts of the same range from two locations. Customers had long become accustomed to having each complete order, no matter for what mix of models, delivered simultaneously. As it was unlikely that despatches from two factories could be harmonised, it was decided to create a new brand name. It was in this way that the name of 'Cornwell-Norton' entered the trade, registered as a separate company to sell the output from the Chipping Norton factory.

By coincidence, there is a village named Cornwell only a few miles from Chipping Norton. It was also the second christian name of Thomas Cornwell Parker — TCP — after his maternal grandmother in Hull. A separate selling organisation was now required. The Directors asked Dane Baskerville, previously Sales Office Manager at Parker Knoll, to set this up and appointed him Sales Manager for Cornwell-Norton Ltd. His replacement was Simon Young Jamieson.

At Chipping Norton, progress in building was swift, enabling operative training to commence in the new factory by December 1962. Trial batches of both chairs and settees were made until all the snags had been ironed out and the labour force had reached an adequate standard. Involved with the project from the beginning was Mike Harvey, who had been running the Chair-making Shop. He was now appointed Factory Manager at Chipping Norton.

The new suite which was the reason for all this activity was called Novella and all sales literature, pattern books of covers, tickets and labels displaying the new company logo were ready by the time trial production was completed. By simply dividing the country in half, north and south, Dane Baskerville recruited two salesmen, Ian Brewster and Phillip Byers, who joined in December 1962 as representatives. He set off with them to introduce and sell the new upholstery brand.

Priced at between £135 and £147 for the three pieces, the suite was well received. The launching of the Novella took place when the furniture trade was in the grip of depression, but retailers were interested in the novel construction methods and their application to a new suite.

Gradually the momentum built up, but everybody knew that the break-even point would not be reached until the factory was despatching a regular weekly flow of fifty suites and at the beginning that seemed to be a long way off.

LEFT: Baker's dozens sold the Ringwood. RIGHT: The Novella.

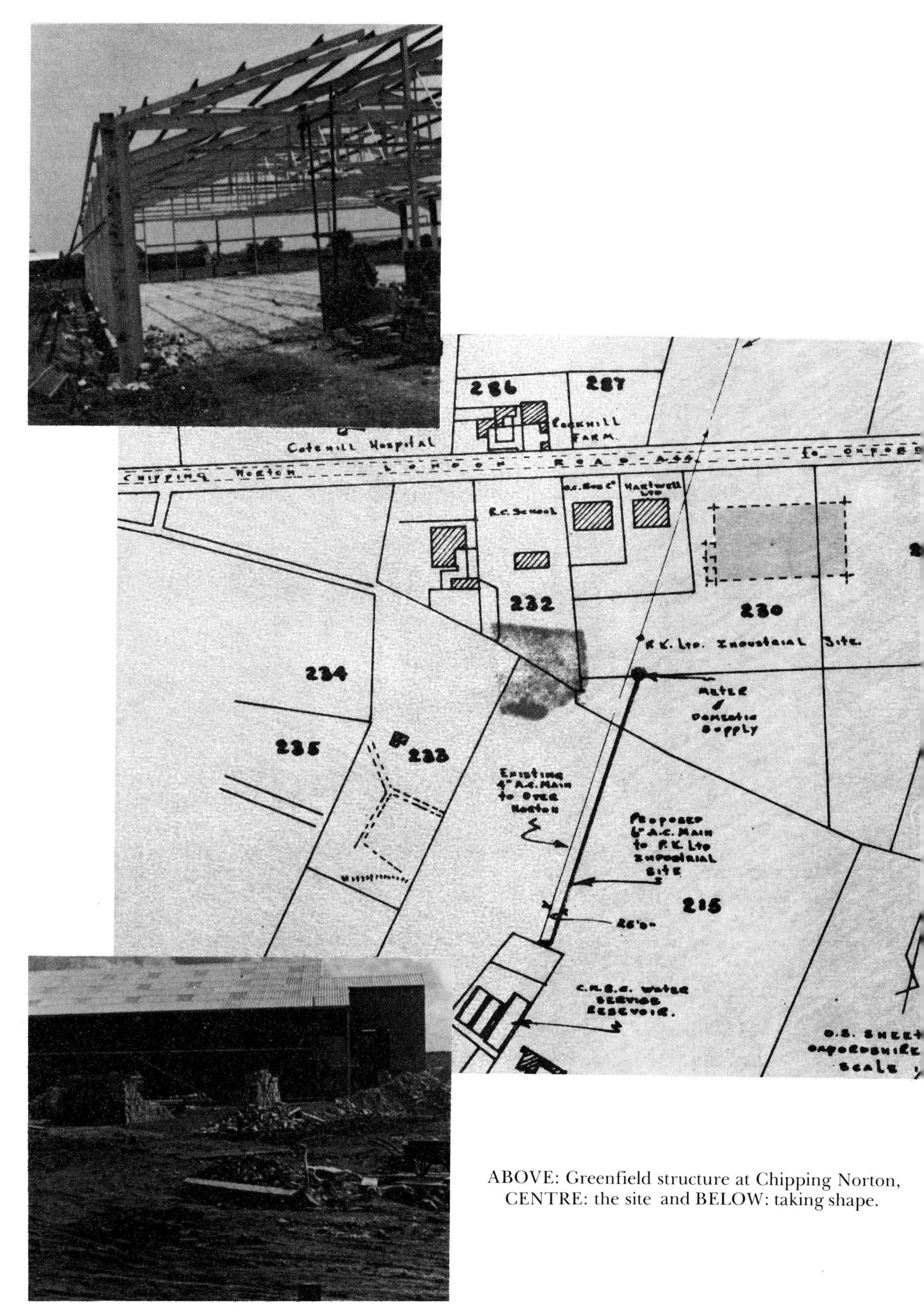

ABOVE: Greenfield structure at Chipping Norton, CENTRE: the site and BELOW: taking shape.

Centenary

While a lot of attention and effort was inevitably focussed thoughout 1962 on the new Chipping Norton factory, the routine business of making and selling chairs from High Wycombe continued in an increasingly difficult market.

EHC as Works Manager, and John Arnold as Sales Manager, were elected Directors in 1962. All departments were on short-time, putting Geoffrey Alpe and John Arnold under pressure. Retailers were holding reduced stocks and only replacing these as necessary. The only available remedy was to present them with ever more tempting 'special offers' of parcels of chairs in better than normal covers, as they seemed prepared to order these if nothing else.

When business falls away high-geared production lines cannot be kept working normally. Employees often form their own judgement of how serious things are from their knowledge of how other firms are suffering. In 1962-3 it became almost universal. Parker Knoll was often less affected by poor retail trading conditions because of the middle and upper class markets, more resilient financially and not as likely to postpone buying when credit is short.

When 51% of the total national expenditure (1962) on furniture and furnishings is concentrated in the hands of a mere 30% of the population, it does make sense to concentrate the marketing effort towards that relatively small but extremely worthwhile group of potential customers.

The 'Family Expenditure Survey' for 1962-3 provides a guide to where the greatest fall in spending on furniture occurred during the 1962/3 depression. This indicates that the sharpest cut-back was made in the most affluent customers whose spending dropped by 50%, while the fall in the middle market was much less severe at about 17%. The decline in spending by the lower market was substantial at about 35%. Despite the indicated sharp decline by the top spending sector, this nevertheless continued to spend appreciably more on furniture in 1963 than any other group.

Prior to the early 1960s there was a dearth of published information on any aspect of the market for furniture. The Furniture Development Council first published its statistical digest in 1958, and went on to provide a considerable amount of information and economic forecasting for the industry.

Although profits for the first half of the financial year ending January 1962 were down by £18,000, performance targets for the year to come were not reduced when the departmental budgets were compiled in May. The figures for the year from August 1962-July 1963 were set to show a further increase and produce 176,519 chairs, yielding a turnover of £1,995,817. The advertising programme was projected to continue much as before, using the same media schedule at a cost for the year of £66,000. The showrooms continued to attract considerable interest from the public. London showrooms in Tottenham Court Road were now too small to display the increasing range. This was overcome in September 1961 when spacioius new showrooms were opened at 19–20 Berners Street; a much more suitable and central site and conveniently close to Parker Knoll Textile's showrooms, just up the street at number 25.

The Manchester Showrooms at 3, Barton Square were not actually in the Square but just off it in a Victorian shopping arcade, known locally as King Street Arcade. These drawbacks were overcome when the showroom was moved in 1960 to a much better location in King Street, said to be the best shopping street in Manchester.

Looking for ways by which the business could be expanded, the Board during 1960, considered the possibility of merging with Gimson and Slater, the highly reputed Nottingham firm making good quality, well-designed modern upholstery. At the same time, they looked at an amalgamation with the old-established High Wycombe firm of F. Glenister and Sons, whose factory adjoined that of Parker Knoll. However, in the end it was decided not to pursue either, but to expand at Chipping Norton.

Parker Knoll Textiles were also looking towards expansion in their own field when the opportunity came to acqure the old-established and much respected company G. P. & J. Baker. This business, formed in the early 19th century, had developed an extensive knowledge of historic textiles and records, which aided them in producing exotic printed fabrics for the modern market. This history and archive of historic material is described in *East to West*, published by G. P. & J. Baker Ltd in conjunction with the Victoria & Albert Museum, as a guide to an exhibition there in 1984.

For many years, although one of the largest High Wycombe manufacturers, Parker Knoll had been outside the membership of the High Wycombe Furniture Manufacturers Association, and had not exhibited at any of the Furniture trade exhibitions run by the British Furniture Manufacturers Association. As conditions changed and business became more competitive, this independent attitude became more difficult to maintain and the Company realised that it should take space and meet its customers at these annual trade shows. Application was made to re-join the Association in March 1962 and space was booked for the forthcoming August exhibition at Belle Vue, Manchester.

Another exhibition, of a different kind, was visited by Her Majesty Queen Elizabeth during a visit to High Wycombe on 6 April 1962. This included a group of antique Windsor chairs taken from the Parker Knoll collection in which she showed great interest.

The depressed state of the furniture industry in early 1963 had its effect on Parker Knoll as well. For the half year ending January nett profits were 50% down, causing much re-examination. In April the net profit for the month fell to only £7,268 compared with £18,998 the previous year, further emphasising the need for action. The Chairman made it clear that he was unhappy about the effects of the 'special offers'. He pointed out yet again that these were costing a lot of money, reducing margins and seriously eroding Company profits during an already poor trading period. Another effect of these 'Offers' was the unbalancing effect they had on the model mix passing through the factory. Volumes were high on the cheapest models featured as offers, but low on others.

Accordingly John Arnold originated another promotional idea designed to win volume orders for a specific chair and at the same time bring tangible advantage to the retailer. John Arnold's new scheme was designed to give all the benefit to the retailer in the form of higher profit margins, when chairs were ordered in dozens on a planned delivery schedule to cover six months ahead. These dozens were then delivered as 'Bakers' Dozens' of thirteen chairs for every dozen ordered, the free chair when sold increasing the retailer's return on each dozen chairs from 31% to 36%. The scheme was first introduced for the new PK973 Ringwood chair in June 1966. This was a replacement for the long running PK773 Arran and designed and priced to be less expensive than the four-model family group based on the PK964 Abinger. Despite the complexities for both the retailer and the office of scheduling batches of chairs for forward delivery several months ahead, the scheme worked like a charm, with 1,600 chairs ordered in the first three days. After ten weeks 12,000 chairs had been ordered, making it possible to plan production of the model well ahead, at a cost to the Company of only 1,046 free chairs. So successful and popular was this promotional selling technique that it was adopted on many other occasions with similar results.

The differences between production times for different chairs in different workshops were considerable. Chairs like the Penshurst wing chair with only the four legs visible required a lot less time in the Polishing Shops than they did in Upholstery, while chairs like the Arran had more visible woodwork to polish but only needed a short time in Upholstery to cover the chair back. The numbers of Penshursts required each day were far less than the Arrans and it is easy to see how unplanned fluctuations in demand for chairs with different work content could cause serious dislocation. Bearing in mind that all chairs being upholstered had to meet a deadline which was the scheduled departure date for the van on which they were consigned, the workload in each section had to be carefully regulated to ensure that all chairs were complete in time.

It had taken ten long years for the industry to achieve any significant increase in output over the 1954 levels but after two years growth it began to fall back again and continued to suffer from erractic improvements and depressions throughout the '60s. The members of the Branded Furniture Society became increasingly conscious that the size of their markets continued to shrink while consumer affluence was increasing. The Furniture Promotion Council was formed to develop strategy for a national campaign and CHJ became its first Chairman.

Within the Company, Parker Knoll sales during the first half of the decade grew appreciably from 148,867 chairs in the year ending 31 July 1960, to a peak of 178,259 in the year to July 1964. Thereafter they slid back to a low of 149,764 in the year to July 1968. However, this figure takes no account of the additional sales made by Cornwell Norton, which added another 36,238 pieces, lifting the total sales to a record 186,002 units.

New designs, for which Geoffrey Alpe was responsible, were brought into production and were priced to yield full margins. Disappointingly not all the new ranges were successful and some only ran for a short time, adding to the stresses upon a factory tooled up to produce at the forecast levels.

In 1965 the Chairman observed: 'At Chipping Norton we made a loss. Strenuous efforts are being made to raise the level of turnover to achieve a satisfactory return on this investment', but in 1966, 'Turnover for Parker Knoll Ltd was only slightly less than last year but margins were lower. The Chipping Norton factory showed a profit on the year's operations for the first time and we are confident that this will continue'. In 1967 'Sales were higher during the last year due to the success of our sales effort . . . The increased production at Chipping Norton . . . has resulted in the factory making a substantial contribution to group profit', and the following year 'The chairs, settees and tables . . . produced at Chipping Norton have been in strong demand and we had to add a second extension of 15,000 sqare feet to the factory'.

In 1969, 'The High Wycombe factory started off the year with a high order bank enabling us to keep the factory running at a high level of activity. However, by [mid year] it was apparent that the credit squeeze was beginning to take effect and in the latter months of the year, short time working was in operation in some parts of the factory. Nevertheless there was some contribution to Group profits' and 'We started the year [at Chipping Norton] with a high order bank . . . there was a decline in orders during the last six months. The activities of this factory also contributed to Group profits'.

It was now nearly one hundred years since Frederick Parker had started his business in Bracklyn Street, Hoxton and a century later, the modern business which had grown from it, had in the ten years between 1958 and 1968, sold and delivered no less than 1,603,378 chairs from the High Wycombe factory.

LEFT: The Mendip was widely displayed, extensively imitated, but sold slowly, which remains a mystery. RIGHT: The 1963 Quartet group was the first outright sales failure. BELOW: The successful Gavotte was joined by the Giovanni in 1963.

MARGINS AND MODELS

When Parker Knoll furniture was introduced to the British market in 1930, a major feature in its marketing was the Company's decision to sell at a fixed retail price. For the retailer, fixed resale prices assured a pre-determined return on certain leading brands.

When, in 1963, Edward Heath as President of the Board of Trade tabled a bill to abolish Resale Price Maintenance, considerable thought was given to its likely effects upon Parker Knoll. Most indepedent furniture retailers favoured retention of price maintenance on branded furniture. From statements made by Mr Heath it is clear that he considered RPM was an umbrella for inefficiency. Only about 15% of all furniture and floorcoverings sales were subject to RPM, and one wonders why the small number who handled this minority of the market should have been considered inefficient and why the public needed to be protected from them.

The Act did allow manufacturers to publish prices for the resale of their goods. These could be based on whatever margin of profit a dealer required and the idea was floated in the trade of printing different lists for different dealers, but was dropped as unworkable. After extensive consultation with Parker Knoll retailers it was clear to the Company that the great majority just wanted to continue with their branded furniture as before; that is to have a published list of recommended prices which allowed them the normal profit margin. They certainly were not thirsting for any price war.

Since the Act made it illegal to enforce resale prices, a new form of contractual agreement was required. This would define the Company policy on how its products would be distributed and replace the old trade terms folder. It was decided to divide dealers into three categories according to the amount of stock they would carry. These were 'Main Agents' who would always carry a minimum selection of twelve designs on their shop floor; 'Appointed Retailers' who would always carry six designs and 'Stockists' who would simply carry two designs consistent with their style of business. Main agents would be offered the opportunity to replace their twelve display chairs twice a year at a discount to cover depreciation and clearance of the old stocks and have first choice on any other promotional offers.

Retailers were given the opportunity to decide for themselves into which of three categories they wished to be placed, by signing a document which appointed them as a classified Parker Knoll dealer. All other accounts were then closed.

The Distribution Policy was as follows:

'1. Fundamental Policy

It is Parker Knoll's policy to distribute its chairs and settees at trade prices only to those customers who can energetically promote, display and service Parker Knoll products in such a way that they maintain the prestige and good name of those products. The company reserves the right to cease to deal with any customer who in their opinion does not come into the above category.

'2. Policy to Dealers.

Parker Knoll intends to do business at trade prices only with dealers who:

a. Maintain a satisfactory credit rating.
b. Pay on the Company's terms of 2½% discount for accounts due and payable by the 20th of the month folowing date of invoice.
c. Energetically endeavour to promote Parker Knoll products.
d. Are able to and will sell Parker Knoll products in a manner consistent with general good business practice in their trading area, so as to maintain Parker Knoll's goodwill, public confidence and prestige.
e. Resell only from their own premises and do not distribute to associated companies, or to other branches, or to other dealers who Parker Knoll are not prepared to supply direct.

Parker Knoll will supply at non-stockist prices those customers who have neither the space nor the inclination to promote our goods, provided that they qualify under 2(a), (b), (d) and (e). Non stockist prices are 15% higher than normal trade prices.'

After the end of Resale Price Maintenance attention was given to maintaining permanent displays of Parker Knoll in Main Agents, Allan Barnett looked after all aspects of design and installation of such displays working in close co-operation with display specialists who made the equipment. His standard letter to customers, advising them of the date of installation and the number of erections the shopfitters had to cope with each day, became a classic example of the unwitting 'double entendre' which went undetected in the office for many months before being pointed out by a Buyer.

Despite the difficulties of handling three-seater settees in the High Wycombe factory another suite, the Giovanni, was introduced in 1963. The earlier Gavotte suite had been a considerable success. The Giovanni suite was designed to provide a full headrest back, no doubt the most important feature in any truly easy chair or settee and, although still on legs, these were a necessary feature of the design and far less prominent. This suite was priced to sell at £125 retail.

The settled tempo of production at High Wycombe during the 1960s was hardly disturbed by the introduction of new models due to extensive pre-planning and the pre-production allowed for the machining of the first batches of chair parts. Improvements were made continuously. Typical examples were the development by the Company of its own cushion-filling machine, as well as the introduction of pneumatic nailing guns to replace the hand nailing methods for fixing the Parker Knoll flexible webbing to anchor the springs to the seat side rails. Another innovation brought an end to the marking out and nailing of staples by hand to back feet, as anchorages for Parker Knoll springs in chair backs. A high powered stapling machine used in conjunction with a jig, which automatically located the correct position for each staple, fired the half inch long staples deep into the back foot with far better results than the old hand method it replaced.

Another notable development was the introduction in 1964 of an experimental automatic sanding machine purchased at a cost of £12,000. Over forty feet in length, with a tunnel in the centre, sanding brushes and drums were arranged at intervals in an overhead arc through which chair parts moved continuously, allowing each set of drums to move in and out to sand one part of the complete operation. Movement of the sanding arms was controlled by a series of rotating templates of irregular shape around which cams 'felt' the contours and manipulated the arms to bring them into contact with the chair parts by a series of remote control cables. As an ingenious example of pre-computer age controlled machinery it now looks crude, but it worked. Despite the time required to position the sanding heads and set up the control templates for each run of say 2,000 of the same shaped parts, only one man was required to load the parts onto the spigots which carried them through the tunnel, as opposed to a sanding operator handling and finishing each part individually. With experience it was found that the factory batch sizes were too small to justify the considerable time involved in setting up and, because of this, was too inflexible to change from one chairpart to another. It eventually went out of use and was removed.

Another investment in 1968 saw the arrival in the Mill of the first Geiger automatic turning machine. Ever since 1851 the cabriole legs for the Penshurst and all other wing chairs sold by the Company had been turned by Massils of Marshmoor, running into many tens of thousands. The projected introduction of other cabriole leg chairs emphasised that the time had come to machine these parts in the factory.

Many new models were introduced throughout the 1960s — fifty-two altogether — imposing a massive workload on both Design Studio and Production Engineering. Not all were successful, and by definition, this was inevitable. The PK950 Mendip chair was introduced, as an elegant modern armchair of ample proportions, designed to appeal to those furnishing in the so-called 'Scandinavian' style. By comparison with earlier successful high-selling Parker Knoll chairs of this type, the Mendip was a vast improvement. It was well received by retailers and was soon to be seen in all the shops. A well-known competitor concluded that this must be a winner and hastened to introduce a close copy. Sad to say, the reason the Mendip chair was seen so widely was because the public did not like it and it was not selling. It is not recorded how long it was before the competitor realised his mistake, but his version of the design did not sell either.

Several of the new wood armchair designs introduced during the 1960s were replacements for earlier models. This type of chair was always in strong demand by contract user customers, especially in hospitals but, by the end of the 1960s, retail sales were beginning to decline in favour of more upholstered styles. Provision for the wood armchair market eventually became concentrated in the Ashby group of models, which continued into the 1990s and sold a total of 559,651 (until July 1990) across all eight styles.

Another idea developed early in the '60s was for a group of different chairs with a matching settee, any of which could be used together to furnish a room, offering an alternative to the uniformity of a three-piece suite. This was first tried with the Quartet suite. The largest sector of the three-piece suite market which accounted for 40% of all sales was that priced at between £60-90. Most of these would have been inexpensive 'down to the floor' designs, while the style of the Quartet models still related to occasional chair design. The sales objective was to offer an upholstered group at the lowest possible selling price consistent with Parker Knoll quality and comfort. Polyether foam cushioning was used for the first time in the seats, which were tightly upholstered over the foam squabs and designed to simulate the appearance of a loose cushion by projecting at the seat front. This was a radical departure from normal Parker Knoll practice, as until then all PK chairs had been fitted with Parkertex latex foam cushions. Buyers' reaction to the range was cool and they expressed their reservations by not ordering the settee at all. Only 200 were sold during the introductory period in February 1963. The chairs, although bought more widely, only achieved initial sales of less than 1,000 each, a fact which made it clear this group was doomed to be a spectacular failure. Plans for advertising the group during the spring of 1963 were too far advanced and could only be curtailed. Sales of the wing chair fell from 5,185 (barely 100 a week) in the first year, to 2,362 in the second and the lug model fell from its first year high of only 3,114 to 1,423 in the second. A total of only 1,174 settees were sold between February 1963 and December 1964 when the whole project was abandoned.

This episode highlights clearly the cost to all departments of the Company of a mistaken marketing decision. The design work is based upon the sales requirements. When this is completed and the production prototype accepted, the die is cast. Production Engineering have to make a wide variety of production jigs for each machining process and order all

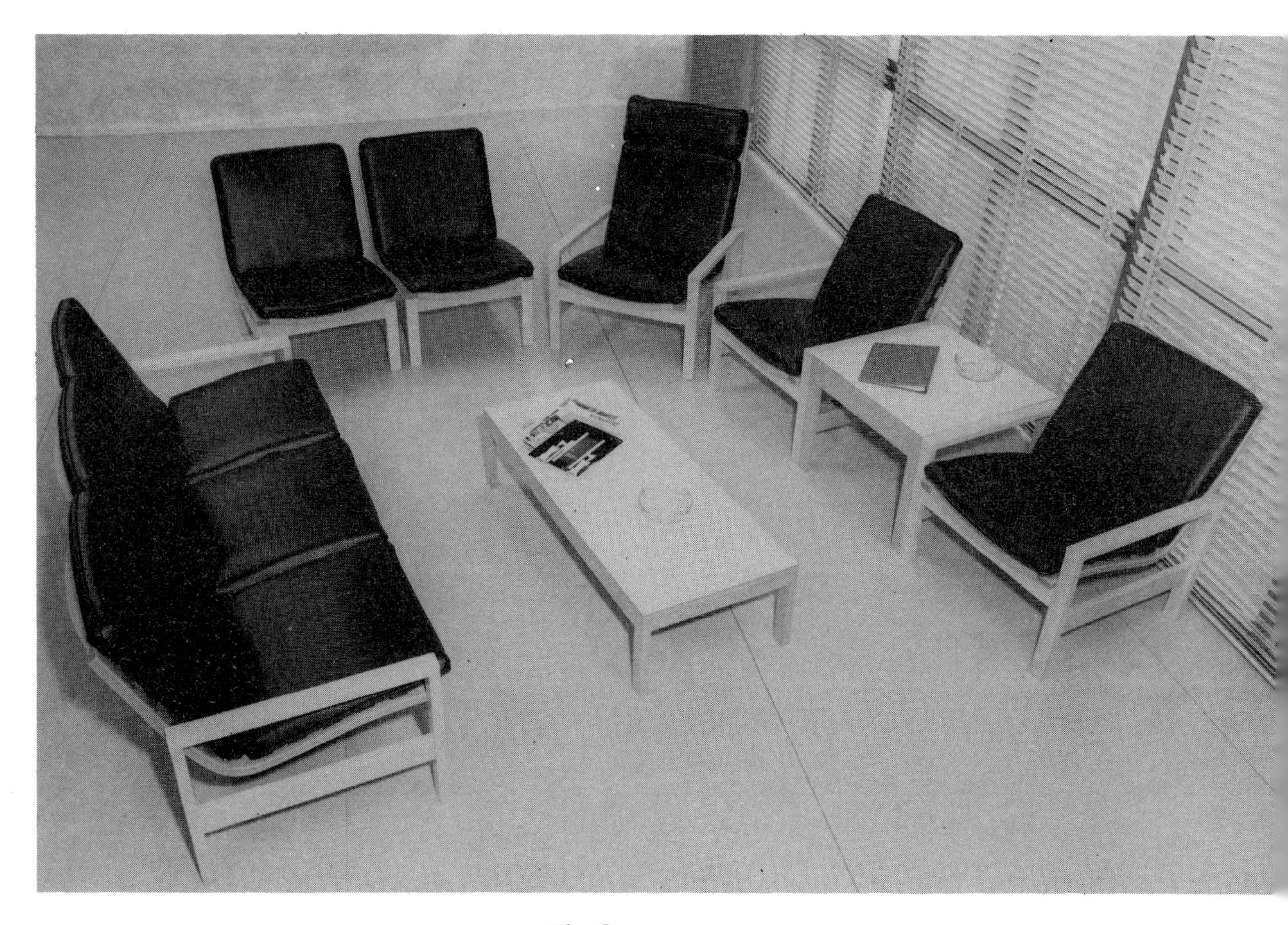

The Compton range.

necessary tools, while Sales provide a forecast of quantities which will be sold during and after the initial introductory phase. Based on this the factory has to order the first batches of chair parts, possibly sufficient for 500 frames of each chair, to be ready in time to meet initial delivery dates. Buying places orders for various components special to the model and moulds have to be made by cushion suppliers for the exact shape required. Quantities of cushions to be delivered weekly are laid down to an exact timetable based on the Sales forecast, while training is carried out by sewing and upholstery departments to familiarise operatives with features of the new product.

In America many manufacturers, when introducing new models, display a prototype at exhibitions to see what reaction is. If sufficient orders are placed the model will then be put into production but if only a few are ordered, the model is scrapped and those who did place orders are told 'sorry we are not going to make it after all'. For Parker Knoll, it had always worked the other way round. Once the decision was taken to produce a new model, an unstoppable chain of events was set in motion despite the fact that no market testing had been done.

Success or failure depended on whether the Company's judgement of both design and market had been correct. It must be said that never before the Quartet Group had such a serious misreading of the market occurred for a new Parker Knoll product.

Breaking the Mould

At the new Chipping Norton factory, production built slowly with great care over quality control. Factory Manager Mike Harvey called on Departmental Managers from High Wycombe who often made several visits a week. Reaction to the Novella suite by trade buyers was good and sufficient orders were available to allow a steady increase in output.

By March 1963 production had reached 40 suites a week, but this was not sufficient to avoid a loss of £17,200. However, indications looked promising and the Board invested a further £42,000 plus £8,000 for plant, to build a second bay, more than doubling the original factory. It was possible to plan for an increase in weekly production of moulded suites to eighty, at the same time widening the selection of models.

The creation of the new and entirely separate brand name of Cornwell Norton made it possible for Geoffrey Alpe and the design team to strike out in new directions, free of many of the constraints which had limited designs for Parker Knoll. The tension springing system imposed its own restrictions on designers. The use of Parker Knoll springing in settees was inhibited unless the springs were attached from front to back in the seat and vertically in the backs. The method prevented a settee from having a soft front edge beneath the cushions which was unacceptable until the problem was partly solved in the 1960s by the Moby Dick. This aptly named technique enabled a small settee to be sprung from side to side using short springs which were anchored in the centre over a deep flexible mounting, similar in shape to the famous whale, supported by the settee frame. This method had proved entirely satisfactory in the small two-seater settee to match the Penshurst wing chair, and was extended for the first time to a three-seater size in the Cornwell Norton Novella settee.

The first departure was the N3 Rossano, a smart occasional chair with a solid teak frame, sprung with the Scandinavian 'Fagas' system. Based on a unit with spring steel side members which attached to the seat frame at only one central point, it carried a mesh of flexible rubber straps; the chair had extraordinary suppleness in both seat and back. The thin slab-shaped latex seat and back cushions were a special feature of the design. A small chair frame shop was set up at Chipping Norton to assemble the machined chair frame parts supplied from High Wycombe. Three more smart occasional and office style chairs were derived from mounting one tub-shaped moulded Novacore shell onto a variety of different base units, ranging from a cruciform teak base or die-cast aluminium castored unit to charcoal nylon finished tubular metal legs. These chairs were of particular interest to furnishing architects and interior designers for whom most conventional upholstered furniture designs held little interest. The fact that they were in regular production and could be supplied in any quantity soon brought orders.

By mid-1964 a second moulded suite had been designed and was put into production. This was the Toccata N7 and N8 which had been test-sold in the south of England and had won approval. Sales of the Novella suite were still not lifting sufficiently, hovering just below fifty a week so introduction of an alternative style might increase sales. The Toccata mouldings were formed in one single piece for both chair and settee, whereas those for the Novella chair and settee were assembled from several separate pieces and sprung with Parker Knoll tension springs. The Toccata models were fitted with a membrane form of suspension in both seat and back which, with latex foam cushions, gave them deep, yielding easy chair comfort, without any of the production complications involved in the Novella.

Another design project was for a range of strong modern seating which would meet the special needs of universities, schools and hospitals. Alan Howard Baker, a member of the Parker Knoll design team, had worked on this brief until eventually both he and Production Engineering were satisfied with the four different pieces which became known as the Compton group. Although of wood framed construction it was decided to include these models in the Cornwell Norton range, supplying frame parts from High Wycombe, and to enlarge the small frame assembly shop already at Chipping Norton. The prototypes of the chairs had been extensively researched with many leading architects and authorities. An important feature of the design was that, although of rectangular outline, which allowed the chairs to butt up closely together in rows, the seat cushions and suspension were supported by an ergonomically shaped, inner frame which added great strength and rigidity due to its laminated construction. All cushions were easily removable, being attached by press studs.

Sales for this range quickly built up into another great success with Contract user customers. Often orders for several hundreds for simultaneous delivery stretched the manufacturing resources of the sewing and cushion-making departments at Chipping Norton to the limits. The Compton range rapidly became a classic in the Contract furnishing world and remained in high level demand for the next twenty-five years during which a total of 240,507 (at July 1987) were sold.

In the year ending July 1965 Parker Knoll sold a total of 167,930 chairs, to which Chipping Norton was able to add some 3,000. By now it had been realised that the original concept, that the Chipping Norton factory would only make designs which required little machine woodwork from High Wycombe, was unduly restrictive and it was scrapped. Initially, arrangements were made to supply chair frame parts to Chipping Norton, enabling them to set up a small frame assembly shop of their own. This was ideal for the Compton range, although it was evident that Wycombe would have to assemble and supply Norton with all their chair frames. This first took effect for the Kings and Queens range but, as larger and more elaborate chairs were put into production there, Wycombe had to shoulder the burden of integrating Norton's need for chair frames with those of the Wycombe factory. This introduced a new hazard into smooth production at Chipping Norton, inasmuch as they could not upholster chairs for which the frames had not arrived. The pressures were increased at both factories, resulting in many acrimonious telephone calls. Norton's requirements increased as new three-piece suite ranges were introduced and had to be integrated into the production plan at Wycombe. The woodworking and frame-making departments there worked to maximum capacity to sustain both factories.

It was soon apparent that the sales force had to be increased. Rather than recruit a new force, it was decided to use the services of the existing Parker Knoll Contracts salesmen, who normally only called upon user customers and not on retailers. These men suddenly found themselves wearing different hats when calling on their Contract user customers and then on retailers in the same town.

Cornwell Norton started to need new and separate office administration. At first this was looked after by Dane Baskerville's own secretary and a small group in the Parker Knoll sales office but, as more models became available and demand increased, the need for a proper Sales Office became increasingly urgent. Before any decisions were made about this the position was complicated by complaints from customers who reported structural failures in the moulded Novella chairs and settees.

The process had relied on laying up the material in the mould and kilning it without using a power press. This had seemed to be quite satisfactory under development and testing, but in production, if the seals around the edge of the moulds were not 100% efficient in creating a perfect vacuum, the bonding was not always perfect and could eventually de-laminate, particularly at stress points. The models were sprung with Parker Knoll horizontal springs which exerted a tremendous tension on the side mouldings when a chair was in use, causing some to fracture. Those which had been moulded in a complete vacuum were perfect and gave no trouble. At first representatives were asked to inspect faulty furniture, but this interfered with their selling. Retailers were asked to collect complaints for repair or replacement, a job which undermined their confidence. Unfortunately the complaints rose steadily and, although all were dealt with to the owners' satisfaction, it became clear that the problem could not be solved unless a power press was used.

Despite the great efforts made to overcome these problems, they were not solely due to lack of vacuum, but also to design features. The inside arms were not an integral part of the body moulding. This proved vulnerable unless the arm moulding was free of laminations, and the method of building a settee by inserting a moulded central section between the left and right hand halves of a chair moulding was prone to fail at the joints. Little trouble arose from the shells for the Toccata models which were moulded in one piece and proved to be much stronger, and none at all on the tub chairs.

The solution adopted was to switch all new manufacture of the Novella models, despite the extra cost, to conventional wooden frame construction which, despite its complexity, completely overcame the problem at no extra cost to the customer. All moulded production for this model was stopped, but the high cost of meeting and servicing complaints on Novella made it impossible for the venture to yield profits.

The problem did not restrict the growth of other Cornwell Norton sales, especially in the Contract field. The small Sales organisation continued at High Wycombe, where all production scheduling was done for the factory at Norton, leaving Mike Harvey and his team to concentrate solely on production and delivery. With almost fifty miles between the two, organisational problems soon arose.

One of these was sample chairs. It had always been a policy of Parker Knoll Contracts department to submit sample chairs to public authorities with tenders. The Cornwell Norton range of Compton models was of immediate interest and sample chairs were made available. The result was rapidly developing chaos at the factory. Not only did the sample chairs have to be delivered, often by a specified date for a committee meeting, but they had to be collected immediately afterwards as the customers invariably had no space in which to store them. This quickly generated hundreds of chairs at the factory which might have suffered damage during their travels to and fro and could not be sent out again without attention. The accumulation of chairs took up valuable space and surprisingly often did not contain the specific model required for the next tender. If so another one was made as a priority! It takes little to imagine the impact of all this upon the small factory organisation, its transport space and lack of resources to keep records. The ensuing chaos threatened to interfere with main line production and deliveries of the Cornwell Norton range.

Attempts to maintain a stock list of chairs involved the author and Ken Sharpe in many hours' work in the factory roof space where they were stored, protected by vast plastic sheets from the thick brown Novacore dust which lay everywhere. Disposal of this accumulated mass of unsaleable chairs became a pressing problem which was solved by Ken Taylor, who arranged to supply whole vanloads at prices well below cost to the residential Jesuit training college at nearby Heythrop Park. They took so many chairs that every room must have been crammed, making it the best Cornwell Norton furnished house in the land.

To relieve pressure on the factory, Dane Baskerville dealt with the less serious Novella complaints by sending a travelling upholsterer to correct them on the spot, reducing the number of items returned to the factory. This was greatly appreciated by customers as their complaint received proper attention and they were not deprived of their furniture. Retailers, too, were relieved by this positive attitude towards their customers, and in many cases previously angry customers were impressed by the Company's policy and service.

This whole disappointing setback prevented sales reaching a sufficient level to fully occupy the extended factory. Although steps were taken to bring forward new models of conventional wood frame construction there were delays. As a stopgap, the Parker Knoll Cavatina suite, designed for production at Wycombe, was switched to Chipping Norton in 1965 and numbered N100/101, The initial distribution under the Parker Knoll brand, supported by an advertising campaign listing names of stockists, went well. However, this new type of production at Chipping Norton required more traditional upholstery skills, for which it had not been possible to train sufficient Norton operatives, and so some initial orders were not delivered until long after the campaign was over. This was disastrous. Many retailers whose names were on the stockist list did not have the suite to show and made their feelings plain. This was not consistent with the reliability of Parker Knoll and left many wondering what was happening.

From the difficulties encountered with the moulding operation at Chipping Norton, a whole sequence of repercussions followed. The Company, which now had two brands and two factories, one totally dependent on the other for supplies of frames, was increasingly drawn into a traumatic situation quite unprecedented in its history. Management skills in all departments, in an attempt to keep both ranges and factories running, were subject to the severest strain. These were initially caused by trying to fill the idle capacity at Norton by transferring the upholstery and delivery of Parker Knoll models there, thereby losing control of delivery dates.

Cornwell Norton sales languished because they had been given no new models to sell and the factory was working well below capacity until, in July 1966, despite the difficulties already encountered, it was decided to manufacture a new model, not for the Cornwell Norton range, but for Parker Knoll. The success of this new chair immediately transformed the situation at Norton and proved the turning point from which the Chipping Norton factory never looked back.

The Toccata suite, Cornwell Norton's second moulded suite, produced in 1956.

LEFT: The Novella went well in the 'black look'. RIGHT: The Rossano was Cornwell Norton's second model — it found favour with architects. BELOW: The Cavatina suite was a Wycombe product switched to Norton.

The fabulous Parker Knoll Recliner — in the *Sunday Times Magazine* in October 1966.

EASY ACTION

During their visits to American upholstery manufacturers both CHJ and John Arnold had been impressed by the large sales and output of multi-position or reclining chairs which were not then made in this country. Greaves and Thomas, famous for 'Put-you-Up' bed settees since the 1930s, had marketed a multi-position chair in the early 1950s described as 'The Bodyline Heart Saver', and did some consumer advertising, but without achieving high volume sales. Apart from a small number of Canadian imports covered in tortoise-shell plastic covers, the market was left undeveloped through the early 1960s. Greaves and Thomas then marketed the American 'Lazy Boy' multi-position chair but, because their 'Put-you-Up' brand, rather than their Company name, was widely known, again failed to make a serious impact on the UK. Undoubtedly the impact of a Parker Knoll recliner would be immensely greater, benefitting from the established public knowledge of the brand and the Company's high reputation.

The reclining chair is really three chairs in one: first the conventional easy chair, second, a chair with a footstool, and thirdly it becomes a chaise lounge, allowing the user to choose any of the positions without rising from the chair. Convinced that this concept would find ready acceptance by the British public, Parker Knoll knew that they had the opportunity to create a new market within the British furniture industry. The Board decided in the early 1960s to commence design and began planning. As a preliminary, Derek Stewart was despatched to the Berkline factory at Morriston, Tennessee to study production.

Most of the American styles were not suited to British taste, so Robin Howland and his design team started from scratch and produced an elegant design in traditional easy chair style, which cleverly concealed its reclining facility. It had no levers with which to operate the action, but simply required the user to apply pressure to the arms to open the chair from the upright position. A major feature, not to be found on many other makes, was the angle adjustment between seat and chair back.

In any chair with an adjustable action it is vitally important that the action itself is of sufficient quality to perform perfectly over a long period. Not only must the gauge of metal used be strong enough, but the friction joints must move smoothly and not loosen in use. The American Company freely provided their advice and assistance and supplied the initial batches of their well-tested actions which Parker Knoll imported under licence. This action had given trouble-free use in the forty-five thousand chairs in which it had been sold by Berkline during the previous 2½ years. Eventually the actions were manufactured in the UK under licence.

There were several reasons early in 1966 for the decision to produce the N30 Recliner chair at the Chipping Norton factory, despite the fact that it would be marketed as a Parker Knoll product. To have sold so important a new chair under the still not widely known Cornwell Norton brand would have risked the public asking 'Cornwell who?'. This was a large and heavy chair which would have been difficult to handle in the Upholstery shop at

Wycombe, whereas the spacious workshops at the Chipping Norton factory were ideal. More important, the shortage of work, which had meant that the extra space in the recently added extension was not being fully used, could be overcome by introducing the upholstery work for the new Recliner there, and then delivering the chairs to retailers direct from Chipping Norton by Cornwell Norton transport.

The Recliner chair was at that time the most expensive model ever marketed by the Company. Retail prices of the Company's chairs, in the lowest cover quality, spread in 1966 between £14 14s 0d and £41 9s 0d. The idea that the public might spend as much as £67 on a single chair was still novel. The 'Lazy Boy' chairs, just introduced by Greaves and Thomas in eleven styles, sold at between £51 10s 0d and £69 15s 0d, while Gomme had some years previously introduced their modern swivel tub rocking chair under the unwieldly description of the 'Most Comfortable Chair in the World' at about £67. Reputedly this chair had been slow to sell and was about to be discounted when it suddenly increased dramatically and became a great success.

Marketing the N30 Recliner chair presented a challenge, not least to the Sales and Marketing departments. A look through the files emphasises the immensely wide scope and detail of the arrangements made, far beyond anything previously attempted. The timetable was set in March 1966, fixing the date of the first Sales Conference for representatives as 14 July, Vernons, the advertising agents, were photographing the chair in May and creating their advertising campaign for which spaces were booked for full colour pages, the first of which would appear on 25 September. Two thirds of the total autumn advertising budget was allocated to Recliner advertising which would appear during October and November. This introduced into the whole plan an element of living dangerously by allowing the absolute minimum of time in which to make delivery to the first shops to order, before the first advertisements appeared. Never before had such tight arrangements been made, but never before had the production and sales departments worked so closely together to make their own contribution to a successful operation.

A series of regional receptions were held during July to which trade buyers were invited, giving them the first opportunity to evaluate the chair away from the distractions of their shops. Special press receptions were also held for editors and jounalists of home interest magazines, at which the attributes of the chair were demonstrated, encouraging them to feature it editorially. *Ideal Home* had previewed the chair in the spring and thought it so good that they decided to feature it in a competition in their November issues with twenty Recliners as prizes. With a circulation of 177,825 and an estimated readership of 2,772,000 this would quickly bring the new chair to a wide audience. Again, arrangements in the publishing world are made many months in advance of publication, and details of the competition were being printed long before any chairs were actually produced.

For the representatives who would present the chair to the majority of trade customers, the author wrote a twenty page booklet. This formed the basis of several Sales Conferences at which the chair was introduced. Normally they would have been equipped with a sample chair, but the weight and bulk of the Recliner prevented that. Nevertheless, from photographs alone it was difficult to adequately demonstrate all the novel features and its action. The author suggested a short colour film. It would have considerable audio-visual impact and capture the buyer's attention. A number of portable projectors could be circulated among representatives, each having the use of this powerful sales aid for a period of two weeks. This, of course, was long before the advent of the video camera.

A budget of a few hundred pounds was set, and the author then spent several hectic weeks scripting, shooting, editing and recording to make a four and a half minute promotion 8mm film. Vernons had already completed the photography and the same background and female model was used. Vic Card assisted at a small studio in the West End usually more occupied with pin-up models. The film proved an outstanding success, both as a means of communication and as a novel method of presentation, which in many shops had the added advantage of being seen by all the sales staff.

Another factor which created considerable trade interest was the introduction of acrylic velvet to the upholstery fabric market. Velvet has always been a sumptuous and expensive fabric, painstakingly woven in silk or wool on hand looms, and had become too expensive and unsuitable on everyday upholstery. Machine woven cotton velvet, introduced to reach the mass market, was far less expensive but unsuitable for use on upholstery as it marked easily, although ideal for curtains where the lack of the traditional sheen of silk was advantageous. Introduction of acrylic fibre made it possible to weave lustrous velvet pile fabrics which had many of the characteristics of silk. The vast Bayer chemical complex at Leverkusen had completed many years of development on the extrusion of acrylics and was finally able to market its fibre under the trade name of 'Dralon'. The Belgian textile industry was quick to see the possibilities and was soon using the yarn to weave strong upholstery velvets. The soft pile had good durability, combined with cleaning properties which other fabrics lacked. Above all it was the attractive spectrum of yarn dyed-colours and the rich sheen of the pile, at affordable prices, which immediately appealed to the housewife.

Of course it was not long before other chemical firms were offering acrylic yarns to the weavers at lower cost than 'Dralon' and as is usual with the loose terminology often used in trade, many of these were incorrectly sold described as 'Dralon' rather than 'acrylic', and were often unsuitable for use on upholstery. Parker Knoll Textiles in 1966 introduced their first high quality 'Dralon' pile velvet under the name 'Draycott' and used it for the first time on the Recliner. The retail price in Draycott rose to £88 15s 6d, well above the lowest price, but such was the appeal of this new fabric that it proved irresistible.

The advent of acrylic pile fabrics in general brought about an amazing transformation in public taste for upholstery covers. For years uncut moquette with a wool pile had been recognised as the hardest and cleanest upholstery fabric, and was widely use in the Parker Knoll cover ranges. However, moquette had been imitated and cheapened. When acrylic velvet appeared there was an almost instantaneous switch away from uncut moquette. Alongside this effect, retailers started another vogue by displaying the N30 Recliner covered in black PVC vinyl, which looked a bit like leather, although it was far removed. A large demand built up for the N30 chair covered in vinyl, mostly black, no doubt prompted by expectation of durability. But why black? There was a time when, in the upholstery shop, the hundreds of Recliners in sight appeared to be entirely covered in either Draycott velvet or black vinyl. The vogue for black vinyl lasted for five years and finished as suddenly as it started, whereas the appeal of good velvets made with 'Dralon' fibres has continued.

Forecasting the required output was a difficult business and 600 chairs were ordered for display by retailers between the mid-July launch and 1 October. So great was the rush that 897 had been ordered by the end of August, and the snowball effect continued until almost 2,000 chairs were ordered by 1 October. This presented the factory with the impossible task of starting output considerably above the original figures. The first 67 chairs were delivered on schedule by 4 September, with weekly production progressively increasing towards the hundred level, but little could be done immediately to exceed factory plans. Consequently delivery delays became inevitable, with retailers being warned in mid-October that they should quote 11-13 weeks for delivery and that no more orders could be accepted before Christmas. On the other hand it would have been a bold spirit indeed who could have assured the factory in April that they could plan from the outset for 200 chairs a week.

Long before the initial distrubution to retailers, another 1,056 chairs were ordered by post during November alone, quite apart from another 781 sold by representatives to replace stocks immediately sold.

The competition run by *Ideal Home* attracted over 6,000 entries by the end of November, after which the twenty prize winners were asked to choose their covering and were presented with their chair.

The demand for the N30 soon began to pose distribution problems. When Recliners were included in orders they had to be separated and sent to Cornwell Norton to be scheduled into production. It was not long before delivery of Recliners failed to synchronise with the Parker Knoll chairs on any order, giving rise to increasing dissatisfaction.

Early in 1967 it was decided that, as the chair was made at Chipping Norton, it should become part of the Cornwell Norton range and be sold under that brand. This dramatic and potentially dangerous remedy of switching brand names, meant that the Parker Knoll sales team, which has successfully launched and promoted the Recliner, now had to abandon it to the smaller subsidiary. Until then, every effort had been made to maintain a separate identity for each Company.

The Parker Knoll Recliner chair was henceforth described as the N30 Norton Recliner in all advertising and promotional literature, production of which was transferred from Vernon's hand and placed with Stillwells, the agency handling Cornwell Norton. The changeover had other repercussions. Retailers were selling the Recliner from the selection of covering materials in the Parker Knoll pattern books, which was larger than that for Cornwell Norton. The Norton models were only available in plain fabrics. Arrangements had to be made to supply the Chipping Norton factory with lengths of any Parker Knoll material specified. Eventually the whole Parker Knoll range had to be put into stock there and endless problems arose when customers, buying Recliners in Parker Knoll covers, also wanted the Cornwell Norton range in the same material. Cornwell Norton had also operated a policy of restricting accounts to only the largest house furnishers and stores, but now had to make supplies available to every retailer buying the N30. This proved an advantage, widening the network of dealerships, creating greater interest in the range.

It was plain that to handle such problems as well as producting planning and customer liaison for Cornwell Norton, an independent administration was required and Hugh Cartwright asked that the author, who was already dealing with the Novella problem, be seconded from Parker Knoll. Until then the Chipping Norton factory had been seen as purely a production unit. The only sales liaison had been that provided by Dane Baskerville during his periodic visits.

Retailers were primarily anxious to obtain delivery of their orders for what had swiftly become the best selling new chair in the trade for years and, once the situation was explained to them, were not unduly concerned that N30 Recliners would in future be supplied by 'another Parker Knoll company', just so long as delivery dates could be given and kept. Assured that all other policies would continue as before, they accepted the switchover with astonishing docility. The factory made valiant efforts with N30 production, ensuring an increasing weekly supply to the hungry market which, happily, wanted more and still more. No longer was the Norton factory short of work.

The appeal of blending the N30 Recliner chair into a comprehensive room furnishing scheme was greatly increased when a matching three-seat settee and non-reclining easy chair were introduced in June 1967. This 'Norton' group was soon featured widely in colour advertising and has been a great success ever since. The Norton Recliner chair celebrated its 25th birthday in 1991, by which time 240,689 had been sold, firmly placing the chair among the Parker Knoll classics.

In Autumn 1969 retailers were asked to choose their own ads.

A CRY FROM THE HEART.

One husband minus Christmas gift
As delivery quoted mid-Jan
For 'recliner' dressed in P.V.C.
Oh, poor unfortunate man !

Ordered for me by small local shop
Davies, Stafford Street, Norwich
Please, please try and expedite
Oh, heck - what rhymes with Norwich !

I know that you will do your best
For that man I idolise
With an empty stocking at the foot of his bed
If my secret doesn't materialise

I can picture him there, lucky dog
Spending Christmas in 'that' chair
Please please please let it be, just for me
And I'll wish you a Prosperous New Year !!

Your plea we just could not ignore
Your plight has struck us to the core
And so with haste we do consign
The means by which you can recline

We hope your gift he will adore
And for many months are o'er
A second one he will procure
For you to join in the rest cure

Your other problem's not forgot
Our Company's poet thought a lot
He hopes that when the "thing's" in Norwich
It won't be splashed with boiling Porridge!

MIRACLE MAKER

ABOVE: Customers often sought fast delivery — especially in November 1966, when the Recliner was in short supply. This customer struck the right chord and the Sales Office responded. LEFT: The Florian won RIGHT: an award and sold for 20 years.

On the Table

During CHJ's partcipation in the Furniture Promotion Council in 1964 and 1965, and when the first nationwide survey of the public attitude towards purchasing furniture was carried out, he came into direct contact with several of the larger market research and advertising agencies, and probably gained a new insight into their philosophy of the 'total marketing concept'.

Hugh Cartwright had expressed his own view soon after he joined the Company on the way in which Sales Department operated: 'efficient in their way, but could be considerably improved'.

The Board decided in July 1966 to re-organise Sales and Marketing by redefining the responsibilities of its Directors and Managers to give the Boad a more direct and centralised control of the complete operation.

Geoffrey Alpe continued as Director in charge of Marketing with responsibility for 'interpretation, implementation and control of policy laid down by the Board on all Marketing activities'. Responsible to him were Dane Baskerville, who was recalled from the struggling Cornwell Norton operation, to take up the position of Marketing Manager to 'exercise overall control of all Marketing activities of the whole organisation (Parker Knoll and Cornwell Norton) including the Chief Designer. Also responsible to the Marketing Manager were the Tapestry Buyer and the author, who became Market Statistician.

Separate Boardroom responsibility for selling, as distinct from marketing, was established by the appointment of John Arnold as Director in charge of sales, responsible for 'creation, organisation and management of all sales forces to carry out the Company's marketing plan'. Both Retail and Contracts Sales Divisions already had their own Sales Managers who, together with the Sales Office Manager, became responsible to John Arnold.

Because so little information existed about the furniture industry, the whole area was almost virgin territory to the researcher, and offered many opportunities.

It was not long before the pressure of events at Chipping Norton forced a change of plan. The author in September 1966 took on the additional job of what amounted to all Sales Office Management functions for Cornwell Norton.

To combine Chipping Norton liaison with Market Statistician, was asking the impossible. Chipping Norton generated forty-eight new complaints during one month with a total of 105 already on hand.

The author was transferred to Cornwell Norton to act as Manager in charge of new Cornwell Norton sales-factory organisation. The first requirement was to set up a Cornwell Norton Sales office. Norton Sales Office was located inthe building at Frogmoor which now houses the Chairman and Company Secretary's offices. Here, a staff of ten was somehow crammed into the limited space. Ken Sharpe joined the Company at Frogmoor in November 1966 and became a member of the small Cornwell Norton team.

Dane Baskerville lost no time in reviewing the model ranges of both Companies and presenting proposals for cutting out weak selling lines to make way for new projects. Several three-piece suites of conventional wood frame construction were already in the pipeline for Cornwell Norton. These were the Cherrywood, the Gitana and Tabor. Unfortunately, by the time they came into production in1967 they had already been overtaken by the Recliner which had rapidly absorbed production resources. Nevertheless, they formed the basis of a regular Cornwell Norton range of modern style upholstery, around which their first colour catalogue was published in August 1967. The modified Novella models were discontinued by spring 1968, while the Cherrywood suite did not sell and was dropped after the first year. The other two suites sold moderately well and made a useful contribution for two years. The strength of demand for the Norton Recliner, and increasingly for the matching settee and chair, required steady expansion of production and transport.

Design and prototype work on several new models for the Parker Knoll design programme was too far advanced to stop and these eventually came into production in 1968 and 1969. Several failed to sell in sufficient quantities and ran for less than two years. Others, such as the Florian Group of three chairs and matching settee, which had such elegant, sculpted lines, became an instant and outstanding success, continuing in production as best sellers until 1989. The Florian chair soon attracted the attention of the design committee of the Furniture Makers Guild who awarded it their Guild certificate of excellence for design and quality of workmanship.

One early step taken by Dane Baskerville in his new position was to bring forward another Recliner chair for Parker Knoll, to compensate for the 'loss' to Cornwell Norton. This was the Novarra PK1006, mechanically the same as the Norton but in a much more modern style, accompanied by a matching easy chair and settee. This was launched in the midsummer of 1967 and achieved substantial sales until 1971. To facilitate production in the confines of the High Wycombe Upholstery Shop, these models were produced in components by the breakdown method and finally brought together on an assembly jig. Gerald Rushby was responsible for this operation. Today he is Production Manager at Chipping Norton.

Also in 1967, the Frith wing chair, first made in the 1950s, was reintroduced, together with a small two-seater settee to match the long-running and successful Froxfield chair. These two extra pieces formed another unique furnishing group in traditional style, which has achieved best selling status ever since.

For a Company with a reputation built on quality and excellence, design limitations imposed by striving for a low selling price can be positively detrimental. In 1966 the failure of the Quartet group was attributed to their having been 'built down' to achieve price. A new group, the Langdale, was created, the design closely resembling the lines of the failed Quartet, but these models were aimed at the top market, without any compromise on cost.

A press preview to introduce the Langdale Group to the assembled journalists from the women's and home interest magazines as well as national papers was held at the Berners Hotel in London on 11 February 1967. They went off to write their editorials while similar previews for trade buyers were staged up and down the country. Colour advertisements had been booked to appear at the beginning of March in the *Observer* and *Weekend Telegraph*, together with black and white insertions in the *Guardian* and *Telegraph*. The whole operation fell absolutely flat. Few trade buyers were prepared to place vital initial orders. By midsummer only 367 wing chairs had been sold and only a handful of settees and other models; barely more than a week's production! This was the most complete rejection of any new models within the Company's long experience. Altogher only 1,765 of all four Langdale models had been sold by July 1968, eighteen months after introduction, when they were scrapped. Recrimininations between factory and sales departments were indeed bitter and the sales force's confidence in management was seriously eroded.

The risks of designing, testing and putting new models into production are considerable. All is staked on the Marketing Manager's confident belief in the new product he has developed. The long run of design successes enjoyed by Parker Knoll over the years are testimony to their usually accurate judgement. Things can go wrong when a Company diversifies into a field in which it has no previous experience. This occurred with the PK8999 dining table.

The concept of Parker Knoll making a dining table was sufficient to raise a few eyebrows in the trade, quite apart from the fact that, for many house furnishers and particularly departmental stores, cabinet furniture was a separate department with its own buyer. The idea evolved from the success of the Florian group, leading to a suggestion by Geoffrey Alpe and his Sales Managers that, by adding dining chairs in the same style, the appeal of the range could be widened still further. Dane Baskerville considered that it would be little use offering dining chairs alone, as this would leave the interested customer looking for a suitable table and sideboard to stand with them. He argued that logically this meant that a comprehensive Florian style dining group should be introduced. Designs were produced which resulted ina table of drop-leaf design, two feet in width which extended to six feet. The drawback of many extending tables is that, when extended, the necessary extra legs are often in the way of the people seated.

The Florian design was intended to overcome this problem by placing the legs supporting the centre section of the table under the centre of the top rather than in the four corners, obtaining balance from full-width runner-type feet. The table was extended to seat six, or more, by raising the flaps and drawing out a single leg from the middle section to support them in the centre of each end, doing away with the more conventional swinging 'gateleg' support. As Parker Knoll lacked veneering and panel making facilities, it was decided to make the furniture in solid beech which looked its best in natural finish. The matching dining chairs reflected the distinctive Florian ladderback style.

These models were presented for the first time to the trade at the 1969 Furniture Exhibition where they were the central display feature of the Parker Knoll stand. It was not long before worried expressions appeared on representatives' faces as buyers, shocked by the unexpected, rejected the philosophy behind the design as too unconventional, pointing out the limitations of achieving acceptable stained finished on beech and positively declining to order in natural beech which most considered unsaleable. Word passed round the Exhibition of Parker Knoll's venture into the cabinet business bringing many manufacturers to see for themselves. Representatives sensed disbelief as well as astonishment at the reactions of their customers and they were understandably demoralised. The table was hurriedly removed from the stand, while the projected advertising campaign to bring the 'Dining Group' to the attention of the public was hurriedly curtailed. The prototype sideboard was abandoned and never produced. Finally, and incredibly, despite the radical approach adopted in the design, nobody had discovered that, when extended, the table was unstable and could be tipped up by leaning heavily on the ends: sufficient to bring any dinner party to a sudden end! And so a veil was drawn over the whole episode, during which only seventy tables and 687 dining chairs were sold. The Company returned to the safety of the market for chairs and upholstery in which it had achieved such remarkable success.

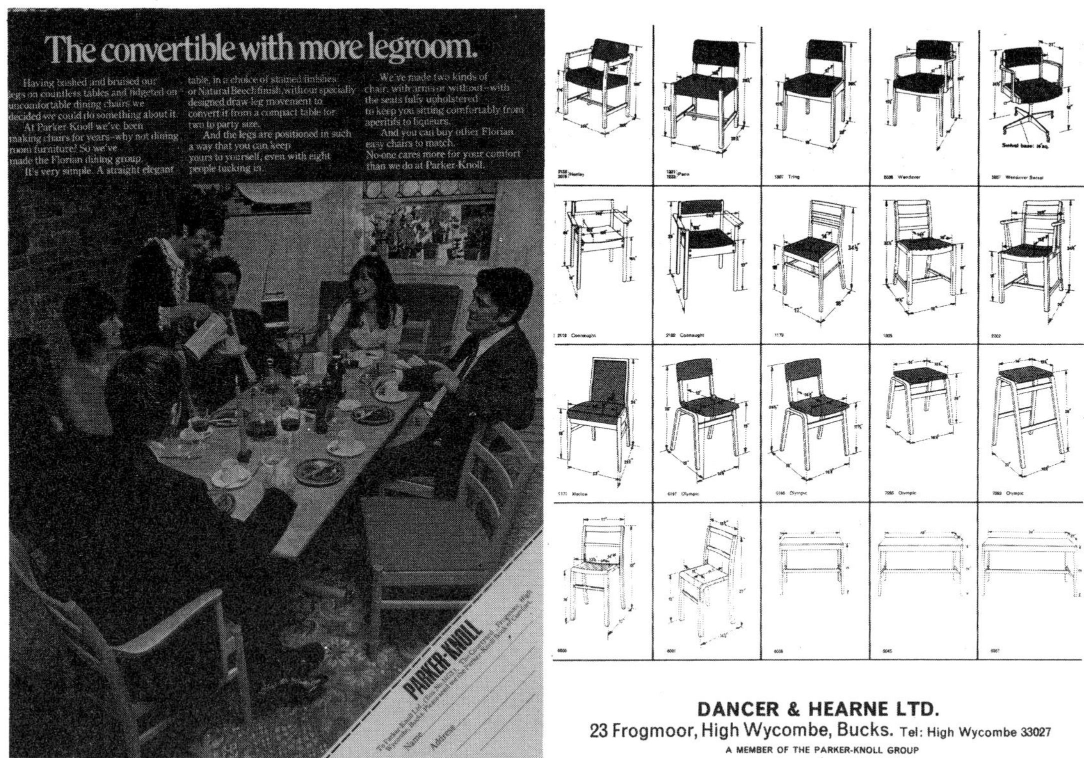

LEFT: The Florian dining group fared badly at the Furniture Exhibition of 1969 — this advertisement never appeared. RIGHT: The Dancer & Hearne Contracts product range. BELOW: The 1950s Frith chair was reintroduced in 1967 with a settee and joined the Froxfield.

Hit and Miss

By mid-1967, although trading conditions were difficult, life at both High Wycombe and Chipping Norton factories had settled down. The Chipping Norton factory contributed 34,306 pieces in the year ending July 1967. The Parker Knoll range was still heavily orientated towards the lighter type of wood arm occasional chairs of lower unit value and contributed 136,785 pieces. Turnover for the Group for the year ending July 1967 reached £3,687,144 and yielded a profit before tax of £215,048 which, although lower than that achieved in 1963-4, was a considerable improvement on the £159,595 of the previous year.

Although the provincial Parker Knoll showrooms provided a useful 'shop window' and linked up with the national and local press advertising, the number of visitors placing orders had declined to a level which made them no longer cost-effective. It was decided to close them as the leases expired and to work more closely with local retailers, many of whom viewed the showrooms with a jaundiced eye. The first to close was Birmingham in 1967, followed by Manchester and Bristol by 1971.

The need to revitalise the Parker Knoll range of chairs had become apparent after the transfer of the Recliner to the Cornwell Norton range early in 1967. For six months retailers' attention focused almost entirely on the N30 Recliner and Parker Knoll representatives found great difficulty in booking orders for even the well established models, putting some departments on short time. Of the new models introduced in 1967 only the Florian chairs were successful while the attempt at a more modern upholstered style in the Merrywood group failed to sell, only achieving 1,975 of all three styles in the ten months before it was dropped. This was no use at all.

As all production at Chipping Norton would in future use conventional wood frame construction, and if the progress being made there with larger upholstered furniture was maintained, there could be a problem. The capacity of the woodworking departments at High Wycombe might limit the chair frame needed for both factories. The answer was another factory. In his report for year ending July 1967 the Chairman commented:
'while the net profit is higher than last year the total dividend is less. This is because your Directors wish to increase the liquid assets of the Company to enable future expansion to be financed from the Group's own resources as far as possible, and this policy must be continued during the year.'

This resulted in October 1967 in a bid for the old-established firm of Dancer & Hearne, who had a large factory at Penn Street between High Wycombe and Amersham. Dancer & Hearne was one of the oldest chair manufacturers in the High Wycombe area, with a history back to the 'chair bodging' days of the last century, but had fallen on hard times, showing losses in 1962 and 1963 and profits of only £9,000 and £14,000 since then, with a nett loss of £35,7699 for the end ending 31 July 1967. Their business lay in suppling large quantity contracts for small chairs, particularly to schools and Government departments. Dining chairs were also made for other cabinet firms in the industry. They still had an impressive facility for moulding plywood shapes, an inheritance from wartime days, when they were fully engaged on production of Mosquito fuselages.

The first cash offer by Parker Knoll, worth £264,000, said by the City press to be not over-generous, was topped by a bid from Yatton Furniture of Bristol of 10s 6d for each five shilling share; 2s 6d above the PK offer. This was recommended for acceptance by the D. & H. Board, but a second bid was then made by PK which was worth almost 12 shillings for each Dancer and Hearne share. This was finally accepted and the process of rationalising the production of the two companies began. Mr A. Cecil Hearne remained on the new Board to which CHJ was appointed Chairman, together with Geoffrey Alpe, Hugh Cartwright and John Arnold, with Company Secretary Peter Bolding to take charge of administration. CHJ expressed the group's intention to expand Dancer and Hearne's substantial business in contract furniture, the bulk of which was sold to the Ministry of Works and Buildings and to schools. The facilities of the Group would also be used to provide additonal production capacity for furniture marketed under the Parker Knoll and Cornwell Norton labels.

The range of models offered and produced by Dancer and Hearne was extensive, including many Windsors — as many as 360 different models. At the Meuropam Exhibition in 1967 they displayed, doubtless to emphasise their long history in the chair-making trade, a Windsor double backed 'chair' which had first been made by them when the firm was founded in 1848, 'to provide comfortable seating for ladies with crinolines'. Had orders been placed for the model they would have been supplied.

An early job was to prune this selection to a manageable level, retaining only items in current demand such as the Knightsbridge chair by Ronald Carter. Tom Jourdan, CHJ's youngest son, had joined the Company in April 1968 after serving an engineering apprenticeship and gaining a BSc at City University, as well as spending six months with IBM in Germany at Sindelfingen. He quickly found himself appointed Production Manager of Conversion and Mill at Penn Street, while Upholstery operations were managed by Derek Stewart. Tom recalls that he found a chaotic situation and what he describes as industrial anarchy, while most of the equipment was out of date and uneconomic. Because of difficult trading conditions generally, orders placed for chairs by dining room suite manufacturers were often delayed indefinitely or simply cancelled outright.

The merging of the two organisations inevitably led to some redundancies in the Sales and Administration of Dancer and Hearne and to several members of their team joining the Parker Knoll Sales force. Among these were Ron Hearne and Derek Thornton who became representatives in the Retail Division, and Brian Gould who joined the Contracts Division early in 1968. Dane Dew, who joined the Company in 1954 as an assistant at the London Showrooms, and moved to Contracts Division in 1958, became Contracts Manager for Parker Knoll in 1958. He was appoined Sales Manager of Dancer and Hearne in March 1968.

When Parker Knoll Ltd took over Dancer and Hearne it was literally a lock, stock and barrel affair. With the factory went the unexpired 967 years of Dancer and Hearne's 990 year lease of the historic Hit and Miss public house at Penn Street. This hostelry had been in the hands of the Hearne family since the days when they turned from 'chair bodging' in the local beechwoods to manufacturing in a modern factory. Once a terrace of cottages, the Hit and Miss, which stands right in the centre frontage of the original Dancer and Hearne factory at Penn Street, has served many generations of chair makers, as reflected by the old chair makers' tools and copper printing plates for Windsor chairs (once used to illstrate the firms catalogues), which now decorate its walls. Geoffrey Alpe was instrumental in broadening the trade of the Hit and Miss beyond the traditional beer and skittles' image of a country pub, by creating alongside the bars, a small but good class restaurant.

A happy innovation occurred early in 1968 when the Parker Knoll Board decided to give recognition to their longest-serving employees by founding the '25 Club'. At that time 32 serving employees had completed 25 years or more in the Company's employ, together with another five who, although retired, had also achieved this distinction. These founding members had between them contriuted some 3,400 years of service to Parker Knoll, Dancer and Hearne and other Companies in the Group. They were all entertained by the Company at the inaugural dinner at the Red Lion Hotel in High Street on 23 May 1968, when all were presented with an engraved gold watch and club membership badge. Toasting the future of the club, the Chairman remarked that the '25 Club' was recognition of the continuity afforded between one generation and the next and he hoped that the club emblem and tie would be worn by an increasing number of people.

The '25 Club' dinner has taken place annually ever since. Membership has continued to expand and over 200 have joined so far, having served the Company for well in excess of 5,000 years.

After early difficulties, sales of Cornwell Norton Upholstery improved steadily, until the Company had finally achieved its status and identity in the trade as an independent member of the Parker Knoll Group. The time had arrived to separate the sales and production services which had for so long been carried out for Cornwell Norton by High Wycombe.

This was done in two stages; first, a separate Despatch Office, managed by Ted Breeze and equipped with a 'Saide' machine was opened at Chipping Norton in March 1969, when it produced all factory documentation from batches of orders and tapes sent down from High Wycombe. The second and more difficult stage of transferring the Cornwell Norton Sales Office from High Wycombe commenced in the summer of 1969 and opened for business on 1 January 1970.

The author started the new Sales Office from scratch with new people. Ken Sharpe was appointed as Sales Office Manager and moved to live in Chipping Norton, while the nine staff required were recruited locally. A portable office cabin was erected at the rear of the factory to be used initially as the training classroom and on 1 January, the fully operating Sales Office.

The office at Wycombe was wound up immediately and the staff absorbed into various parts of the Parker Knoll Sales office.

The Hit and Miss — an unexpected diversion which came with Dancer & Hearne.

ABOVE: Long service members of the 25 Club in 1977 — Ron Styles, buyer; Jack True, wood machining manager; Martin Jourdan, Chairman, John Pryce, Yorkshire and the NE representative; Richard Clibbens, Lancs and Cheshire. BELOW: Standing — S. G. Carter, R. Howland, W. Johnson and Martin Jourdan; sitting — G. Moss, R. Oxlade and R. J. Seaman.

Death and Departure

The last of the four Parker brothers connected with Frederick Parker & Sons and Parker Knoll Ltd, Mr William Parker, died at the age of 90 on 6 May 1969. He joined the original company of Frederick Parker & Sons in 1891. His death meant a sad break with the older generation of Directors.

Breaking new ground early in 1969, Cornwell Norton successfully launched a small drop end sofa, the N42 Codetta, which was reminiscent in many ways, except styling, of pieces with this function in Victorian times. A matching easy chair was available to make a furnishing group suitable for small flats. Once again the author and Ken Sharpe turned to film production. The result was a film entitled *A Quart in a Pint Pot* which emphasised the extra seating which could be obtained when needed in a small space, as well as provision of a spare bed at instant notice. To illustrate this theme many hours were spent filming a quart being poured into a pint jug which had a hole in the bottom. This was fitted with a pipe for drainage, the rate of which was controlled by a person under the kitchen table pinching the pipe to restrict the outflow. After many trials the effect was achieved — for just a few seconds on the screen.

About this time the designers had created a small storage unit in teak veneer which was put into production for Cornwell Norton and, with poetic licence, known as the Canterbury. While this was a useful piece of occasional furniture, it was outside the mainstream of the upholstery business and did not sell, leaving large stocks. It was decided to clear these by staging a promotion to increase sales of the Codetta sofa by supplying a Canterbury free of charge with all orders placed during November and December. The promotion did little to increase sales although all 300 Canterburys were cleared by the end of the year.

At the time of the bid for Dancer and Hearne it was no secret that they were short of orders, with several large contracts deferred by Government Departments due to restrictions on spending. Derek Boult, Works Manager at Penn Street, decided to leave and in July 1969, Tom Jourdan, who had run their Conversion Shop and Mill for the past year, was appointed his successor on 1 October. Before that he took up a different appointment as husband to Sue Rolph. Their marriage took place on 9 September, and Tom recalls that, on return from honeymoon at the end of the month, the first thing he was told by EHC was that Dancer and Hearne was to be closed down in March 1970.

The closure had been under consideration for some time. The Ministry of Education had decided to abandon wooden, plywood seated school chairs. It had purchased many hundreds of thousands each year, but now favoured metal-frame chairs with plastic seats, so the decision was made. Loss of orders for these highest volume lines could not be readily replaced.

The cost of this abortive operation had been considerable, heavily draining the Group's profits for the year to July 1969. These fell to £218,404 from the previous year's record £296,007 despite an increase in turnover of almost £800,000, resulting in no final dividend compared with 15% the previous year. Redundancies began in January 1970 and all machinery was auctioned in February. A potential purchaser for the site had been found but was delaying completion. The final decline of Dancer & Hearne was another drain on Group profit. When the half year results to 31 January were announced they revealed a severe drop to £156,000 from £218,000.

In two short years, expectations from the successful acquisition of Dancer and Hearne had been completely shattered. Parker Knoll had expanded considerably since 1946. The furniture division now included the separate subsidiaries, Cornwell Norton Ltd, Dancer and Hearne Ltd and still operating with extremely difficulty, Parker Knoll France SARL. Additionally, Parker Knoll Textiles Ltd and G. P. & J. Baker Ltd formed a separate Textiles Division. The ordinary share capital in each of these companies was wholly owned except in France, where 75% was owned by the Company. The Chairman believed that the time had arrived to re-structure the Group by separating control of the operating companies from the 'Head Office and accounting functions'. To this end a new company, Parker Knoll Furniture Ltd, was formed in July 1969 to control sale and manufacture of Parker Knoll Furniture Ltd, which became a separate profit centre within the Group.

As a result the Joint Managing Directorship under which Parker Knoll had operated since 1946 could no longer continue. C. H. Jourdan became Chairman and sole Managing Director of Parker Knoll Ltd and proposed that Geoffrey Alpe took integrated control of both Sales and Production operations of the furniture company as Managing Director of Parker Knoll Furniture Ltd. Unfortunately the reconstruction could not be agreed unanimously among members of the Board. So strongly were feelings expressed that, despite every attempt made to restructure the Company in a way which met the view of all, an impasse was reached. Following a long and successful period of harmonious working, it was difficult for Geoffrey Alpe to accept the major changes. Attempts to resolve the situation continued for some months without success until Geoffrey Alpe formally resigned his directorship and left the Company in November 1969. An extraordinary general meeting on 27 November 1969 asked him to accept the title of President for five years and Hugh Cartwright was appointed Managing Director of Parker Knoll Furniture Ltd.

As no statement was made to the staff until the new Board was appointed, the upset inevitably created a strained atmosphere which was apparent to all Managers in both Sales and factory. This episode was an unsettling and depressing end to the sixties, particularly to those in Sales who had worked closely under Geoffrey Alpe for over twenty years. His creative flair had influenced both advertising and the choice of covering materials, and particularly designs for the whole chair range, many of which had enjoyed tremendous success. At the same time, his departure had little disrupting effect upon day-to-day business, leadership of which Hugh Cartwright now took over. He saw his first job as the 'liberation of the Sales department' as he put it, and its unification with Production by bringing the two departments together in meetings where the views of both could be discussed. To bring this about Dane Baskerville was appointed Marketing Manager and moved into the office adjoining that of EHC.

Another change, small but significant, soon became apparent in Sales Department, when Managers and staff realised that their new Managing Director always addressed them by their Christian names rather than their surnames as in the past. This simple change, in line with modern attitudes to staff relationships, did much to ensure acceptance and respect for Hugh Cartwright from many Sales staff with whom he had had little previous contact, which to them, made him something of an unknown quantity. Hugh Cartwright moved his office from the factory to the Sales building at Frogmoor.

Blow for High Wycombe furniture industry

250 LOSE JOBS IN FACTORY CLOSURE

THIS IS OUR VERY VERSATILE CHRISTMAS PRESENT
THE CANTERBURY WORTH £25-10s.*
which is given free with every Codetta Sofa ordered before Christmas for normal delivery

More than 250 workers at the Penn Street factory of Parker-Knoll Ltd., the High Wycombe furniture manufacturers, will lose their jobs by the closure of the factory—due to a sharp decline in orders.

Axing of the factory — formerly owned by Dancer and Hearne Ltd. — comes at a time when extensive areas of the furniture industry in Wycombe are in the doldrums.

There are already 421 men and 106 women unemployed in the Wycombe area and 167 furniture workers on short time — with very few vacancies in the industry.

And Mr. C. H. Jourdan, chairman of Parker-Knoll Ltd., told the 'Free Press' that taking on of any of the men from Penn Street at the High Wycombe and Chipping Norton factories of the company was "virtually ruled out."

DIVIDEND BLOW

The company announced this week that it would not pay a final dividend, and the interim dividend of five per cent was all the shareholders would get.

The century-old works at Penn Street were taken over by Parker-Knoll Ltd. nearly two years ago in what Mr. Jourdan described as a "rescue operation". But this had been defeated by the drop in orders.

"The Penn Street factory had a fall off in the high volume areas of the market, such as school furniture, where the trend is towards metal and plastics," said Mr. Jourdan.

"In these areas we have come down sharply in profit. We did increase sales in the models designed by Dancer and Hearne, their catalogue models, and we also put work into the factory, required for the rest of the organisation.

"But that increase and the in-

Mr. C. H. Jourdan

feed of work nowhere near compensated for the very heavy cut back in orders in the high volume area.

NO ALTERNATIVE

"We do not want to get into a position where we could sink ourselves, and there was no alternative but to close the Penn Street works.

"We had to cut down before there was any chance of an adverse effect on our other sections at High Wycombe and Chipping Norton, and our textile section, which are all strong.

"It is a tragedy for the men that this had to come at a time when things are pretty bad for the industry."

REDUNDANCY PAY

Many of the men at Penn Street — they come mainly from the Wycombe and Amersham areas — have worked there for a long time, and are getting on in life.

It was a blessing, said Mr. Jourdan, that there was a redundancy payments scheme which would ease the burden on the workers.

It is expected that redundancy payments will total in the region of £80,000, to be paid half by the company and half by the government.

Mr. Jourdan said that the company had been in touch with the unions before the closure was announced, and it was co-operating with them and the Ministry of Employment in efforts to place the men in new jobs.

No definite date has been fixed for the closure of the factory, and there were orders to be completed, said Mr. Jourdan.

As each department completed its work it would be closed, and it would be about four weeks before all the departments were closed.

"DIFFICULTY"

Mr. Stephen Brook, of the Ministry of Employment office at High Wycombe, said that it was feared that most of the Penn Street workers would find some difficulty in getting other work in the area.

Arrangements had already been made to interview them and officials would be going to the works. Some of the men might be able to re-train for other jobs under the government scheme.

To qualify for redundancy pay a worker must have been employed continuously by the firm for two years.

The rate of redundancy pay is: for each year between the ages of 18 and 21, a half-a-week's pay; for each year between 22 and 40, one week's pay; for each year between 41 and 64, 1½ weeks' pay.

ABOVE: Jobs went in the recession of 1969, along with dividends.
LEFT: The firm made determined efforts with the Cornwell Norton Codetta drop-end sofa and a free Canterbury with every sale.

mid-week

No 77 February 25 1970 4d.

FREE PRESS

RAG WEEK PICTURES ARE FEATURED ON PAGE 2

THE £750,000 GLARE THAT LIT UP WYCOMBE

Airborne lion

Parker-Knoll chairman says—

'FULL PRODUCTION IN FIVE WEEKS'

FOLLOWING LAST WEDNESDAY'S DEVASTATING BLAZE at the factory premises of High Wycombe's noted furniture firm of Parker-Knoll Limited, Mr. C. H. Jourdan—chairman and managing director—has stated that the company hopes to resume full production within the next four to five weeks.

RONALD GOODEARL took these pictures at the height of Wednesday night's blaze at the Parker-Knoll factory. Technical note for other photographers: he used Ektachrome Professional roll film in an old Zeiss Ikonta camera, giving a transparency of 3¼ by 2¼ inches. The exposure was one second at f 4.

County budget up nearly £5m.

A RECORD BUDGET for 1970-71 of £43,769,830 — a massive increase of £4,975,330 on the 1969-70 estimates — will go before Bucks County Council tomorrow (Thursday). If approved, as it almost certainly will be, it will send up the county rate by 6d. to 9s. 4d.

ABOVE: The news was apalling on 17 February 1970 — fire destroyed the factory but not the firm. BELOW: The despatch office and loading bay were ablaze in this dramatic shot.

Burning Issues

The 1970s started well for both Parker Knoll Furniture and Cornwell Norton when they both introduced new models displayed for the first time at the annual Furniture Exhibition at Earls Court. Trade buyers were quick to indicate approval by their readiness to place orders, creating that tingle of excitement, familiar at Exhibitions, which senses the beginnings of a best-selling success. For some considerable time, although Parker Knoll had introduced a large number of new designs most failed to achieve the necessary high volume, repeating sales vital to sustain production.

The innovative new Statesman chair, PK1028 was a departure from conventional wood frame construction, built on a moulded polyurethane shell. For some time the Company had shown interest in the supply and manufacturing facilities for solid foam shells and had visited factories in Scandinavia and Germany. Plenty of shells were available 'off the peg', but they were sold generally and could not be exclusive. A valuable market was being opened up, but no manufacturer was interested in confining a shell design exclusively to the Company and still less in moulding shells to the Company's design.

A stimulant was provided by Vivian Card, the senior representative, who met the Management to report the anxiety of the Sales force that a newly introduced shell chair by Vono was already sweeping the market and selling several thousand a month, while buyers were asking why PK had nothing to offer. To make his point Vivian arrived at the meeting armed with the competitor's chair, which he had purchased himself. Coincidentally Jacksons of Bourne End, also anxious to supply this new facet of the market, had recently equipped themselves to manufacture moulded shells. As long-standing suppliers to the Company they were prepared and able to work closely with it to produce a shell to Parker Knoll design in expanded polyurethane foam, reinforced with glass-fibre: hardboard and plywood inserts provided attachment points for the base unit and upholstery.

Nearly all the chairs already on the market were mounted onto a chromed metal base, but these were generally disappointingly finished and of indifferent quality and engineering, which made them unsuitable. The Company decided to make its own, with five solid afrormosia feet but using a standard swivel and tilt box unit.

Because normal upholstery fabrics had insufficient stretch to allow them to be tailored to fit the contours of the shell, a fabric of knitted construction was needed, although experience showed that fabrics of this type were unlikely to prove durable. A new type of paper-thin plastic surfaced material has recently been created, and was becoming available from several different manufacturers. The trade used the name of one brand — 'Airskin' — as a generic term to describe them all. The technology was new and untried, but Parker Knoll decided to use 'Buckflex' which was made by heat-laminating modified polyurethane films onto a warp-knitted, nylon base cloth. This combined the stretch factor of the cloth with the plastic surface to give the fabric as much durability in use as many of the heaviest upholstery cloths. It also had many desirable traits which the housewife had long wanted, such as easy cleaning with soap and water, anti-static properties which did not attract dust, resistance to hair grease which affected PVC plastic materials and, at the same time, was soft and warm to sit on in contrast to the 'cold' feel of vinyl coverings. This cloth was adopted for the new chair and named 'Astral', available in five colourways, but initially was the only fabric in which the chair could be sold.

From this combination of materials and techniques which were new to the upholstery trade, Parker Knoll had created a best-seller which not only was a different shape, but also a comfortable chair at an economical price.

Over on the adjacent Cornwell Norton Exhibition stand, the excitement was caused by the new Sonata three-piece suite. It was an accepted complaint from representatives and trade buyers that, although many of the smartest suites were designed with low-backed settees because they looked less bulky in small sitting rooms, the majority of the public wanted high-backed settees that provided a full headrest. Very careful thought had been given to the design of the high-backed Sonata suite. Trade buyers at the Exhibition quickly confirmed the Company's thinking. The Sonata suite became another best-selling model and continued so for fourteen years.

Both factories now turned their attention to overcoming teething problems. After the despressed profits and depressing events of the year to July 1969, the Company looked forward to greater success in 1970. Only a few weeks passed before these expectations were rudely shattered.

All was quiet at the High Wycombe factory soon after work finished at 5pm on 17 February 1970. There had been a heavy snowfall the previous night followed by a rapid thaw which left rooftops snowcovered. Elsie Cambray managed the Accounts Department, and stayed late to clear up some work. Arthur Rush, the Security Officer, had just completed checking all factory departments.

'About 6.30 pm I returned to my office by the main gates and came in to have a cup of tea. I looked in my external mirror (which gave a view of the yard) and saw some smoke which I though was steam, (from the boiler house out of sight to the right). I went outside to make sure and saw that the factory was on fire. I immediately called the brigade, but in fractions of a second the factory was going up in flames.'

So began one of the biggest and most disastrous fires in the history of High Wycombe. The town was no stranger to fires in furniture factories, which were full of highly combustible liquids and materials, but the County Chief Fire Officer, Mr William Ward, said it was the biggest fire in the County since the Bucks Fire Brigade was formed in 1948. Twenty appliances and 100 firemen were quickly on the scene but the conflagration swiftly became an inferno, which devoured almost the whole factory, reducing it in two and a half hours to a smouldering ruin. CHJ had arrived home at Lacey Green and was unpacking some new fishing waders, when at 6.30pm Arthur Rush telephoned to tell him the factory was on fire. Together with his son Martin he drove the seven miles back to Wycombe in ten minutes with horn blaring, to find that the whole town centre had been cordoned off by the police to restrain crowds of sightseers. When CHJ persuaded them to let them through on foot and reached the factory it was totally ablaze.

He thought there might be a chance to save the accounts from the top floor of the three storey building, which the flames had not yet reached. He was surprised to find that Elsie Cambray was already trying to do this. The heavy drawers had to be carried down three flights and away from the factory, and it was impossible; they left just before the flames engulfed the block. By this time many employees had arrived to give what help they could, such as driving fully laden vans out of the blazing loading bay, and carrying all the working drawings from the Drawing Office over to Joe Bedwell's house opposite but, with the flames reaching 60 feet in height and the intense heat, they were removed by the police for their own safety.

Initial estimates of damage were put at £700,000, but the threat to jobs was what concerned most who viewed the wreckage the following day. Part of the Machine and Assembly Shops, which had concrete floors, could still be used. The vital Timber Drying Kilns, Conversion Shop, Mill and Spring Making departments were untouched, but the workshops dealing with Polishing, Upholstery, Sewing, Fabric Cutting and Issue Stores, renovations and repairs as well as the loading bay and several loaded vans were all totally destroyed. In addition, all the offices which were located at the factory, those of Accounts, Buying, Company Secretary, Directors, Chairman, the Parlour, and Despatch were lost, the Drawing Office being the only one to escape. Although the subject of much complaint in the past, the fact that the Sales Offices were separately located at Frogmoor, and were untouched, was one small mercy to be thankful for. Another was that the collection of antique chairs had been removed from the factory to release space for production, and stored in Reading only a few weeks previously.

It is thought that the fire started in the upholstery shop or Kapoc store due to spontaneous combustion, and most accounts agree that it spread with incredible speed. The polishing shop was located on the top floor of the three-storey building with the frame making shops below. These were all connected by overhead conveyor which moved assembled chair frames up through the floors to Polishing Shop and, when ready, down two floors and through a tunnel which crossed above the yard, delivering them to the Spring Fitting shop which then passed them on to Upholstery. This section was housed in a large single-storey building which was separated by the yard from the main buiding, but connected to it by the conveyor tunnel. It is throught that, soon after the fire became established inthe Upholstery Shop, the tunnel acted as a chimney through which the heat and flames spread rapidly into the three-storey building. The conveyor space up through the two upper floors enabled the fire to swiftly reach the top floor and the volatile fluids in the Polishing Shop exploded, blowing the walls outwards and the roof off. By this time the flames could be seen for miles around and it was a miracle that no firemen were injured by the collapsing brickwork.

All the Company's Managers had come to the scene during the evening, making it possible for them to attend an emergency meeting with the Directors at the Frogmoor Sales Offices at 9.30 pm. Although everybody was stunned by what they had just witnessed, the Chairman was quick to dispel any gloom and apprehension by focusing thoughts on immediate plans for recovery and starting production. After agreeing the most urgent courses of action by individual Managers they dispersed, arranging to meet and report progress at 9am the next morning. A team from Bovis was called in, arriving in less than an hour to survey the wreckage and organise demolition of all dangerous structures. They also took immediate action to re-roof surviving buildings to provide temporary working accommodation.

During the night a leaflet was produced for all employees, which emphasised the essential need to restart production and deliveries to customers. Stressing that all employees would be kept on the payroll, detailed instructions were given on how to report for duty on the massive clearing up operation, as well as information about plans for the future. Arrangements were made for the payment of wages to continue, calculated on consolidated rates plus the average shop, group or individual bonus.

First thing next day CHJ was able to confirm that immediate salvation was at hand. Production could be restarted at the Dancer and Hearne factory at Penn Street, which was now empty, all machinery having been sold and removed. Everything was swept and clean, awaiting sale of the buildings, negotiations for which were complete, only awaiting the purchaser's signature on the Contract. This was providential, and allowed the Company to withdraw from the sale so as to restart all the destroyed workshops there in the shortest possible time. CHJ even forecast that limited deliveries to customers from Penn Street would be resumed in less than three weeks.

Tom Jourdan, who was designated Works Manager of the now defunct Dancer & Hearne, had completed the rundown and closure of the Dancer and Hearne factory only eighteen days prior to the fire and now had unique responsibility for opening it up again. Not many Works Managers experience such a sudden reversal of fortunes! Together with Derek Stewart as Upholstery Manager, with a team of other Managers from relevant departments and twelve maintenance staff, he moved immedaitely into the main office block at Penn Street to set up his recovery headquarters.

Lists were made of immediate requirements for both equipment and materials which Ron Styles, Buying Officer Manager, had the daunting task of locating and obtaining. Meanwhile the empty workshops were appraised and spaces allocated and marked out.

At High Wycombe the first priority was to get the Machine and Frame Assembly Shops back into operation. The Maintenance Manager and his team worked without a break to re-connect steam, compressed air and electricity supplies, enabling the Conversion Shed to continue normally and the Machine Shops to restart ten days after the fire. The Chair Frame Assembly Shop was working on a limited scale, being held back by some piece parts that had to be machined. A first delivery of 150 assembled chair and settee frames went to Penn Street on the Monday after the fire, increasing the next day to 300, compared with a normal 550 to 600 a day. Within two weeks a temporary building was erected at the end of the Machine Shop, making it possible for still further machining operations to restart.

Generous offers of assistance were made by other manufacturers, both in the town and further afield, while suppliers gave immediate assistance by supplying replacement Spray Booths, Sewing Machines, Upholstery Benches and the mass of other equipment and materials necessary, and production restarted almost as if nothing had happened. It was far from that simple and that it was accomplished so swiftly was thanks to prodigious efforts by everybody in the Company and trade. Inspired by CHJ's dynamic attitude, a tremendous spirit imbued the whole management and workforce, resulting in almost non-stop working by many factory managers.

Only two weeks after the fire, the Polishing Shop restarted at Penn Street and some sewing machinists were at work, but here production was limited by shortage of machines. The forty required were not available and finally had to be purchased in Germany and took three weeks to arrive. Upholsterers started work in their new location three weeks after the fire, completing about 10% of normal production that week. It was hoped that 50% of normal capacity would be achieved by Easter and that all orders currently on hand would be cleared within 13 weeks, with delivery time gradually reduced.

Meanwhile Bovis were busy clearing the spaghetti of twisted girders from the site at Temple End and plans were being formulated for the future. In an exchange of letters with the National Union of Furniture Trade Operatives, Hugh Cartwright wrote of his 'appreciation to the General Secretary and all members, for [their] consideration to people at all levels at Parker Knoll for getting this moving so quickly'. The General Secretary, A. G. Tomkins CBE expressed its 'admiration for the speedy, confident and efficient way the Directors of Parker Knoll have tackled the stupendous task of restoring production after the disastrous fire'. And he added the 'wish to specifically acknowledge the care and regard the Directors have had for the welfare of their workers and the generous financial arrangements made at a time when the management had to face severe financial and technical problems to ensure the continuation of the firm'.

Bert Llewellyn on behalf of the Union Shop Committee also wrote: 'The way the Company has tackled the job has laid the foundation for future Labour Relations. We are sure Parker Knoll will survive this disaster and once again, play a leading role in our Industry'.

The ashen aftermath — total devastation.

ABOVE: The successful Statesman with its matching stool created much excitement at the 1970 Exhibition, but fire stopped work until the Penn Street premises of Dancer & Hearne were resurrected. BELOW: 1970 saw the birth of the Cornwell Norton Sonata suite too.

Rebirth

There was more to it than reopening Penn Street. The Accounts Department was rehoused at Frogmoor. All their records had been destroyed so the first job was to write to all customers asking for a copy of their January statement, from which the ledgers could be re-constructed. All suppliers also had to be asked to do the same, as well as to give details of all unexecuted orders. Over 12,000 letters were mailed and brought a sympathetic and excellent response. From the customer record cards in Sales Office it was possible to extract lists of work in progress, passing through the production at the time of the fire, to make sure they were not overlooked. Sales had to ensure that customers understood Parker Knoll Textiles and Cornwell Norton had not been affected. Very few orders were cancelled. Retailers were also asked to notify any chairs returned for renovation as these had been destroyed.

Offices were reshuffled to economise on space and to make room for Hugh Cartwright, while the Chairman and Company Secretary moved into the small Frogmoor building which had only recently been vacated by Cornwell Norton. Although the ground floor showroom had initially been cleared to house Elsie Cambray and her accounts staff, the space could not be spared. It was needed for the Tapestry Buying Office, which had been ejected in the reshuffle. Parker Knoll Textiles came to the rescue with space in their newly completed warehouse at West End Road, to which Accounts moved. 'Space' it was, consisting of twenty four square feet platforms which formed landings between floors in the warehouse, a vast space filled with racks of materials. Accounts staff desks were scattered only one or two on each landing without telephones and little heating. The 1920s half-timbered three-storey building erected at Frogmoor by Frederick Parker as an extension to his original factory was sublet at the time, but immediate arrangements were made to get it back and convert it to offices. This was completed by the end of May and the long-suffering accounts staff moved back to the top floor where they remain to this day. Contracts Department moved into new offices on the middle floor, which backed onto Sales Office and was connected by an opening in the common wall.

The old Penn Street factory was a godsend, but the Company had to consider its options for the long term. Once the temporary woodworking operations at Wycombe and the finishing and upholstery sections at Penn Street were up and running, the Board and Company Managers embarked on an intensive and detailed study. As Derek Stewart recalled, there was a lot of midnight oil burnt at the Penn Street offices in planning what to do. The factory buildings at Penn Street were large and all on one level, but they were quite old and unsuitable. Derek Stewart as Upholstery Manager had gained wide experience and many ideas on upholstery production from his visits to factories in Sweden, France and the USA. He had worked in eight different places to study floor layouts, production methods and the way they were controlled. He saw that the Company was now in a position to plan a new factory from scratch, an ideal opportunity.

It was decided to extend the Chipping Norton factory to carry out all the finishing and upholstery operations lost in the fire, retaining only the wood machining and chair frame assembly department at High Wycombe. The key to this plan was Derek Stewart's conviction that it was possible to break down the upholstery of any chair into separate operations and train green labour to do repetitive work to the requisite high standard. The Union and shop floor objected to the proposed move to Chipping Norton. Hugh Cartwright went to see A. G. Tomkins and J. R. Stanley at Union headquarters, and the Union tacitly agreed, on condition there was acceptance on the shop floor. Hugh Cartwright met the upholsterers at Penn Street and explained the relationship necessary between machine and making shop at High Wycombe and upholsterers at Chipping Norton, who would be interdependent. He asked for help and was pleasantly surprised when, despite the fact that most of them would become redundant, they gave him a standing ovation.

By the end of April the plan became public. In a statement to the *Bucks Free Press* on 24 April CHJ stated that 'First consideration had to be the long-term financial viability of any plan' and 'The re-building of the premises lost in the fire at Temple End was not financially possible . . . building on this site will be limited to that necessary to reinstate the kilning of timber, the production of finished machine parts and the assembly of these parts into frames . . . 'after having introduced deep stuffing upholstery to High Wycombe 73 years ago, we shall no longer be producing upholstery in this town, and much more important, we shall no longer be able to give employment to polishers and upholsterers. A number of the staff will be asked to transfer to Chipping Norton'.

Work now went ahead. Permanent rebuilding commenced on 20,000 sq ft of factory space at the Wycombe factory, and site clearance started at once for a 50,000 sq ft extension at Chipping Norton, doubling the size of the factory. A small ceremony signalled this when the Mayor, Cllr P. J. Leech, with Mrs Leech and watched by Directors of both Parker Knoll and the contractors, Bovis Ltd, and members of Borough and County Councils, cut the first turf. Staff would be increased during the next few months by an extra 100 men and 30 women, all recruited locally.

The whole change-over operation was complex and planned to a tight schedule. The first phase of 13,000 sq ft for upholstery was scheduled to be in full operation in October. As one factory expanded, the other gradually ran down, until Penn Street finished in February 1971.

One memento from these traumatic times is the brass nameplate of Frederick Parker & Sons. Originally on the front door of the offices at Temple End, it was retrieved from the rubble after the fire by Martin Jourdan. TCP's daughters had presented him with a silver cigar box to mark his retirement and this was destroyed in the fire, but Bill Crane made a cedar-lined rosewood box to replace it and fitted the old nameplate in its charred and stained state onto the top. This was presented to CHJ on the first anniversary of the fire by EHC and at the same time CHJ presented EHC and each of his Managers with a heavy brass ashtray which he made personally in his own home workshop.

The cigar box now circulates after the loyal toast at Company dinners and reminds many of the events of that fateful night of 17 February 1970.

One of the first post-fire priorities was the new Statesman chair, so successfully sold at the January Furniture Exhibition; 2,612 were in the shops by the end of July. After production was transferred to Norton, output increased, helped by the moulded shells, which were bought in. A full page advertisement in the *Daily Telegraph* made the chair a major success. As with the Recliner in 1966, the majority were covered in black Astral,

At Cornwell Norton, the new Sonata suite depended on Wycombe frames. The first 400 were delivered by the end of July and it became the most successful suite to date, in production for fourteen years.

Another Parker Knoll model introduced just before the fire, its Victorian style derived in part from chairs in the collection, the Waverley PK1022 (and PK1027 matching settee), became best selling classics.

To test the market for a modern suite, the Stockholm was introduced — a Scandinavian design on a moulded polyurethane shell, and covered in polyurethane — the so called 'wet look'. At about £325, the trade was not at all interested and orders were booked for only 33 suites.

In June 1970, a third Parker Knoll Recliner chair, the Snoozer N60, joined the range, incorporating a rocking action. It was demonstrated on film by the author with three characters, among them Margot Boyd, who played the part of Grandma and who continued to be heard in BBC radio plays for many years. The chair was successful at between £95 and £130, manufactured at Chipping Norton and added to public awareness of Parker Knoll as 'the Recliner people'.

The annual report for the year ending 31 July 1970 showed Group profit before taxation as £196,846 compared with £218,404 the previous year. Although at the half year no interim dividend was paid, the Directors recommended a final of 6%. Both in this year and in that end July 1969, when the furniture industry was in the grip of recession, the major contribution to Group profits had been made by Parker Knoll Textiles. Due to the fire, the number of chairs from High Wycombe fell by 26,000 during the year ending July 1970, while turnover fell by a dramatic £1,000,000. The Chairman, commented on:
'The loss of practically all of the accounting records . . . we have had to make estimates . . . [and] . . . we had not completed our negotiations with the Insurance Companies . . . amounts due under various policies have had to be estimated'.

There was a new appointment to the Board, Mr L. N. OLsen on 30 April 1970 and, as a result of the fire, the capital expenditure not provided for had risen from £79,000 to £400,000.

Another newcomer was John Mason, Group Accountant and Transport Manager Len Cox moved to Chipping Norton in September.

With the establishment of two separate factories — Woodwork at High Wycombe, and Finishing and Upholstery at Chipping Norton — Production Engineering coordinated all departments concerned with manufacture. A unit run by Norman Stewart was set up attached to the Prototype Shop and this worked closely with Designers, making and modifying all development models and producing design prototypes for costing. Once accepted, a second prototype was made from which all necessary assembly jigs for frames and upholstery were produced.

The fire encouraged computers. Simon Young-Jamieson, Sales Office Manager, was appointed Data Processing Manager in October 1970. In July 1971 he inherited his family fortune and left to run his estate in Cornwall. Henry Watson replaced him as Data Processing Manager and the author took over Sales Office management.

Another fully upholstered suite was added in 1971. Attitude surveys frequently indicated that Parker Knoll had little appeal to the younger generations who saw its styles as 'dated'. The new Buccaneer suites, for which there was a matching Recliner chair, addressed this market. This unfortunately proved illusory, despite an extensive campaign. Only 500 suites were sold in two years, by contrast with the Statesman group which sold more than 10,000 units.

By the summer of 1971 Chipping Norton had overcome most teething troubles and was making two separate ranges — Parker Knoll and Cornwell Norton — under the same roof. Trade buyers saw this as an inconvenience 'unnecessary as they are both the same Company anyway'. Retailers felt that there was no justification for retaining the Cornwell Norton name as an independent brand, as few believed it enjoyed any real recognition. Cornwell Norton had, as a result of the fire, been absorbed by Parker Knoll. The survey reported that the two ranges should be amalgamated under the Parker Knoll brand name, removing the need for separate Sales forces, literature and offices. At the same time it would make it possible to broaden the public image of Parker Knoll, thought of as a maker of Queen Anne winged chairs.

ABOVE: Cllr J. P. Leech, Mayor of Chipping Norton, cuts the first turf on 6 May 1970. LEFT: The Waverley chair and settee were introduced in 1970 and RIGHT: so was the Snoozer recliner.

The two ranges were merged in August 1971 under the Parker Knoll name. The Company circulated a poetically worded brochure and a new catalogue, entitled *The Book of Comfort,* with a comprehensive price list. Forty-one models were identified by the PK prefix and twenty-seven former Cornwell Norton models by the N prefix (to identify former Cornwell Norton models which could not be supplied from the wider selection of materials in the PK ranges).

Cornwell Norton tickets, labels and pattern books went out of use and were replaced by those of Parker Knoll; the Sales force representatives were re-deployed between Retail and Contracts areas; the delivery van fleet was repainted in the new Parker Knoll burnt sienna livery and the seven year Cornwell Norton operation faded gently into history.

Parker Knoll
Parker Knoll
Parker Knoll
Cornwell-Norton Limited
PARKER KNOLL
fter seven years of
living together
we decided
to get married.

ABOVE: The van fleet in 1975. BELOW: The factory's experimental Scandinavian Stockholm suite of 1970 — the wet look was not well received. INSET: A marriage is arranged.

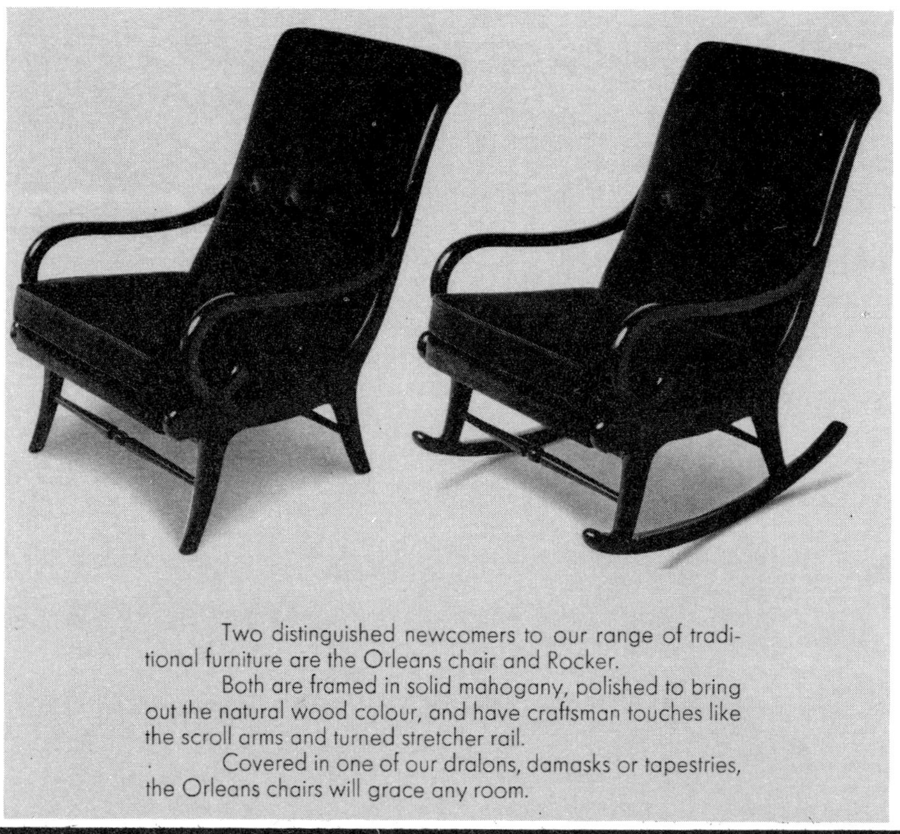

Two distinguished newcomers to our range of traditional furniture are the Orleans chair and Rocker.
Both are framed in solid mahogany, polished to bring out the natural wood colour, and have craftsman touches like the scroll arms and turned stretcher rail.
Covered in one of our dralons, damasks or tapestries, the Orleans chairs will grace any room.

The space-saving Maxi sofa
from Parker Knoll

ABOVE: The Orleans chair and rocker and BELOW: the space-saving Maxi sofa.

Setting the Pace

Transfer of production from Penn Street to Chipping Norton was completed in February 1971, only one year after the fire at Temple End. Within a week the Penn Street factory, together with the Hit and Miss, was sold.

All insurance claims had been agreed but estimates in the previous accounts had proved conservative and understated profit before tax by some £50,000. After including £108,000 recovered under consequential loss, pre-tax profits for the year to 31 July 1971 recovered to £347,236, paying a dividend of 12%. A. J. Faux retired — he had been a non-executive director since 1959.

It was clear more space was needed and another extension to the factory at £138,000 was planned. Further building was also done at Wycombe, to extend the store for finished chair frames and provide a new loading bay. New office accommodation was also built to house the Board Room, Drawing, Personnel and Production Offices.

The model range was almost completely composed of individual occasional chairs; Dane Baskerville wanted to increase its appeal by adding a selection of three-piece suites. The success of the Norton Recliner had enhanced the image of Parker Knoll, but it had not drastically altered the idea that they made 'single chairs and high backed Queen Anne be-legged wing chairs'. Tastes had moved steadily towards upholstered suites for a number of years, albeit with demand at lower prices. At the same time, Contracts Division was mainly concentrated on sturdy wood armed chairs for the hospital and university world, long after domestic interest had moved away from them.

During the first half of the 1970s the range progressively broadened to include all types of chairs and upholstery.

The autumn of 1971 saw the introduction of the Maxi sofa and then the Orleans chairs. The sofa replaced the original drop-end Codetta built to a high standard, reflected in the price. The Maxi was designed at a lower price and created steady demand. The Orleans chairs were inspired by those sold by Parker Knoll France, where the frames were entirely hand-made. Adapting the design for quantity machine production made new demands in manufacture, in that the side frames were not only flush jointed, but the curves ran though the joints to form one free flowing shape. The chairs were well liked, no doubt because there was nothing else on the market of such high quality and style, and they continued to sell well for the next seventeen years.

A second attempt at selling a lower-priced reclining chair was made with the Skomer in June, at a starting price of £78.

Ian Brewster had been Sales Manager of Cornwell Norton prior to the merger; now he became Sales Manager of Parker Knoll Furniture, working closely with Marketing Manager Dane Baskerville. Andrew Wighton joined to administer advertising and promotion, while John Arnold devoted his energies to the Contracts Division. The organisation was jolted in May 1972 when Mike Harvey, Works Manager at Chipping Norton since 1963, suddenly resigned. He had made a solid contribution to the establishment of Cornwell Norton and played a key part with Derek Stewart in developing an efficient factory. Derek Stewart, Group Upholstery Manager, lived between High Wycombe and Chipping Norton; as Deputy Works Manager at Chipping Norton he provided continuity.

Another new arrival at Chipping Norton in July 1972 was Allan Barnett. He opened and managed the extensive new showroom and had managed the London showroom since Henrietta Place was opened in 1952. Graham Dean now took over management in London.

By July 1972 Parker Knoll Ltd had become a holding company only — transferring all furniture production and selling activities to Parker Knoll Furniture Ltd, a wholly owned subsidiary. Martin Jourdan, Works Manager at High Wycombe, now joined the main board as a Director of Parker Knoll Ltd together with J. N. Kitching from Parker Knoll Textiles. As the same time, a separate Board was formed for Parker Knoll Furniture Limited. Hugh Cartwright became Managing Director, with John Arnold as Contracts Director and Martin Jourdan as Works Director. Newly appointed Directors were Peter Bolding, Company Secretary, Dane Baskerville, Marketing Director, and Robin Howland, Design Director. This achieved CHJ's objective — a Board of Directors whose members were each responsible for one aspect of the Company's production.

Turnover had reached an all-time record, with profits for the year at £754,896, more than double those for the previous year. Furniture sales had set a new record. The forthcoming introduction of Value Added Tax in April 1973 would require additional working capital of over £100,000.

During 1972 the Company decided to buy for £1,500 Pace Furniture Limited, at Henley on Thames, a small firm selling mostly imported flat-pack furniture by mail order. This offered a Mail Order Division to the furniture company. Pace, however, was the subject of devastating and critically hostile publicity both in press and on television, for its failure to deliver goods ordered and paid for many months before. It was out of character for Parker Knoll to become involved but Pace heaved a sigh of relief to be bailed out by so prominent a Company. The amount it owed creditors was £111,000. Seven months later, the Board wrote off as an extraordinary charge the £103,892 cost of the 'goodwill' of Pace Furniture Ltd and then set about trying to turn it round, even putting a group of flat-pack furniture into production. After re-organisation put the operation on a stable basis, sales could still not be raised to satisfactory levels, and the business was sold in 1975.

Dane Baskerville joined the main board on 1 January 1973. At the same time T. C. R. Jourdan (Tom) and Derek Stewart were elected Directors of Parker Knoll Furniture Ltd.

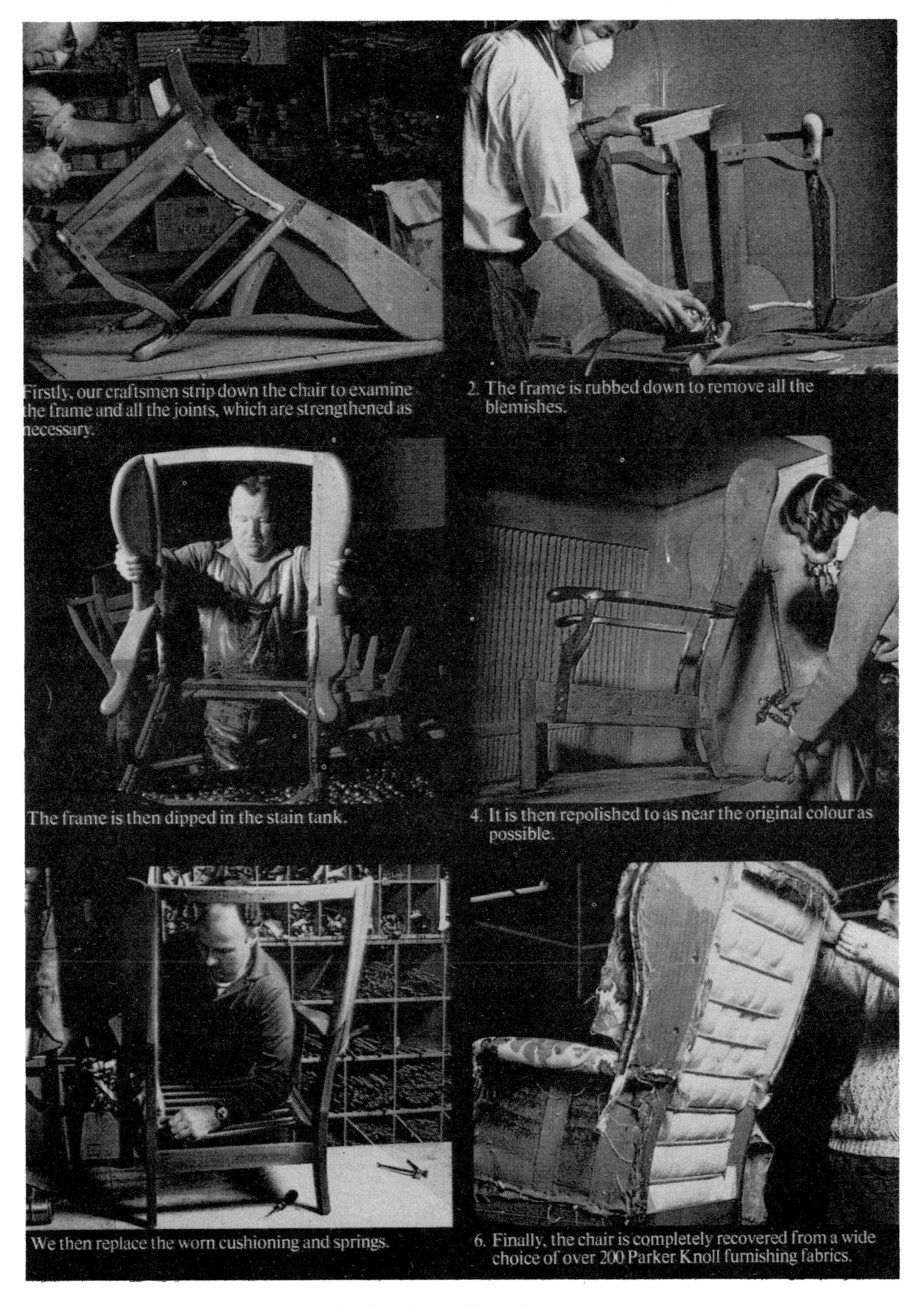

irstly, our craftsmen strip down the chair to examine
he frame and all the joints, which are strengthened as
ecessary.
2. The frame is rubbed down to remove all the
blemishes.
The frame is then dipped in the stain tank.
4. It is then repolished to as near the original colour as
possible.
We then replace the worn cushioning and springs.
6. Finally, the chair is completely recovered from a wide
choice of over 200 Parker Knoll furnishing fabrics.

Showing the world how it was done.

Area representatives for the Contracts division gather with head office management for a sales conference in 1976 — standing: Andrew Wrighton, Colin Eke, John Arnold, Mitchell Bray, Peter Young, David Penny, Tony Falkingham, George Moss, Steve Bland, Dermot Delaney, Roger Hawkins, Tony Trown, Arthur Rose, Ricard Carruthers and Ian Brewster; sitting: Raymond Billington, Joyce Bedwell, Peter Lee and Brian Gould.

THE FIRST MILLION

Annual consumer expenditure on furniture and floorcoverings was rising by the mid-1970s – 56% between 1964 and 1970.

The Company took advantage of this welcome public interest. For the first time, group profit before tax rose above a million pounds to £1,032,823, and a record number of 187,830 pieces were delivered from Chipping Norton, averaging almost 4,000 each working week.

During March 1973 it became possible to re-start the Renovation Service discontinued when Penn Street was closed, welcomed by many customers in the Contract field. A separate workshop was opened. Len Cox handed management of the transport fleet to Selwyn Williams and became Manager of the new Customer Service Department, in which Ken Sharpe was Manager of the Service Office.

Experience had taught that one of the major appeals of Parker Knoll upholstery was its moderate styling, of 'comfortable and homely' furniture, rather than more advanced design, catered for by specialists. The major factor controlling manufacture of any design by the Company was its potential for volume sales over a long period.

There were exceptions, like the Libertine chair of 1973 Robin Howland had put a lot of thought into this striking design which was an extension of the Meriden and Malton concepts of the 1950s.

Many novel construction features were embodied. The main expanded polystyrene shell carried a rubber seat diaphragm and was mounted onto a high-density enamelled polyurethane base with a rock and swivel mechanism, evolved and patented by the designer. Without metal pivots, springs or attachments, but using a pair of rubber 'springs', it was completely silent. The whole structure and rocker mechanism had been tested by FIRA to grade 4 – the most severe test for Contract use. Deep buttoning of the upholstery over the resilient filling, of a single piece cold-cure polyether, shaped to fit the shell, not only gave the chair a luxurious appearance, but allowed the concave shape to be fully resilient, at the same time avoiding too many tailoring seams which might have caused trouble under strain.

Sad to say, only 494 chairs were sold. Of these 277 were delivered in June and July 1973, but only another 120 in the following year, tailing off to the final 90 after that. It served to confirm that the retail trade and public in general were not yet ready to depart from convention and invest in furniture of advanced design.

More staff changes took place in September 1973, when Arthur Newell retired, Tapestry Buyer since 1964. He was succeeded by Dane Baskerville's son, Vincent, who moved from Parker Knoll Textiles. By this time the factory were cutting up in the region of ten thousand metres of fabric each week, making the stock-keeping operation difficult. Parker Knoll Textiles provided a warehouse service, taking delivery and holding all bulk stocks of Parker Knoll materials, delivering to Chipping Norton each day as required.

The Contract Division rarely hit the Company headlines but nevertheless made a significant contribution. This had always been achieved by selling standard chairs. By the early 1970s attention was turning to standards of fire retardence for coverings in public institutions, bringing a new dimension to product performance and suitability. The Company was one of the first to provide Contract customers with results of fire tests.

In mid-1973 the first group of new models for many years was designed expressly to meet the needs of Contract customers — the Evesham group of assorted chairs and integrated tables, enabling any arrangement of the different pieces to remain unified and co-ordinated with modern architectural surroundings. At the same time further development took place of high-seated chairs for institutions, hospital wards and day rooms. This was the N73 Cornwell chair, especially for use by elderly, infirm and post-operative hospital patients, who required a high seat with upright back with firm rather than softly supporting upholstery.

In the early 1970s, 80 different models were being sold, each of which could be supplied in any of seven different cover ranges, which meant that the product file had to hold 560 different pricing possibilities. In addition there were about 200 different materials in which any chair could be supplied, a total of 1,456,000 options. The model numbers and prices in each cover quality were held on disc in the computer and each one of the 6,000 customers was identified on the name and address file by the account number.

Computers were introduced, finally coming into their own by 1977. Valerie Buckingham had moved from Sales Office in 1970 to become the Company's first Computer Operator. When Simon Young-Jamieson left, she became the only link between a bewildered Sales Office and the increasing pressure in the Computer Department.

Peter Hill joined the Company as Data Processing Manager. He later moved to Parker Knoll Textiles and is now Managing Director of Monkwell Fabrics, a subsidiary of the Group.

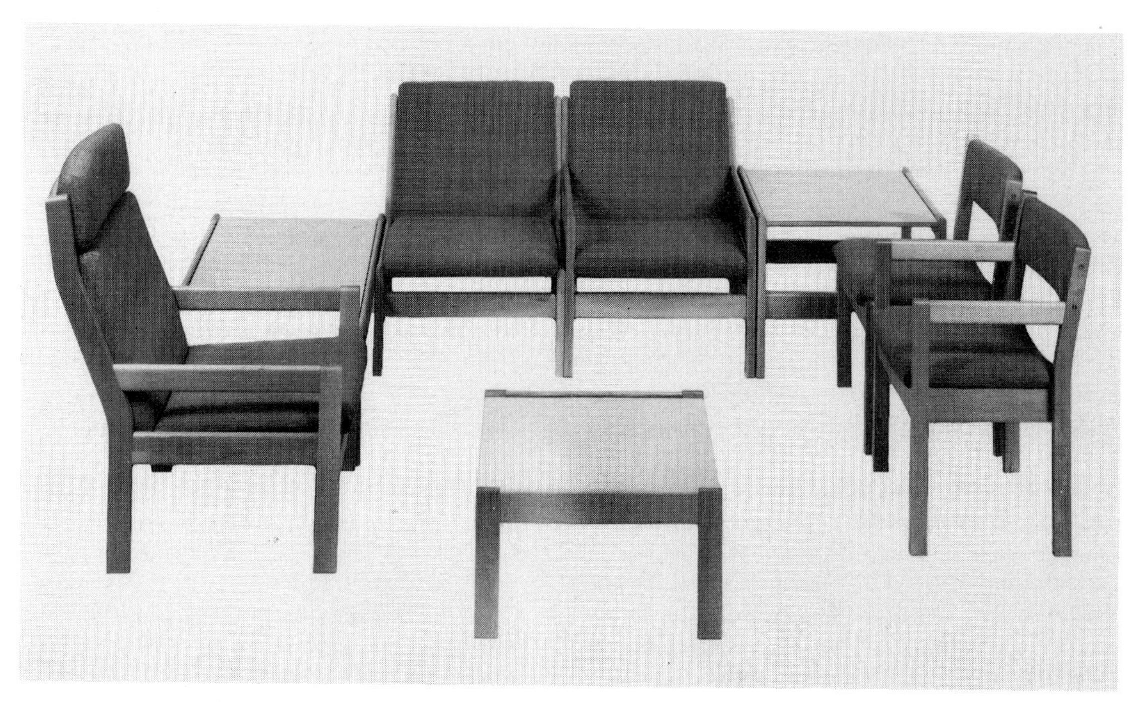

The Evesham group of co-ordinated chairs and tables was introduced to the contract market in 1974.

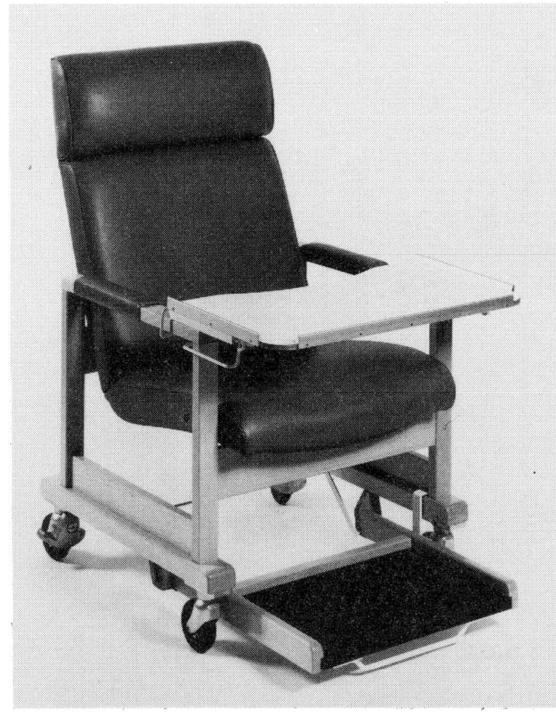

LEFT: The Cornwell chair was adapted and made mobile for hospitals. RIGHT: The Libertine was not a major seller. BELOW: Upholstery at Cornwell Norton in the seventies.

The Cornwell Norton sewing shop.

WARP AND WEFT

Parker Knoll Group activities were broadened into a new field of furnishings when Mercia Weavers Ltd, manufacturers of high quality Wilton carpets, joined the Group on 1 January 1974. This profitable Company continued independently, without changes, under the Chairmanship of F. G. Patterson, while D. J. and J. N. Kitching, Directors of the Textile Division, joined their Board.

At both Parker Knoll Furniture and Parker Knoll Textiles, younger executives were beginning to take over senior positions. Hugh Cartwright, Managing Director of the Furniture Division since 1970, decided on grounds of age that it was time for a successor, and Martin Jourdan succeeded him.

Douglas Kitching, who first started Parker Knoll Textiles twenty-four years previously, also retired in 1974, was succeeded as Managing Director by his son, J. N. Kitching. Another appointment was that of John Mason FCMA to the Boad of Parker Knoll Furniture Ltd.

These were troubled times for business; rising inflation and unemployment saw unions showing their strength. A fourfold increase in the price of Middle East oil in 1973/74 fuelled inflation. A successful miners' strikes in 1972 resulted in the Heath Government imposing a three-day working week to conserve power supplies, as well as extensive power blackouts. The factory at Temple End was equipped with its own generator and continued working but Frogmoor offices were not. Sudden breaks in power seriously affected the computer causing dislocation. Frogmoor was later equipped with its own generator. Industrial unrest continued with a second miners' strike in 1974, leading to a general election.

Ted Heath was defeated, and a Labour Government returned. The miners won their demands, but the Government's majority of three was too narrow and another election, the second in 1974, was called. Labour won a slightly higher majority and tried to woo the unions with the Social Contract.

The Government burdened industry with limitations of profits, increased corporation tax, and payment in advance of some taxes and import duties. A popular referendum in 1975 confirmed British membership of the Common Market and in 1976 economic crisis forced the Government to apply to the International Monetary Fund. The furniture industry uncharacteristically rode out these storms, increasing its volume.

Annual inflation throughout the 1960s was about 3%, but in 1970 it reached 6.4% and continued to rise through 9.4% in 1971 to 15.8% in 1977 before it slowly fell away, not to reach 5% until after 1982. The impact of this on business and employment was traumatic. In all companies, 1974 will be remembered as the year of the continuous price increase. At Parker Knoll, after an increase in September 1973, new lists were issued on 1 January 1974; 1 April; 20 June; 1 November, followed in 1975 by new lists on 1 April; 1 July and 12 November. During 1974, Parker Knoll prices increased by about 25% overall, although some models were not affected, and by a further 10% during 1975. During 1976 they again increased by about 20%, making an increase of 65% in three years. This kept them slightly below the cumulative average inflation increase for the three years, which was an overall rise of 68% for the same period.

The volume of all furniture delivered by manufacturers between 1970 and 1975 increased by 55%. At the same time, prices rose far faster than output. Value of deliveries increased from about £204 millions in 1970 to £577 millions in 1975. It is estimated that the 55% increase in volume achieved in 1975 would, at 1970 prices, have raised sales value to £361 millions. The remaining £216 millions for 1975 presented a substantial increase in sales, albeit at the higher price levels.

It was a long time since the industry had enjoyed such a surge in activity, but it appears that the largest benefit went to firms supplying the middle and lower ends of the market. Parker Knoll factories in 1973 were working flat out, particularly in the wood machining department at High Wycombe. Hugh Cartwright had warned in 1972 that, if demand rose above budget, he would face difficulty in supplying more machined chair parts. By mid-1972, output had fully recovered from the fire, although numbers declined between August 1974 and July 1977 when prices rose most rapidly. The important factor was not the number of units sold, but the changing model mix and increase in items with higher values. For example, twice as many high value Norton Recliner chairs (21,855) were sold in 1975/76 than in the previous year. Emphasis in the domestic market was swinging towards the heavier, higher value, upholstered items, but this was offset by rising Contracts Division sales of the smaller wood armed chairs at lower values. The number of chairs sold of all types improved rapidly after the fire and then fell back to a plateau around which it stayed until 1976, dropping sharply in 1977 and rising substantially again in 1978. Just over one million chairs were sold between August 1970 and July 1975.

Rising prices were a factor in lifting the Group's furniture turnover by 29% in the year ending July 1975 when an extra 5,590 units were sold, but the further increase in turnover by another 22% in year end July 1975 may, in view of the 3,596 less units sold, have owed something more to increasing prices. Furniture Division profits reached an all-time record in 1976.

The Parker Knoll collection of antique chairs had remained in store since the fire, but in 1974 an opportunity arose for it to be housed at one of Somerset's fine historic houses, Brympton d'Evercy near Yeovil.

In 1967 the house, then occupied by a school, was acquired by Charles Clive Ponsonby Fane. He took up residence in his ancestral home and started to restore it. He had to refurnish it in appropriate period style from scratch, so Martin Jourdan suggested that the Company provide the chairs on loan from the Parker Knoll collection. Ultimately the whole collection went to Brympton, using as many pieces as necessary to furnish the staterooms on display to the public. Arthur Newell was living close to Brympton, and supervised the collection at its new home.

In the year to July 1974 the dividend at 2.462p per share (previous year 2.450p) was the highest permitted under the counter-inflation legislation. The final dividend would have produced a higher cash payment to shareholders but for the increase in personal taxation introduced in the budget.

Almost all new designs during the 1970s were upholstered three-piece suites, while consumer research continually showed that the image of Parker Knoll was almost totally determined by the familiar winged back chair. This fixation derived, no doubt, from the tremendous success of the Penshurst chair since the 1950s and the Camden wing chair in the Utility period.

Changes in pubic taste and pocket, however, displaced individual chairs in favour of upholstery. Parker Knoll was in a good position, with a new modern factory, and the strongest brand name, to correct this imbalance.

Early indications were encouraging. The Sonata three-piece suite had sold well since 1970. Although the Statesman had been introduced as an individual chair, both high and low-backed matching settees were soon added enabling weekly sales of suites to exceed fifty, with another 500-600 individual chairs.

Some difficulties developed throughout the trade in 1972/3 with many types of polyurethane covering materials, including Astral, which had been used on the Statesman models. This was due to plasticiser migration which caused the top polyurethane surface to separate from the knitted base.

From its introduction in 1970, the Statesman group sold well, only declining substantially in 1975 and being discontinued in 1976 after reaching a total of 65,572 chairs, 10,763 stools, and 11,130 settees. To follow this was difficult, especially as the vogue for this style had probably run its course, but another suite based on moulded shell construction was introduced in 1975, just as the Statesman was coming to an end. This was the Ambassador, plainer in shape and without wings, but otherwise similar. Although sales at about a dozen suites a week plus additional chairs were not large, they continued to make a contribution for another six years.

The Buccaneer suite was designed for Cornwell Norton and was launched in 1971, but was dropped in 1972 after only 526 suites had been sold.

At a conference in February 1972 Dane Baskerville outlined his marketing philosophy — the greatest scope lay in the three-piece suite market. The first of this programme was the Concorde suite, designed to sell at the lowest price which the Company could possibly reach. The box construction gave the frame great rigidity and strength at an economic price, but was, as always with upholstery, a hidden asset which only the retail salesman could fully exploit. Sold in a 100% wool covering at a retail price of £114.50, the suite was calculated to appeal to at least 1,600 Parker Knoll stockists. This distribution was achieved, with deliveries of about 140 suites a week between April and July, during which national press advertising appeared. Repeat sales settled to a level of about thirty a week in 1972/3 and dropped to twenty the following year. The Concorde remained in the catalogue for three years and continued in production for a further five.

By mid-1972 another suite was launched, this time accompanied by a matching Recliner chair. The Lexington was another modern style with clean, simple lines but of higher quality than the Concorde, at a retail starting price of £198. With one Recliner chair in place of the standard chair the price became £238, or with two Recliner chairs, £278. Only 967 suites were sold in the first year, dropping to 340 in the second after which it was discontinued.

The next venture came in February 1973 and was designed to build on the established success of the Norton Recliner and its matching upholstery at the top end of the market. This was the attractive VIP group, made up of a three-seater settee, an easy chair and the unique Stowaway chair. In appearance the easy chair and the Stowaway recliner were identical but, in addition to the extending footrest, the Stowaway incorporated a cleverly concealed 'pop up' headrest, emerging and retracting as the action was operated. This made it possible for the lines of the matching settee and fixed chair to be less tall, in a design which was much less bulky and better suited for use in smaller rooms.

The secret lay in the Recliner action, which fitted into the dimensions of a compact easy chair but, when operated, extended not only the footrest but raised the head support from within the outside chair back. Stowaway aptly described this function, but inevitably the chair became known as the 'pop-up-back chair'. Priced at between £351 and £500 for a suite including one Recliner chair, slightly less than for a similar combination from the Norton group, this was the same high-quality upholstery in the traditional Parker Knoll manner. Unusually elaborate marketing arrangements were made — including another short film.

Retail price for a group made up of one Stowaway chair, one matching fixed chair and the three-seater settee in the basic cover range was £351 — or £405 in a middle grade cover.

About three hundred stockists initially ordered a suite, but more were prepared to stock the Stowaway recliner chair on its own, accounting for an additional 1,000 chairs. Disappointingly, repeat sales of the suite only totalled 400 in the next full year, (about eight a week) but three-piece suites from the Norton group were running at over 1,000 a year and rising, quite apart from an additional 8,000 separate Norton Recliner chairs. By this time the 'Norton' models had been available for eight years and had become firmly established as market leaders. Widespread national advertising captured the interest of purchasers which the retailer could convert into sales by featuring the range in his showrooms. Not all buyers were inclined to stock a second group, which fulfilled a similar function.

The third suite in the development programme was the Roskilde, introduced in mid-1973. This was intended to counter several similar suites sold by competitors. The Melissa suite by Gommes had become one of their best-sellers and it was not long before other makers were offering their own, often close, copies. In pursuing the market for suites of around £300, the Company tried to avoid visible similarity between their products and its own new designs.

The Roskilde suite was the largest of the three, with generous mock cushions, providing a full head-rest back. First offered to the trade in June 1973, the retail price in basic cover was about £315. The price of the Roskilde was evidence of rising costs, considerably higher than for the Lexington only one year previously. Most buyers were cautious about buying another of Parker Knoll's 'modern offerings' when there were already so many on the market. Only 261 suites were sold in the introductory period and only another 290 in the next twelve months, after which it was discontinued.

Marketing policy of penetrating the middle-priced upholstered suite market had so far met with disappointing results. Possibly the Company expected too high a sales volume from each design, or perhaps marketing and promotional activities had been inadequate, or perhaps the designs and prices were adjudged uncompetitive despite carrying the Parker Knoll name.

In cabinet furniture, the public were most aware of Gomme's 'G Plan' brand. This had been cleverly and successfully extended to include upholstered suites. Designed to harmonise, these enabled them to promote sales by the concept of 'a home completely furnished with G Plan'. It was more difficult for Parker Knoll to do anything like this in reverse. By simply expanding the range of Parker Knoll chairs to include upholstered suites, which most retailers would not stock, was alone not enough to win public recognition.

Ironically, the Cornwell Norton business was just becoming established as a manufacturer of good modern upholstery, when the fire at High Wycombe in 1970 forced a change of direction, and eventual closure of the Company as a separate entity. The original concept to enter the market for three piece suites with its own plant and brand looked correct at the time. Since the 1980s new model ranges, mostly of traditional styles, have successfully won retailers' enthusiasm and wide consumer support. Had there been no fire at High Wycombe in 1970, it is probable that the Cornwell Norton business would have accomplished this, while the traditions of the original business in occasional and upholstered chairs would have continued separately at High Wycombe.

In the 1970s advice from staunch retail friends was increasingly that Parker Knoll should stick to what they did best — designs in traditional styles of upholstery for the higher price markets.

Striking out in a different direction, the topically named Apollo range of unit seating was introduced in 1974, designed to offer a fresh approach to the living room. By contrast with the formality of the three-piece suite, Apollo units, with or without arms, could be grouped together with the corner unit to work out a variety of schemes to suit the room and space available, or they could be broken apart and used separately. Both high- or low-back units increased the flexibility of the system. Constructed on a rigid polyurethane moulding, the units increased upholstery output without making demands on hard-pressed frame making or polishing facilities. Each piece was remarkably light in weight for its size and fitted with a linking device.

A five unit group was priced at £400, equivalent to the cost of a similar three-piece suite. From the outset buyers showed enthusiasm for the idea. Sales reached over 5,500 pieces in the first year and the high-backed models outsold the low by three to one.

Another interesting unit group, Comus, was introduced experimentally, intended mainly for the Contract market. Each seat was built from a solid block of load-bearing polyether foam, stiffened by a plywood back and base. This Continental idea was new to this country, and to be reliable in use the foam had to be carefully engineered. Working in close co-operation with Dunlop, a satisfactory method of upholstery and construction was devised and thoroughly tested. Simple and neat in design, it was light in weight and easy to move, had no sharp edges and was itself difficult to damage. Because of its construction Comus was economically priced. A corner unit with three single units sold for as little as £91.75p plus VAT. Comus units, although an experiment, found a niche in the market and remained in production for five years.

The Howard suite, introduced in 1975, was much more in the Parker Knoll manner. This good-looking full-sized suite featured mock buttoned-back cushions and made up equally well in plain or patterned covers. It quickly found favour. It was now clear that the Company could not capture high volume sales with suites selling at £200-£300 because their styling was nowhere near what the popular market could obtain elsewhere at these prices.

Priced at between £540 and £750 according to cover, the Howard suite quickly became an established part of the range, continuing for more than eleven years, during which over 7,000 suites were sold. At the time, the long-established practice, of placing two settees one each side of the fireplace in large rooms, was given publicity by home magazines. The Howard settee was ideal, resulting in a disproportionate level of settee sales in addition to regular three-piece suites.

From the wide variety of designs marketed during the last five years, only the Sonata, Norton and Howard, each selling steadily and continuously at around thirty a week, had successfully emerged. Their quality characteristics and appeal were to the top end of the market, whereas designs looking to a lower priced sector had failed. Despite this, one final attempt was made in 1976 to extract some worthwhile sales from the volume market.

The Elsinore suite had plain, simple lines making it suitable in modest rooms without seeming to monopolise available space. Special attention to cushion interiors made sure it was extremely comfortable and priced at between £400 and £600, it had a lot to offer. Although supported by advertising, it failed to make an impression, reaching 865 suites in thirty months. It was dropped in 1977.

Design work had been in progress for some time on another suite and a matching Recliner chair, using the same 'pop up' action as the Stowaway. Marketing Department decided to use the suite to test the market for printed covers. Many suite manufacturers found that printed materials were colourful and stylish and much cheaper than multi-coloured jacquard woven materials. Colour and pattern caught the customer's eye in the showroom, when price then became a serious factor in relation to other merchandise. Representatives had long pressed for a suite of suitable design on which printed covers could be used.

The new Miami suite, rectangular in style, was covered in a modern printed fabric. When they saw the Miami suite Representatives were not impressed. Their instinct proved correct; during the eighteen months of its catalogued life, weekly sales averaged five suites, with no more than an additional three Reclining chairs.

Meanwhile forty thousand catalogues were sent out that year to respondents to advertisements, with as many again to retailers. The catalogue had always been important.

A 1970 attitude survey found that 'Parker Knoll's awareness and reputation has extended far beyond its original core market during the decade. Every study during the 1970s suggested that awareness and appreciation of, and desire for, Parker Knoll furniture was sprading to younger and more mass market consumers. Although these newer potential buyers would often say that Parker Knoll, for them, was unaffordable or impracticable, nevertheless they ultimately claimed to see Parker Knoll as the ultimate to which they aspired'.

Such reports defined the type of consumer for whom Parker Knoll furniture held the greatest appeal and against which success or failure could be evaluated. They also indicated that, if more work was done to produce suitable designs, the interest of a new, younger generation of affluent furniture buyers might still be won.

The VIP group and the Stowaway recliner.

ABOVE: The Buccaneer in Airskin. CENTRE: The Concorde introduced in 1973. BELOW: The Roskilde, also introduced in 1973, was intended to compete with the G-Plan Melissa.

LEFT: The six Managing Directors of the Company since 1946 gathered for this portrait at Chipping Norton — Hugh Cartwright, Geoffrey Alpe, Martin Jourdan, now Chairman, Dane Baskerville, Tom Jourdan and seated, Hans Jourdan, Chairman 1969-1976. RIGHT: Ian Brewster and John Arnold have a word. BELOW: Geoffrey Alpe, Mrs and Mr Gordon Abram, Mrs and Mr Reg Hopkins — at Chipping Norton.

New Faces

The Furniture Division of the Company had another good year in 1975. Orders and despatches showed substantial increase over the previous year, with turnover up by 29%. Pressures on profit margins continued, but the production cycle at High Wycombe and Chipping Norton had settled down. The trauma after the fire was now behind them and the benefits from intensive training programmes were beginning to show results.

Dane Baskerville and advertising agents C. Vernon and Sons took the Company's advertising into television. Not a lot of furniture had previously been advertised in this way, due no doubt to the high cost, as well as the difficulty of presenting the product. In the case of the Norton Recliner, its popularity was not in question, but could be drawn to the attention of a far wider selection of consumers. The versatility of the chair itself and the fact that it 'opened' made a visual impact.

The message was delivered within the thirty second spot by a skillfully made film which humourously showed husband returning home at the end of the day to be met in the hall with a recitation by his wife of all the disasters which had happened while he was away. Not appearing to pay much attention, he takes his paper and makes for the lounge while his wife says she will make a cup of tea. Husband sits in his Recliner and, after a few seconds, extends the chair until he is fully reclined. By the time his wife enters with his tea he is fast asleep. This was something with which every viewer could identify, and drove home the message in less time than it takes to tell.

In preparation for the promotion retailers had been encouraged to increase and maintain their stocks, and to be sure to display them prominently. The benefit was almost immediate, increasing sales to 21,885 in the year ending July 1976, more than double the previous year's figure, and rising still further in following years as the promotion continued. The level of public awareness of Parker Knoll increased dramatically to long term advantage.

Group profit for the year to July 1975 was £1,169,171 with turnover at £12,591,782, both higher than previously achieved.

In preparation for the Chairman's forthcoming retirement in July 1976 the Board appointed Martin Jourdan Deputy Chairman in addition to his duties as Managing Director of Parker Knoll Furniture. At the same time Tom Jourdan, Production Director of Parker Knoll Furniture, was appointed to the Board of Parker Knoll Ltd. Ian Brewster, who joined the new Cornwell Norton company in 1963, became Sales Director when he was appointed to the Board of Parker Knoll Furniture and was soon to take up the duties of Marketing Director.

C. H. Jourdan retired in July 1976 after 21 years as Chairman. Geoffrey Alpe retired as President of the Group on the same day.

It was now 107 years since Frederick Parker had completed his apprenticeship and started to make chair-frames at Bracklyn Street, Hoxton. Control of the Company had remained with the Parker family and their descendents through three generations, during which time its products had mutated from fine, hand-crafted cabinet furniture and upholstery to upholstery for the modern age, produced by high technology methods in quantities not dreamt of in 1869. Throughout this time, Frederick Parker's feeling for quality and the right way of doing things, as well as his principles of fair dealing, had been handed down to those who worked with Harry, Tom and Will Parker and then through Hans Jourdan and Geoffrey Alpe.

When CHJ joined the Company as Joint Managing Director in 1946, it was up for sale, employees numbered 200, the turnover was £100,000 and the Company made a loss that year of £5,582. In 1976, the number of employees was 1,089 and the remuneration paid them was £3,069,714. Turnover had reached an all-time high of over £14.5 millions, yielding record profits of £1,747,265.

CHJ died in 1989. Some of his proudest achievements during this thirty years with the Company were summed up in a tribute by his son, Martin at the thanksgiving service on Friday 21 July 1989. They were: bringing about the end of the Utility Furniture scheme; his partnership with Douglas Kitching in Parker Knoll Textiles; the establishment and growth of the factory at Chipping Norton; his part in the promotion of generic advertising for the furniture industry under the 'Old Furniture Must Go' campaign, for which he was awarded the BFM Gold Medal; his work with the CBI as Chairman of the Southern Region; his founder membership of the Furniture Makers Guild in 1973, and his year as Master of the Worshipful Company of Furniture Makers; the foundation he laid for the future growth of the Company by modernising and re-equipping the factory during the 1950s, and again after the disastrous fire of 1970.

In 1976, Martin Jourdan and his brother Tom became the fourth generation to accept responsibility for the future of the business and of shaping it to meet the changing demands of the late twentieth century.

Geoffrey Alpe talks to Harry Jones, area representative.

ABOVE: Quality control at Cornwell Norton in the seventies. BELOW: The factory in the summer of 1976.

ABOVE: Looms at Raymakers and BELOW: Nathan's factory.

THE SUM OF THE PARTS

Naturally, one of Hans Jourdan's principal objectives was to ensure that, when he retired, he left the business in the hands of the family, but a family trained for the purpose and with an experienced team to support them.

In the early 1960s, he had sent John Arnold, his nephew, and one of Tom Parker's grandchildren, to work in Kroehlers, the largest manufacturer of furniture in the United States. At the same time, he sent one of his two sons, Tom, to learn German in Vienna. He sent his other son, Martin, to Paris to work at Sieges Parker and arranged for John Kitching, the son of Douglas Kitching, the founder of Parker Knoll Textiles, to learn Italian. This ease with languages was to prove invaluable as the Common Market became home territory for the business.

In 1972, when John Kitching and Martin Jourdan joined John Arnold on the main board, their training was incomplete. Both were sent to the Harvard Business School and Martin also worked in the City branch of ICFC now 3i (Investors in Industry) through Nigel Olsen, who had joined as a non-executive Director in 1970. Nigel had married Rosemary Kies, Harry Parker's grand-daughter – and was an astute and tough banker; there needed to be someone on the outside who could guide, support and develop the team Hans was building on the inside.

In 1973, John Kitching took over from his father, Douglas, as Managing Director of Parker Knoll Textiles, which now incorporated G. P. & J. Baker, purchased in 1964 for £110,000. At the same time, Martin Jourdan took over Parker Knoll from Hugh Cartwright, whose influence, like that of Hans Jourdan and Douglas Kitching, endured during the next decade.

Company Secretary Peter Bolding had joined Parkers in 1959, succeeding Edwin Down, Peter was also its link with High Wycombe through his local activities and, when he retired in 1990, that link was not replaced which was sad both for Company and town.

The financial side of the business had been badly overstretched and undermanned in the '60s and the decision was made to appoint a Financial Controller who would, in due course, join the Board. John Mason had been brought up in cost and works accountancy and joined Parker Knoll in 1970, just after the fire. He was, therefore, able to build his department from scratch and, with the purchase of the first computer, to install a fast, responsive and accurate management information system.

In September 1975, when Tom Jourdan joined the Board, Les Packer became a director of Parker Knoll Textiles, responsible for administration and exports. With Martin as Deputy Chairman, and the intention that he would take over as Chairman in August 1976, the team for the next fifteen years was in place.

In 1975, Margaret Thatcher became leader of the Conservative Party, and the first North Sea oil was brought ashore. Electricity prices, however, had risen by a third and inflation had soared to 27%. Wilson, who had been Prime Minister since 1963, apart from the Heath interregnum, was about to surprise the country with his retirement in favour of Callaghan.

The Labour Government had not damaged the furniture industry. Increases in public spending had accelerated the construction of universities and hospitals, and this cavalier disregard for prudent financial policies had increased inflation to Latin American proportions. Parker Knoll, through its Contracts Division, led by John Arnold, became the leading supplier of chairs to the National Health Service and furnished many new universities. In the domestic market, inflation encouraged people to buy — 'It would be more expensive next month'. The success of television advertising pushed Norton Recliner sales to over 400 per week.

There were difficulties. The prices and incomes policy restricted an individual company's ability to increase prices, and wages and dividends were pegged to nominal levels of increase compared with inflation. The 'prices' part of the policy proved helpful in increasing margins. So long as Parker Knoll could justify price increases to the Price Commission, they could be passed on.

Parker Knoll can mean two quite different entities; the upholstery company, whose history largely reflects this, and the Group which, in additon to Parker Knoll Upholstery, comprised Parker Knoll Textiles, (incorporating G. P. & J. Baker) and Mercia Weavers, a carpet weaving company supplying the contract market. Effectively the upholstery business is Parker Knoll and the overall company, the Group.

Parker Knoll, during this period, had added further space at Chipping Norton which, together with capital expenditure upon machinery, had added significantly to capacity. Nevertheless, demand exceeded supply and plans were considered for a new factory at Swindon, Milton Keynes or one of the financially attractive development areas. These all had disadvantages: the more financially attractive, the more disadvantages. Metra Proudfoot, an American consultancy firm specialising in increasing productivity, claimed with reasonably convincing evidence that it could improve productivity by a minimum of 15%. Their estimated fee of around £200,000 was a difficult pill to swallow, particularly since that would be paid before the benefits were enjoyed. The Parker Knoll management team swallowed hard and, with the support of the Board, commissioned Proudfoot.

John Mason, by this time Finance Director, was sceptical but, to persuade him to back the project, he was invited to establish the benchmark against which Proudfoot's programme would be measured. The management team met for its inauguration at the Shillingford Bridge Hotel by the Thames, where Proudfoot put the team through its paces prior to getting to work in the factory. This was the start of an intensely difficult twelve months but, at the end, John Muir, the Proudfoot Director, together with the support of the Parker Knoll team, delivered the productivity gains forecast. This put in place a production management and control system that endures. It also saved the cost of a new factory.

In the year the Proudfoot project was completed (1978) the year-on-year increase in profit achieved since 1975 was broken. It fell back £300,000 to £1.94m.

Parker Knoll Textiles had substantially developed its export business, particularly in Europe with G. P. & J. Baker. Mercia Weavers was contributing to profit but proving more difficult to integrate with Parker Knoll Textiles than expected. Mercia was sold to Stoddard Carpets for £2m in 1988.

By and large, the business was doing well. Sales and profits were on the increase; much time had been spent on modernising production facilities and establishing the fabric business in Europe. However, there were signs that markets were slowing. It was time to broaden the business base.

K. Raymakers & Sons had been suppliers of cotton velvet (velours), to Parker Knoll Textiles for many years. Raymakers had been established in Padiham, Lancashire, in the early thirties by a Dutch family, who had an identical business in Helmond, Holland, originating from the

18th century, with substantial sales to the British market. Realising that with Britain off the Gold Standard, their exports would become less competitive, William Raymakers' grandfather sent his son Karel, together with Mr Gijsbers, a bright young man in the office and a weaving master, Theo Phillipini, to set up a velours business in Lancashire. In due time, William Raymakers, aided by his brother-in-law, Victor Keunen, had taken control and, with the assistance of Mr Gijsbers' son, Anton, built the most modern and efficient pile fabric weaving mills in Britain. By the late '70s, however, it had become apparent that the active involvement of the family in the company, at that time owned by the four children of Karel, would cease upon William's eventual retirement and that a buyer would not be unwelcome. Several suitors had already been turned down, but when Parker Knoll Textiles, one of Raymakers' biggest customers over many years, made overtures, the negotiations that followed with Martin Jourdan, Nigel Olsen and John Kitching resulted in a deal being struck whereby the group paid £2.7 million for the business and the takeover was completed on 1 August 1979, when at the same time William joined the board of Parker Knoll.

Raymakers had a second weaving shed in Colne, a few miles away from the main factory in Padiham. In the Colne shed were 66 of the old-style shuttle looms, the design of which had changed little since the nineteenth century. Some of these looms had been sent from Holland in the thirties. They ran at half the speed of the Guskin rapier looms in Padiham but produced good-quality cloth at a cost that gave a reasonable profit, until the recession in 1982 and the consequent fall in demand required the Colne shed to close. It was the end of an era and, although Martin wanted William to keep one of the old looms going, for some reason he refused. Both of them regret that decision to-day.

At the time William Raymakers joined the Group Board, Martin Jourdan relinquished his position as Manager Director of Parker Knoll to Dane Baskerville to concentrate on Group development.

The winter of 1979 was subsequently dubbed 'the winter of discontent' and marked the end of the Labour Party's seventeen-year reign. Mrs Thatcher became Prime Minister, with the task of bringing inflation under control and restoring to the Government the power to run the country. It was not an easy time; the first of the post-war recessions was about to begin but the Group was well prepared. In the four years since 1976, profits had doubled to £3.5 million; considerable work had been done to make both Parker Knoll and Parker Knoll Textiles more competitive. In addition, Raymakers had joined the Group to broaden the product base and inject a new voice and view at the Board table.

Despite the famous brand name, Parker Knoll was small in the furniture market with less than 4% share of the upholstery market alone. The Board noted with concern the increasing power over manufacturers exerted by the multiple and generally out-of-town retailers. While they were trading one or two price points below Parker Knoll, they were bound to trade up as time went by. It was not difficult to envisage Parker Knoll coming under pressure. Cabinet making had been in the Company's blood until just before the war and, when B. & I. Nathan ran into difficulties, the Group made an offer of 34p per share, amounting to £660,000, which was accepted by 90.7% of the shareholders. B. & I. Nathan joined the Group on 3 August 1981.

Nathan had been founded at the turn of the century by two brothers, Isaac and Barney, and run by the family ever since. They had two factories, one on the North Circular Road in London since 1932, and another in Worcester, opened during the boom in the mid-seventies. In their previous financial year, they had lost around three-quarters of a million pounds so, although Nathan was acquired cheaply, there were substantial problems.

Tom Jourdan was sent to Edmonton as Managing Director. He had run both Parker Knoll's factories for a number of years. He welcomed the challenge but no one could have foretold how much of a challenge Nathan would be.

Nathan lost £622,000 in the first six months and the decision to close the Worcester factory was taken in June 1982. The full year loss, including the closure costs, turned out to be around £1.5m and Group profit fell to £2.0m.

Just as the Falklands War was the turning point of Mrs Thatcher's first Government, so the consolidation of Nathan into the London factory was the low point in the restructuring of Nathan. New ranges were launched to complement Nathan's best-selling teak range; the massive discounts which the previous management had been compelled to concede to powerful retailers were cut to more commercial levels. A fresh management team included Ian Brewster, Sales & Marketing Director of Parker Knoll. Gradually, sales improved and losses reduced, so that, by the mid-eighties, Nathan was one of the top brands in the cabinet sector and making acceptable, if not spectacular, profits.

On the first day Nathan was acquired, Martin arrived early at the factory in Angel Road on the North Circular. He believed you could judge the temperament and enthusiasm of a workforce by the speed with which the factory started up each day. Reaching a double end tennoner machine in the top end of the mill, he saw a man sitting on a partly-completed pallet load of parts smoking a cigarette — at Parker Knoll an offence calling for instant dismissal in the high combustible environment of an upholstery factory. He needed to establish discipline but did not know the local rules. Approaching the man, Martin said:

'Are you allowed to smoke here?'

'No,' repled the man.

'Then report immediately to your foreman' Martin said.

He did not know any foremen either but approached the nearest man in a white coat.

'That man on the double end tennon has been smoking. Deal with it, please!,' he said.

He had put the matter out of his mind when, later that morning, there was a knock on the door and the foreman came in:

'Er, Mr Jourdan,' he said. 'About that man smoking. I've sacked him!' Martin, somewhat take aback said: 'Good. Well done!' but was fearful this might, in the prevailing climate, result in a strike. It did not and it was the first of many steps in convincing the Nathan workforce that the management from Parker Knoll was as good as its word.

Profits of the Group rose, albeit slowly in each of the years to 1986, when E. Lock Ltd was acquired for a consideration of £1.5m. Lock of London was a cabinet business, manufacturing and importing Tudor oak reproductin furniture. Amazingly, it had been run by Bert Lock since he had been invalided out of the Royal Mechanical Corps in 1917. Bert was 91 when he sold the business.

Bert volunteered and enlisted at an Army recruitment post in the City of London in 1914, and was wounded in the right hand at the Battle of Ypres. No longer fit for active service he did not wish to be transferred to the Pay Corps, preferring to return to the family business. Just before attending a Medical Board, in November 1916, he pushed his maimed hand into an ice-cold bucket of water, kept in those days to douse fires, and left it there, in great pain, for five to ten minutes. When the rather pompous doctor saw his blue mangled hand, he discharged Bert on the spot! The next day Bert returned to the business to find his uncle gravely ill and working in the office from a bath chair. His uncle left the business that evening, never to return. Bert ran the business from that day until his retirement in 1988.

Lock was probably the first furniture company to imported fully assembled cabinet furniture from countries destined to be behind the Iron Curtain for almost half a century. In the early 1930s, Bert with his brother, Fred, travelled into Eastern Europe by train, but sometimes with the car. They were frequently memorable journeys. By the 1980s, Lock's principal source of supply was from a factory in Tega Mures in Central Romania, which used to be part ofthe Hapsburg Austro-Hungarian Empire. Travelling there in the mid-1980s, one took as currency Kent cigarettes, Dior tights and Fortnum & Mason coffee. Almost better than

US dollars, these commodities bought taxis, dinners in smart hotels and the officials, without whose permission travel was most difficult.

Lock prospered until the overthrow of Ceausescu. With him fell the established order. Discipline both from a quality and scheduling standpoint collapsed and the Group merged the Lock business into Nathan and sold the factory site in London. It was a profitable acquisition.

The purchase of E. Lock coincided with some important changes in the management of Parker Knoll. Dane Baskerville, who had been Managing Director since 1979, reached 65 and retired. At the same time, two long-serving Directors also retired. Derek Stewart, who had started as an apprentice at Parkers and who rose to be the Production Director, hung up his upholsterer's tack hammer. Len Cox, whom Hans Jourdan had taken on as a labourer in the Tapestry Stores in 1947, retired as Director in charge of the Chipping Norton factory. The retirement of these three, coupled with the retirement of Robbie Howland, the long-time Director of Design, marked a major change in the character of the Company.

Tom Jourdan had turned Nathan's losses into a profit and it was time to move on. Tom returned to Parker Knoll as Managing Director, bringing with him Ian Brewster. While Parker Knoll had survived the recession well, their range of products had not developed at the pace of their market. Parker Knoll had remained the leader of the fireside chair and recliner market but not found a position in the fashionable three-piece suite sector. Tom and Ian put this right with the result that, in the five years to 1991, profit grew fourfold from £1m to £4m. Much of this was due to Ian Brewster's determination to introduce the right products, and the flair of Richard Carruthers, the new design director.

During this period, on the fabric side of the business, Parker Knoll Textiles, now known as Parkertex and incorporating G. P. & J. Baker and K. Raymakers, profits had grown substantially. G. P. & J. Baker, who had celebrated their own centenary in 1987, had become established as a leading designer and converter of printed cottons, linens and unions. Exports to continental Europe had continued to increase and strenuous efforts had been made, without success, to buy into the large and high margin market in North America.

It was against this background that William Raymakers arranged for the Chairman, Martin Jourdan to meet Richard Gloyn, Managing Director of Semple & Co, a competing wholesaler of curtain and upholstery fabrics, wallpapers and wallcoverings.

Richard's father had joined Semple after the war, when the Semple family had decided that a medical career was more to their liking than trade. When Richard joined the business, it was located in London and dealt principally with the low end commodities of the fabric business: grey cloth, moquette in three colours, brown, green and gold and an assortment of auxiliaries of little relevance to the fashionable fabrics business. Richard introduced style into Semple and created the brand name 'Monkwell', taken from their address in the City of London. He also moved the business to Bournemouth, principally because it had same-day rail connections with most parts of England but also because his passion for sailing was more easily and time-effectively pursued nearer the south coast. The business prospered in Bournemouth but, as so often happens in private firms of this type, increasing profitability brought its own pressure. The business needed cash to expand but the Semple family saw only a capital asset and not the pound notees necessary to support and educate a growing family. Richard, who with his father had around one third of the equity, decided to seek a buyer and, knowing William Raymakers, decided through him to approach the Group. It is a remarkable tribute to both parties that William, who had sold his company to the Group, was able to recommend one of his long time customers to do the same.

Early in January 1987, Martin Jourdan and Christopher Semple sat down in the High Wycombe offices to sign the deal. At that point, Martin saw that Christopher's full name on the Sale Contract was Christopher Greenhill Semple. Martin asked Christopher whether he had ancestry conected to-day with Kings Langley in Herts. Christopher was surprised and asked how Martin knew of the connection. Martin produced the family tree that the Drawing Office in Parker Knoll had been re-drawing for some time, to find that the Semple 'Greenhill' was also the Parker 'Greenhill' and that, going back to the eighteenth century, the families were related. Thus started a happy and profitable union with an unexpected pedigree. Richard Gloyn joined the Group Board and Monkwell, as the company was now known, contributed significantly to the profits of the Group.

Later that year, 1987, Mrs Thatcher began her third term in office. In October, a hurricane hit the south of England, destroying 15 million trees and, during the same week on 13 October, a record fall on the New York Stock Exchange caused the collapse of the London Market on what has become known as 'Black Friday'.

The hectic expansion of the Group over the previous five years had attracted considerable interest from the investing community but this was not without benefit to the employees. In 1979 the Board had launched a Savings Related Share Option Scheme whereby eligible employees could take up options in Parker Knoll shares. Of those eligible employees, 50% had participated in the scheme, taking up 247,000 shares which was over 70% of the shares made available by shareholders. It was an outstanding success and the option price of 97p had by 1988 increase to £8.50 giving an 876% gain to all those with the foresight to back their Company.

But this success had, as in previous times, brought its problems. The investing community in the City of London thought that the Group only manufactured upholstered chairs and settees; they could not grasp that the Parker Knoll brand, made famous for its upholstery, was also the holding company for a number of other enterprises in their own way equally well known — Nathan for its dining and living room furniture; Lock for its Tudor Oak range; Parkertex and G. P. & J. Baker for their fine range of curtain and upholstery fabrics and Monkwell for the entrepreneurial mirror image of Baker and Parketex; K. Raymakers, the lowest cost producer of cotton velvet velours in Europe.

The Board decided to change the name of the holding company but made the mistake of commissioning a well known design company to investigate suitable names and logos. Of course, the Board had no intention of changing the Parker Knoll brand. Indeed the change of name for the Group would enhance the prominence of Parker Knoll in the upholstery market. The Board went through a series of psychological gymnastics that irritated more than educated. The new names put forward were banal, pompous or ridiculous and the accompanying logos surreal in the extreme. Many doubted the wisdom of a change but Martin, supported by his brother Tom and Nigel Olsen, insisted on continuing, though without the design company. At its meeting on 4 August 1988, the Board resolved to change the name of the holding company from Parker Knoll to Cornwell Parker. To preserve the tradition and ensure continuity 'Parker' was vital but 'Cornwell'? To the outsider, this was no more than a name but one that carried with it the integrity and reputation for quality and service that was encapsulated in Parker Knoll. To the insider, Cornwell was a small village, only a few miles from the main factory of Parker Knoll at Chipping Norton, now employing over 400 people. To the family Cornwell was TCP's middle name Thomas *Cornwell* Parker. After one hundred and eighteen years, the company, founded by Frederick Parker in 1879 and, with his great-grandchildren still on the Board, was about to enter a new era. If we had known we were on the brink of the worst recession for sixty years, we would not have celebrated our new name in quite the same manner as we did. If we had at all times possessed the gift of foresight, we might never have dared to build the Company as we did!

ABOVE: The Monkwell range on show. BELOW: Craftsmanship continues at Wycombe — contemporary frame making.

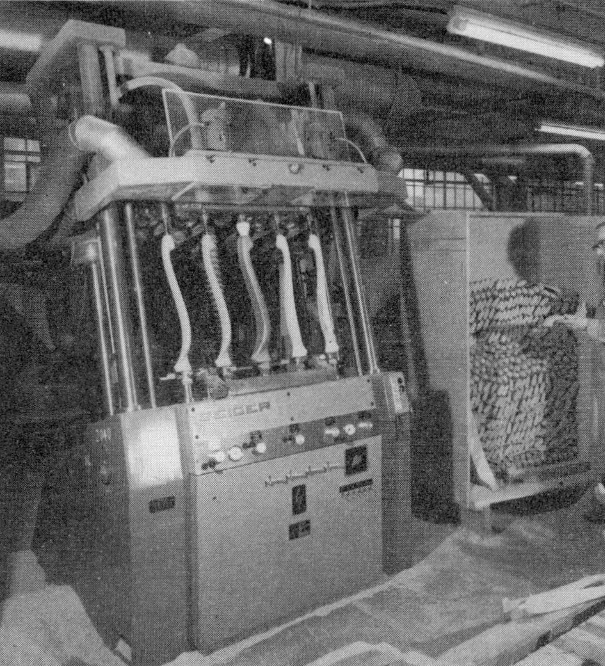

LEFT: The Rye shaper produces curved parts at High Wycombe and RIGHT: the Geiger shaper supplies cabriole legs. BELOW: The polishing shop.

ABOVE: The end product — in the despatch bay at Chipping Norton
and BELOW: Parker Knoll, High Wycombe today.

INDEX

All figures in *italics* refer to illustrations

SUBSCRIBERS

1 Cornwell Parker plc
2 The Worshipful Company of Furniture Makers
3 Marion Arnold
4 Peggy Jourdan
5 Nancy Alpe
6 The Cornwell Norton Library
7 The High Wycombe Library
8 High Wycombe Local History and Chair Museum
9 Lucian Ercolani
10 S. C. Bland
11 Clive & Carolyn Birch
12 Jonathan Arnold
13 Christie's
14 Dr Paul & Mrs Sue Spice
15 John & Margaret Postle
16 Ronald Rawle
17 Stephanie Woolcott
18 Betty B. Howland
19 Dr & Mrs John Preece
20 S.W. Boreham
21 Mr & Mrs J.S. Gore
22 John Weeks
23 Leonard William Hughes
24 Anthony John Campbell Scaife
25 Miss T.E. Vernon
26 Alan E. Brain
27 John M. Towner
28 E.R. Denton
29 Sandra I. Glander
30 Keith Pinn
31 M. Reeve-Parker
32 Alan Watkins
33 Christopher G. Gilbert
34 Dr C.D. Edwards
35 Stephen J. Hearn
36 William Baldry-Vincent
37 B.E. Chapman
38 Colin J. Seabright
39 Peter Legg
40 Trafford Boughton
41 Mrs R. Kewnen
42 Oliver E.P. Shanks
43 Graham Haines
44 Treen Antiques
45 Bertram Claude White
45 Ronald A. Green
47 A.W. Adams
48 Hazel Chandler-Simmons
49 J.J. Grantham
50 J.P.H. Werner
51 Brian C. Treby
52 Glyndwr Price
53 Anthea Marshall
54 Eric Lovegrove
55 A.F. Swain
56 Jeremy Reynolds
57 Donald G. Douglas
58 V.B. Card
59 Audrey Duck
60 Richard J. Brett
61 A.P. Newell
62 J.P. Bravington
63 Diana R. Billingham
64 P. Flecknoe
65 Raymond Gibbins
66 Gordon Thomas Belson
67 Margaret F. T. Young
68 Anne Elliott
69 Miss K.B. Jourdan
70 Miss M.C. Jourdan
71 M.C. Blackshaw
72 Robert Church Branch
73 John English
74 E.D. Crofts
75 Alexander John Jemmett
76 Elaine Smith
77 Derek Frank Skinner
78 Ken Matthews
79 Pamela Styles
80 Sheila Leonard
81 K.D. Wright
82 Donald Frank Jackman
83 Ron Ridgley
84 Ted Pick
85 Mrs K.A. Scott
86 James J. Hackett
87 Ronald Leslie Styles
88 John Hales
89 Mike Bowen
90 Elsie K. Cambrey
91 Peter Roy Bolding
92 I.W. Baldwin
93 Violet E. Vickery
94 Kenneth Jones
95 Karen Tolhurst Neil
96 Aubrey Saunders
97 Henry H.T. Mason
98 C.F. Gardner
99 Mrs Pat Richards
100 Brian H. Ludlow
101 Margaret Clark
102 John Black
103 David Wallace
104 William Towlson
105 Ernest Bartlett
106 Mrs V.I. Buckingham
107 Patricia M. Tinnelly
108 Edie Bailey
109 Harold L. Brown
110 H.C. Liddle
111 Mr & Mrs James Murgatroyd
112 Mr & Mrs Cooper Park
113 Miss Lara Jourdan
114 Mr & Mrs M.H.T. Jourdan
115 Mrs I.C. Tomlins
116 Joan E. Gray
117-121 Phyllis M. Jourdan
122 Mr & Mrs C. Arenson
123 Bernard Sharp
124 D.F. Candler
125 Kenneth Gordon Sharpe
126 R.E. Clibbens
127 G.L.M. Pipe
128 E.H. Cartwright
129 Lionel C. Baker
130 D.J. Kitching
131 Graham Dean
132 M.G. Mason
133 Mrs D. Woodcock
134 Allan Barnett
135 Doris I. Hammond
136 Leonard George Cox
137 R.A. Hopkins
138 Jack True
139 William Arthur Reynolds
140 L.W. Robson
141 Jozef Wieczorek
142 J.P. Boddington
143 Mrs R.M. Warr
144 Susan Walker
145 Robin Howland
146 Daphne Middleton
147 Peter Grantham
148 Kathryn Gill
149 Mrs J.M. Baird
150 Dayton House of Blackpool
151 F.J. Wilson & Son -Upholsterers
152 L.J.P. International
153 W.H. Griffiths
154 R.K. Parsloe
155 H.J. Foster
156 Keith Hunt
157 Shirley Read (née Rowles)
158 Terry Cox
159 Donald George Baker
160 William Raymakers
161-163 Witney Antiques
164 Mr & Mrs R.H. Thomas
165 Mr & Mrs P.E. Thomas
166 Audrey M. Lampard
167 Peter Willers
168 Ken & Gwen Ranklin
169 Richard & Irene Ranklin
170 Mrs W.H. Heaned
171 Mrs Pamela Bartlett
172 Flemming Hvidt
173 Dane Dew
174 Raymond A. Shard
175 John Newman
176 William H. Watson
177 L.E. Dane Baskerville
178 Terence Pearce
179 Philip George Souch
180 David Learmont
181 Peter Lacey
182 Harry Leech
183 Max E. Ott
184 Derek Ingram Stewart
185 George H. Gilbert
186 George Neville
187 Glyn Barry Paradise
188 A.A. Green
189 Peter James Pearson
190 David Edward Barnes
191 A. Carter
192 Ian Grant
193 William Henry Green
194 N.E. Walker & Son
195 Packbourne Ltd
196 Barsleys Department Store
197 Bernard Wyne
198 W.G. Hart & Son (Clapton) Ltd
199 Lorimer & Beetham Ltd
200 Lancaster of Sherborne
201 Fred Winter
202 Peter Bancroft Standish
203 F. Butterworth
204 Simpson & Hill
205 J.W. Donovan
206-207 Vitafoam
208 A. McGreevy
209 Beard Bros Ltd
210 Susan Carr
211 Doreen Newell
212 Robin Waning
213 Russell Warren Advertising
214 S. Gascoigne & Sons Ltd
215 Peter Longland-Lee, Longland Co, Birmingham
216 Townsend Associates Ltd
217-218 Bennetts Family Furnishings
219 W. & J.R. Thompson (Woodturners) Ltd
220 Fairway Furniture
221 E. Langton & Co Ltd
222 William Bedford PLC
223 Peter J. Sharpe
224 Bailey Wighton Ltd
225 Hazel Williams
226 Rosalind Musselwhite
227 Butlers (Furnishers) Ltd
228-229 Calverts (Taunton) Ltd
230 Hampton & McMurray
231 William G. Gibson
232 South Beach Hotel
233 Harpers of Bath

234 W.A. Buckland & Sons Ltd
235 M.E. Johnson
236 R.D. Wates
237 Garry Frederick Janes
238 Robert George Easden
239 John Robinson
240 Terence Norman Austin
241 David Charles Bustin
242 Antony Charles Foster
243 Thelma Burrus
244 Mary Farwell
245 H. Chare & Son Ltd
246 Jeffark Engineering & Metal Pressing
247 Judith Anne Livingston
248 R.H. Glossop
249 Mrs Nancy Hawkins
250 John Keil
251 Haydn Gabb
252 Flo Beith
253-254 Cobham Furniture Centre
255 Martin Fear
256 A.J. Kaye
257 Blodwen E. Jeskins
258 Geffrye Museum
259 Culver & Son
260 R. Stevens
261 Windlestrae Hotel Business & Leisure
262 Pirelli Limited
263-264 Stanton Davies Ltd
265 Roy Sirs
266 Hairlok Ltd
267 Peter Loftus
268 Anneke C.H. Hofstede
269 Southons of Salisbury
270 Jonathan Lee
271 Smyth Patterson Ltd
272 McClenaghan Gilhooly Antiques
273 H.G. Scadgell Ltd
274 Isaac Lord Ltd
275 Abbot Brown & Sons Ltd
276 Raymond Raynor
277 Lesty Hardwoods Ltd
278 Cheshire Textiles Ltd
279-280 N.H. Chapman & Co Ltd
281 R. Barbour & Sons Ltd
282 Chiltern Springs Ltd
283 Doorway to Value
284 Malcolm John Purslow
285 Steven Hickman
286 David Wood
287-288 Production Tools (Oxford) Ltd
289 C.T. Haynes
290 A. Davis & Sons Ltd
291 Kimstyle Furnishing
292 Bobbie Xuereb
293 Bryan Gowans
294 Sheila Moore
295 Sheila Allen
296 Joyce Cornwall
297 Sheila Whittaker
298 Gill Bettison
299 Fords of Lymington
300-301 William Burke
302 Christine E. Bily
303 Michael P. Humphery
304 Vernon Walker
305 John Pargeter & Son Ltd
306 Michael Tilbury
307 John L. Robertson Ltd
308 Smith's 'The Rink' Ltd
309-310 K. Raymakers & Son Ltd
311 M.A. Jones (Furnishers) Ltd
312 Carpenter PLC
313 Meyer, London
314 James Mitchell Parker
315 Higham Tong Ltd
316 B.A. Wyllie
317 David Morgan Ltd, Cardiff
318 Caroline Rimell
319-320 Peter Marino
321 F. Richards & Sons Ltd
322 Barry & Sylvia Kraushaar
323 Coba Plastics Ltd
324 Murmar Fabrics PLC
325 Firsteel Cold Rolled Products
326 David T. Allcock
327 Dr Sherlaw-Johnson
328 H.J. & D. Webb & Sons
329 Roger Keith Smith
330 Gordon Busbridge Ltd
331 Foam Engineers Ltd
332 Glenmere Timber Co Ltd
333 Malcolm Wilson
334 A.E. Bate
335 Meubles Home Furnishings
336 Fibretrent Ltd
337 Jake Kaner
338 W.N.H. Chick
339 House of Shah
340 Warden Bros Ltd
341 Brenmark Engineering Ltd
342 Cookes Furniture Ltd
343 Philip Eavis
344 Mrs P. Thornton
345 University of Brighton
346 BeA Fastening Systems Ltd
347 Brian Gwinnell
348 Mrs Mary V. Oddie
349 Christopher B. Prosser
350 Cyril Gall Ltd
351-352 J.E. Beale PLC
353 Dominic Reynolds
354 The Winterthur Library
355 Standard International-London, UK
356 Molteni Spa-Como, Italy
357 Pullmaflex U.K. Ltd
358 L.J. Alliston & Son Ltd
359 Jonathan Garrard
360-361 Portways/Vitaluxan
362 A.R. Stockton & Co Ltd
363 A.E. Deller
364 Russell Bush
365-368 Imatex Spa/Italy
369 Denise P. Bearne
370 David Neville (Furnishings) Ltd
371 Winchester School of Art
372 Colonial Williamsburg Foundation
373 Samuel Ramsden
374 Paul D. Tapping
375 A.P. Walters
376 Peter E. Johnson
377 Randalls of Uxbridge
378 Simon C. Evans
379 Mr H.L. Atha & Dearlove & Atha
380 Jobs of Deal Ltd
381 V.R. Flowers & Son
382-383 Keith Robinson
384 Mrs T. Price Zimmermann
385 P.V. Radford
386 Glasgow University Library
387 Peter Silver
388 Monica Elliott
389 Pauline Williams
390 Alan Jeskins-Powell
391 Wendy Brayne
392 Rebecca Sanderson
393 David King
394 Colin Greenland
395 Vale Interiors, Evesham
396 Furnishing Flair
397 Maureen Bennett
398 Jean Scofield
399 Graham Child
400 Peter J. Hill
401 G. Pounce (Furnishers) Ltd
402 G. & R. Clarke Ltd
403 Vineys of Abingdon
404 Keith Dawson
405 John M. Cross
406 Deborah Humphrey
407 Hugh Johnson
408 C.N. Baker
409 Ian Watson
410 Barbara Quinn
411 Terence Shirley
412 Mrs V.M. Ridgley
413 Clark's Press Equipment Ltd
414 Arthur C. Abbott Ltd
415 County Archivist, Bucks County Council
416 Jack Marsden
417 Frank Reginald Way
418 W.R. Stephenson
419 David Howling
420 Alex Donaldson & Son Ltd, Larne
421 Geoffrey Wynne-Jones
422 David Vokins
423 Douglas Story
424 Hugh Garforth-Bles
425 Linton & Robinson Ltd
426 Richardson Library, St Louis Art Museum
427 Donald Bennett MBE, Broadmoor Hospital
428 Lister Mouldings Ltd
429 David Simpson
430 Kingston University
431 James Hunt
432 Gloria Clemson
433 M.J. & F.V. Fletcher
434 Tim Povey
435 Stephen Prudhoe
436 John Brice
437 Gerald Stefanovic
438 Bentley H. Burrows
439 T.L. Howie
440 G.S. Hirons
441 Ronald Frank Lloyd
442 Stephen Thornton
443 Bill Johnson
444 R.E. Jarvis
445 Ivor R. Terry
446 Nigel Jones
447 Catherine Claridge
448 G. Wright
449 Peter Julian Harrison
450 Christopher Wilk
451 Maurice William Peachey
452 Dr John Everalls
453 Marian Ross
454 Roy S. Watmough
455 Ian T. Cramond
456 Ann F. Lynch
457 J.L. Hart
458 Kaymetzeler Ltd
459 Nicholas Somers FSVA
460 W.R. Stephenson
461 Andrew J. Brewster
462 Guildhall Library
463 Philip J. Crouch
464 John & June Scarsbrook
465 M.J. Palmer
466 Alex Copland
467 Martin Williams & Gillian Darby
468 Hugo Van Zazzara
469 Keith Burton
470 Paul Hancock
471 Keith Cooper-Harris
472-473 SCP Jean Romfort
474-476 Mrs Nancy M. Reid
477 Hafren Furnishers Ltd
478 R.H. Malthouse
479 Mary Winch
480 Barclays Bank PLC
481 Sally Rose
482 Jane Rose
483 Mathew Rose
484 Colin E. Greenfield

485 Mrs Russell
486 K.T.C. Arnold
487 Mrs Dorcas King
488 Andrew Fursse
489 David W. Vernon
490 Marigold Honey
491 Kenneth Hodgins
492 Association of Master Upholsterers
493 Luke Honey
494 W.L. Massil
495 Charltons
496 Stuart M. Golding
497-498 Alain Larche
499 Arthur G. Fountain
500 Nick Shears
501 Theodore Wissink
502 The London Library
503 Kenneth Hodgins Ltd
504 Sotheby's Educational Studies
505 Stewart Linford, Chairmaker
506 Janet Potton
507 Mayers & Shaw
508-510 Elizabeth M. Davey
511 Rosemary Olsen
512 Vivien Kies

Remaining names unlisted